Baking for Breakfast:

Sweet and Savory Treats for Mornings at Home

A Chef's Guide to Breakfast with Over 130 Delicious, Easy-to-Follow Recipes for Donuts, Muffins and More

By Donna Leahy
Photography by Robert Leahy

Baking for Breakfast: Sweet and Savory Treats for Mornings at Home

A Chef's Guide to Breakfast with Over 130 Delicious,
Easy-to-Follow Recipes for Donuts, Muffins and More

By Donna Leahy

Photography by Robert Leahy

Food Arts Fusion LLC

ISBN 978-1-942118-14-5

© 2015, Donna Leahy

Disclaimer

The information contained in this book is based on research and personal experience unless otherwise stated. While every care has been taken in compiling the recipes for this book, Food Arts Fusion LLC or any other persons who have been involved in working on this publication cannot accept responsibility for any errors or omissions, inadvertent or not, that may be found in the recipes or text, nor for any problems that may arise as a result of preparing one of these recipes. Health-related information provided in this book is for educational and entertainment purposes only. The author and publisher disclaim responsibility for any adverse effects that may result from the use or application of the recipes and information within this book. The publisher and the author make no representations or warranties with respect to the accuracy or completeness of the contents of this work, and specifically disclaim all warranties, including, without limitation, warranties of fitness or health for a particular purpose. This work is sold with the understanding that the publisher and author are not engaged in rendering medical or other professional advice, and that neither is liable for damages arising from it.

Also by Donna Leahy

French Toast, Waffles and Pancakes for Breakfast: Comfort Food for Leisurely Mornings

Eggs for Breakfast: Delicious, Healthy Recipes to Jump-Start Your Day

Morning Glories: Recipes for Breakfast, Brunch and Beyond from an American Country Inn

Recipe for a Country Inn

Cover - Cinnamon Rolls Recipe p. 290

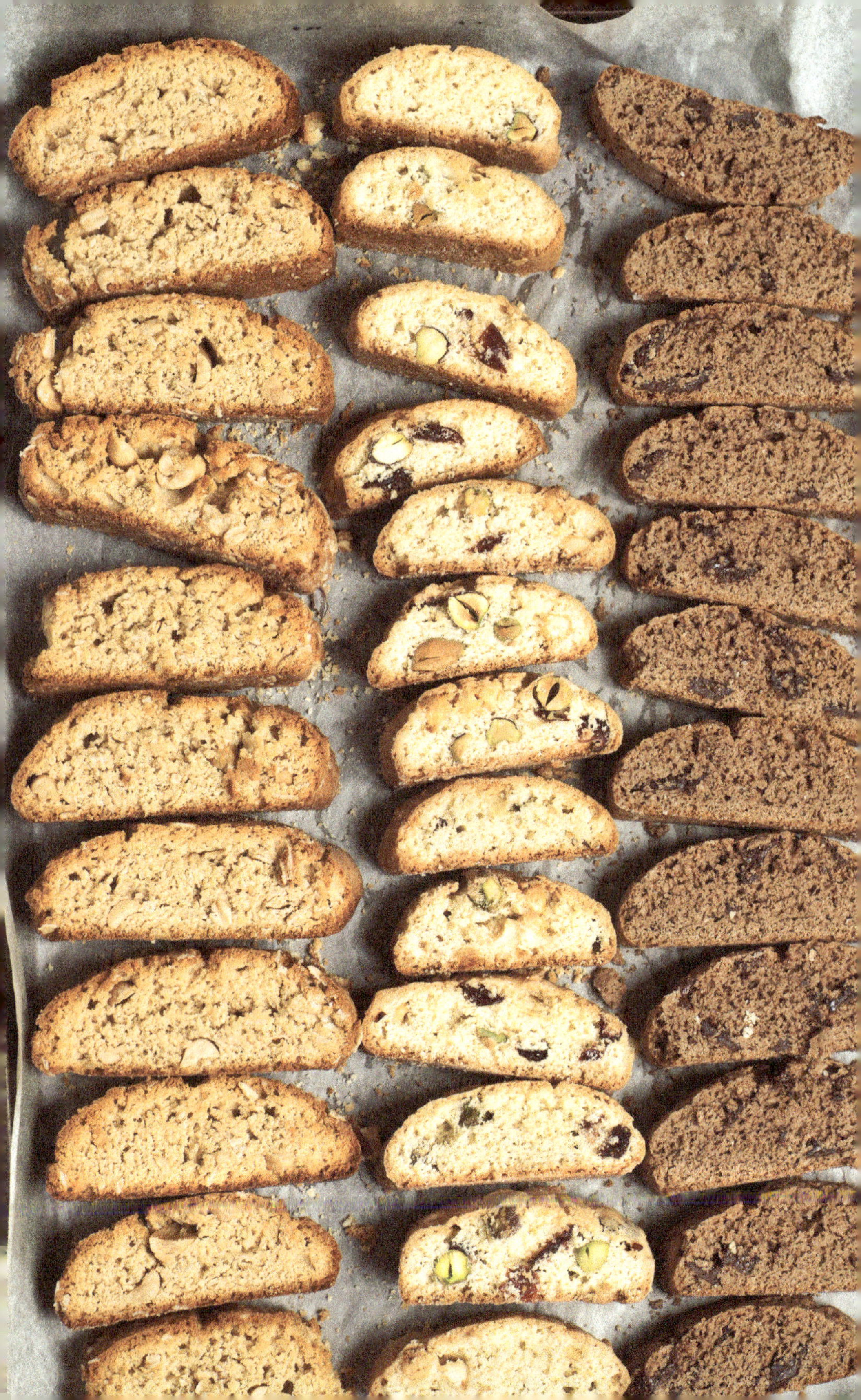

Thank you!

I appreciate your purchase of this book and hope you will enjoy these recipes. I know you could have picked dozens of other cookbooks, so to show my appreciation I'd like to offer you a bonus: *Ten Delicious Donut Recipes*. Simply sign up on my website www.donnaleahy.com to receive my monthly newsletter, and I will send you the PDF.

Finally, I need to ask you a favor. If you have a moment to post an online review on a book retailer site, I'd really appreciate it. This type of feedback will help me continue to write the kind of cookbooks that you want to use. If you have any direct feedback, please contact me through my website.

Thanks again. I look forward to hearing from you.

Chef Donna

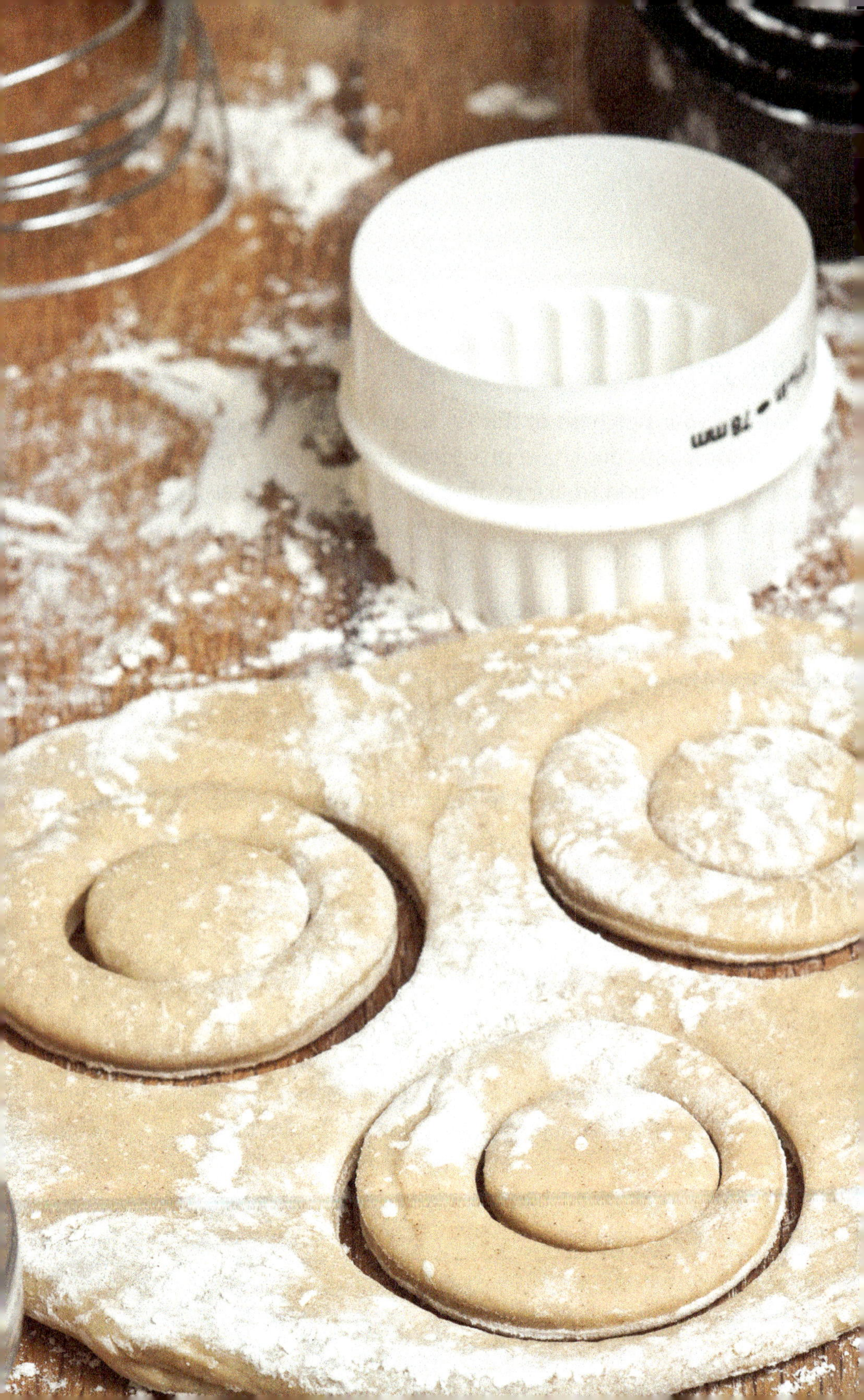

Table of Contents

CHAPTER TWO
COFFEECAKES, SWEET ROLLS AND DANISH............87

CHAPTER THREE:
COBBLERS, CRISPS, TARTS AND TURNOVERS..........153

CHAPTER FOUR
DONUTS, BISCOTTI, BARS AND GRANOLA................205

CHAPTER FIVE
CLASSIC BAKED GOODS, BREADS AND DOUGHS.... 261

CHAPTER SIX

BONUS CHAPTER SEVEN

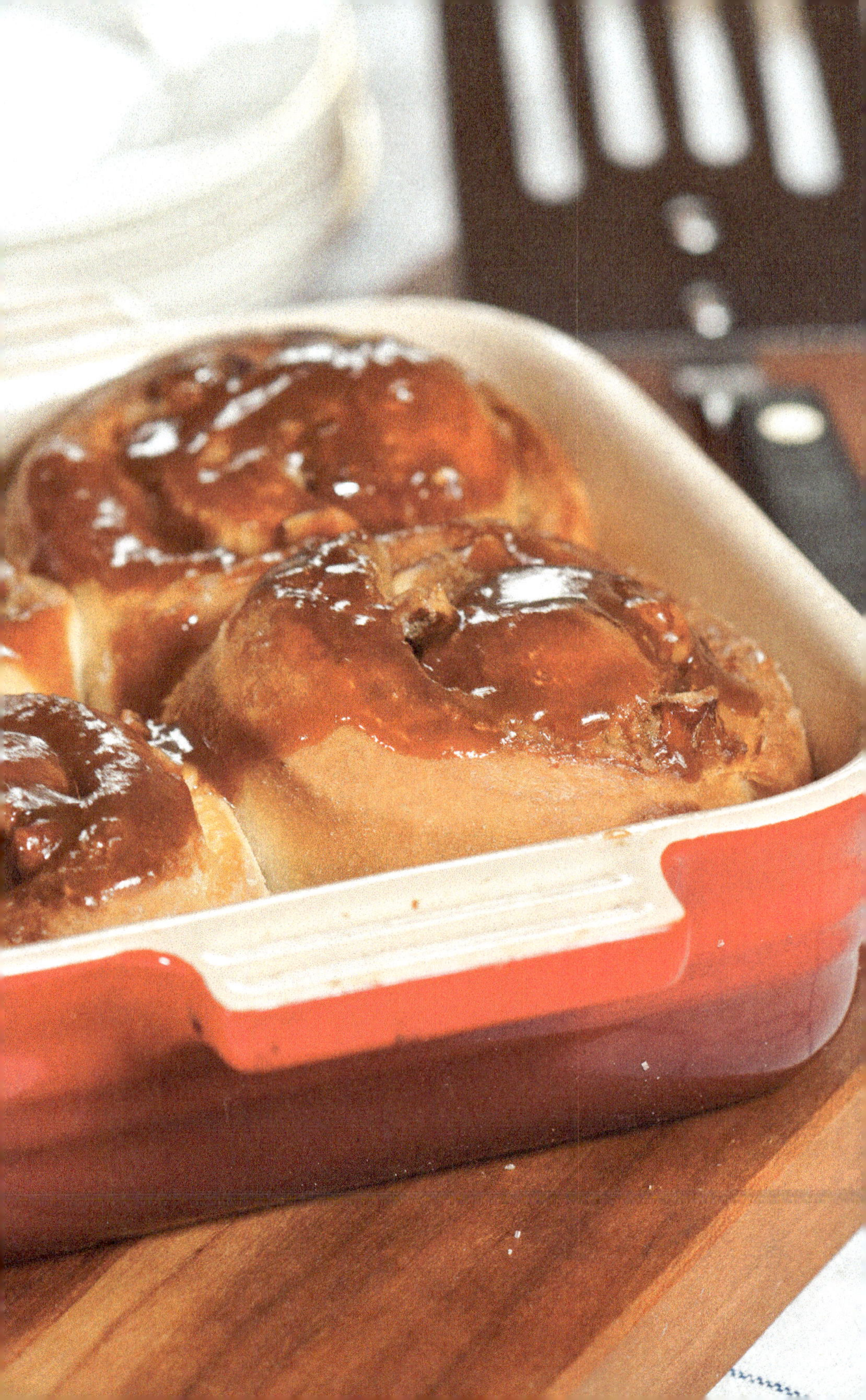

Introduction

What could be more comforting than waking up to the fragrant aroma of freshly baked coffeecake or muffins? Spending a leisurely morning at home, sipping a steaming coffee or tea and nibbling on a warm-from-the-oven pastry conjures the very essence of relaxation and renewal. Breakfast is a meal for savoring time alone or enjoying casual interactions with family and friends, where comfy pajamas and cozy robes are standard dress code. For me, breakfast has always had a special meaning, both as a lover of good food and as a culinary professional. In my years as a chef at our country inn, baking for breakfast was the starting point for the delicious, nourishing morning meal that would follow. It was the first step to helping our guests begin their day happy and content.

Baking is actually quite an amazing accomplishment, much like creating a work of art. Bakers combine various ingredients that turn into something completely different and unique—ideally, something delicious. In recent years there has been a trend in baking to make it less of an art and more of a science. There is no doubt that baking requires accuracy, but accuracy is the means to an end, a tool that is used to create. In this book, I want you to be able to share the happiness of baking for breakfast, with creative recipes that are easy to prepare and share. Nowhere did my professional baking bring more happiness than first thing in the morning.

As a chef, making breakfast was always my favorite time at the inn. During our dinner service, there was off-the-wall pressure to get 10 things right at once. Executing a multitude of different menu items at once could be a daunting task. Since one mistake could ruin someone's evening, I felt an incredible amount of responsibility for making that experience perfect. In contrast, breakfast was like a deep breath of fresh air. The menus I created for breakfast were simpler, but still interesting and inventive. Compared to the hectic scene in the restaurant kitchen each night, mornings in that same kitchen felt leisurely.

People expect dinner at a fine dining restaurant to be perfect. But they often don't expect that same care and consideration in the morning. Breakfast was my chance to take them by surprise. Our breakfast menu always included one special baked item, presented to the guests at the onset of the meal service. It always brought a smile to their faces, and often a gasp of "wow!" Sharing the joy of baking is a powerful feeling. With that kind of reaction, it's no wonder I love breakfast.

In larger restaurants, there is a dichotomy between the line chefs and the bakers. Bakers arrive in the early hours before the meal prep begins, sometimes only a few hours after the line chefs have left once dinner service is complete. But in our country inn restaurant, I did all the cooking. I started baking early in the morning as part of the breakfast menu. Baking continued later in the day for afternoon tea service, plus breads and desserts for the full-service fine dining restaurant. So as a chef, baking was not a separate activity for me—it was part of my daily cooking routine. Today, I continue to develop new breakfast baking recipes for clients, as well as for sharing with friends and family.

If you're imagining having to get up in the middle of the night to enjoy a baked good at home for breakfast, I want to reassure you that, for these recipes, that won't be necessary. From juggling many aspects of cooking throughout my career, I've learned to divide more complex preparations into manageable steps. Many of these recipes, like Blueberry Peach Cobbler or Strawberry Muffins, are easy to assemble and can be on your breakfast table in under one hour. When the recipes are a little more involved, like the Croissant Cinnamon

Rolls or Coconut Almond Bear Claw Pastries, I've noted special "make ahead tips" at the bottom of the recipe so you can spread out the preparation over a few days.

When possible, the number of servings is kept as low as possible to accommodate baking at home, although in some cases it is simply not practical to reduce the yields. I also know that the time we spend at home is best spent with those we love. The point of making these comfort foods at home is to allow you leisurely time to enjoy them with family and friends, not to spend the morning hours alone in the kitchen. These recipes are designed so you can enjoy breakfast treats along with your guests.

Although I baked in a professional capacity, my baking was much more like your baking at home. Maybe you're making a holiday dinner and you want to bake biscuits as part of the menu. Perhaps you are sending your kids at college a care package with the cookies they loved as children. Or maybe you have company for the weekend and want to make muffins for breakfast. There's a good chance you don't have time to work out the kinks in a recipe. You probably have a limited amount of time to get the baking done, so you need those recipes to turn out 100% of the time.

When I arrived in my restaurant kitchen to begin prepping for breakfast, I needed my baked goods to turn out as well. How could I start breakfast service by telling my guests there were no croissants that morning because they didn't rise? I had to be fairly certain a recipe would work, so I would work out the details of recipes in between other things throughout the day. I was constantly coming up with new ideas and recipes, ensuring that my returning guests would be able to enjoy their favorites as well as indulge in new treats. Seeing smiles on their faces each morning made it all worthwhile.

In the chapters that follow, there are a range of recipes for breakfast treats that will suit every schedule and time constraint. From muffins to cobblers, many of the recipes can be easily assembled and baked off the same morning. Coffeecakes and tarts can often be made a day or two ahead, so there is little to do in the morning except to enjoy them with guests. Biscotti, bars and baked donuts are delicious portable baked goods, able to be enjoyed at home by a glowing fire or outdoors at a sunrise picnic, depending on the season. While some classic breakfast treats like croissants and brioche may involve a few extra days of preplanning, I've also developed some simpler versions that require less time to prepare. Either way, they will be worth the effort. In the pantry section, there are recipes for components of dishes like applesauce and jams, and also some alternate glazes and toppings. While this book concentrates on baking for breakfast, I've also included some recipes for fried donuts in a bonus chapter.

Mornings at home should be a time for leisure and enjoyment. These appetizing recipes will inspire you to create breakfast treats that will bring joy to your family and friends. Come into my kitchen and let's get started.

MEASURING

Accurately measuring ingredients is imperative to successful baking. Although there has been a recent trend among some home bakers towards weighing ingredients, most still measure in volume, such as cups. So while I have included weights for the dry ingredients, these recipes were tested specifically with measured ones. During this testing, I found the use of measuring scoops to be the most accurate for dry ingredients. Because the scoops are easy to level off, they give the most consistent result. But if you don't have the scoops, double check your measures in a cup. (There is a saying in woodworking— measure twice, cut once. The same idea applies here.)

Measuring spoons in various sizes (¼ tsp. to 1 tbsp.) also ensure greater accuracy. Dry ingredients like flour should be sifted *after* measuring. Because it is prone to clumping, brown sugar should be packed into the measuring scoop or cup before leveling to eliminate air spaces. For wet ingredients, I use 1- and 2-cup Pyrex glass measuring cups. Be extra careful measuring wet ingredients by setting the cup on the counter so the liquid levels. Do not measure spoons of liquid ingredients over the bowl to avoid splashing extra into the mix.

INGREDIENTS

Where specific ingredients are called for, they are described in detail in the recipes. However, here are some general guidelines for the more generic ingredients used.

Flour

Professional bakers keep a larger variety of flours on hand. They can be confident they are used consistently and maintain freshness, but that's not always practical at home. For this reason, the recipes were developed using unbleached, all-purpose flour (with a few exceptions). Some recipes include bread flour (which has a higher amount of gluten), important in yeast breads and some baked goods like bagels. You can also purchase gluten separately and add it to your all-purpose to up the gluten ratio. (If you go this route, follow the directions on the gluten you purchase for how much to add.) Since I almost never have pastry flour on-hand, I add cornstarch to all-purpose to soften it for certain recipes. This is noted in those specific recipes, but if you prefer to use pastry flour, substitute it for an equal volume of all-purpose.

Sugar and Sweeteners

These recipes were tested with granulated sugar (in lieu of superfine, which is often used by professional bakers), because it is readily available. I also like the texture it gives to the finished product (basically, when combining granulated sugar with butter, it helps incorporate more air and allows the butter to "fluff up"). I typically use light brown sugar because it has less molasses (strictly a matter of taste), but if you only have dark on hand, it won't affect the end results other than by altering the flavor profile. I have purposely not used corn syrup in these recipes to avoid the high fructose type. In cases where honey is used, please invest in a good quality product (my favorite is Savannah Bee Tupelo because of its delicious taste, and because it doesn't crystallize). Low quality, commercial honey can add an off-flavor to baked goods. Ditto on maple syrup—buy the best you can afford (I like the darker Grade B Kirkland brand from Costco for its rich flavor).

Dairy

Where butter is used, the recipes include unsalted sweet butter, the standard type available in U.S. groceries. In certain recipes that require laminating or layering butter (for example, croissants or Danish pastry dough), the amount of butterfat in the butter can make a big difference in the lift of the dough layers. Sometimes this butter is referred to as European-style because the European standard for the minimum amount of butterfat is higher than that in the U.S. In short, less butterfat means more water. Flavor, however, is less a matter of butterfat and more dependent on the quality of the cream. Flavor is increased through a process called culturing, the addition of which allows the butter to ferment before churning. I like this added richness, so I recommend using a cultured butter, especially for laminating (if possible). Kerrygold is my first choice for laminating (also from Costco), and I also love the cultured butter Vermont Butter and Cheese (it is not as widely available, but is just plain delicious). If you are fortunate to have access to a local dairy, check to see if they produce a higher fat, cultured butter. The most common brand of higher butterfat butter in U.S. supermarkets is Plugra. If you don't have access to any of these, the recipes will still work. I recommend tossing the lower fat butter with a few tablespoons of flour when laminating to absorb some of the excess moisture.

When dairy products like milk, sour cream, yogurt and ricotta are included, they are full-fat. Cream cheese is the dense version (not the whipped), and buttermilk is by nature lower in fat—although I use the minimally processed 2%.

Eggs

The recipes were tested with large eggs and yolks from large eggs. The eggs were from chickens that were cage-free but not free range to keep the color of the yolks consistent. (If you need a more detailed explanation of the nuances of how eggs are produced, please check out my *Eggs for Breakfast* book. You will be amazed, as I was when researching it, on what the labeling on eggs really means.)

Shortening and Oil

Solid shortening has a negative reputation because it typically contains trans-fats, also called partially hydrogenated oils, which have been associated with increased health risks. Trans-fats are created when hydrogen is added to vegetable oil to make it more solid. There are now many brands of solid shortening available that don't include trans-fats, even the old standards like Crisco. Nutiva-brand coconut and palm oil-based solid shortening was used for testing (it has a natural golden color that adds a nice, natural hue to baked goods). Olive oil used in baking should be a lighter style (although not "light"), not an extra virgin oil, so as to not dominate the flavor profile. When liquid vegetable shortening is called for, whether for baking or frying, canola oil was used.

Salt

Finely ground sea salt is used in these recipes. An equal amount of table salt may also be substituted. Although I prefer not to bake with kosher salt because the coarser grains do not always dissolve, use a conversion chart if you choose to substitute kosher.

Yeast

Instant dry yeast was used for all recipes that call for yeast. I prefer it over active or fresh yeast, mainly for its versatility and added fermentation qualities (i.e., faster rise with instant yeast, although active dry eventually catches up). Instant yeast can be added directly to the mix, with no proofing or rehydration required. However, it should not contact cold ingredients directly, so I generally whisk it into the flour to distribute it evenly, and/or slightly warm any liquids in the recipe before combining them with a dry ingredient/yeast mixture. The recipes were tested with the SAF brand, which I purchase in the vacuum-sealed package and keep in the refrigerator (it can also be frozen). Their Red Label is the standard instant dry yeast.

I also sometimes use the SAF Gold Label (osmotolerant) for sweet breads like Danish pastry. The sugar in sweet breads attracts water and can starve the yeast, essentially inhibiting the rise. SAF Gold works best when the amount of sugar is between 10% and 30% of the amount of the flour. If you commit to baking a number of the sweet yeast recipes, purchasing the osmotolerant yeast is a worthy investment. However, it is not necessary. The recipes were tested with the standard Red Label.

If you are an experienced baker and prefer to substitute fresh yeast, instant dry yeast is used at 33–40% of the weight of fresh (check with the manufacturer's recommendations). Instant yeast and active yeast are typically substituted on a 1:1 ratio. Keep in mind that there are many variables when dough is rising, so timing is less important than how much it has actually risen. Ambient temperature, barometric pressure, how you knead the dough and many other factors affect dough rising times. As mentioned earlier, this is part of the art of baking that I hope you'll embrace.

Chocolate

When a recipe calls for cocoa powder, I prefer Valrhona Dutch-process unsweetened cocoa powder. For dark chocolate, the recipes were tested with Guittard bittersweet and semi-sweet chocolate baking wafers and chips. For white chocolate, Ghiradelli was tested (my personal favorite is Callebaut, but I can't get it reliably shipped to me in southern Florida). Substitute your favorite brands.

Nuts and Dried Fruit

Freshness is really important with nuts, so if you have some hanging out in your pantry that you don't remember purchasing, throw them out! The dried fruit in these recipes has no added sugar, comes in a sealed pouch and is moist. If your dried fruit is not moist, submerge it in warm water for 10-15 minutes to soften the fruit and drain off the water before using. (Note: There is a recipe for candied citrus peel, which is not dried, on p. 73.)

SPECIAL INGREDIENTS

Diastatic malt powder is the not-so secret ingredient commercial bakers use to promote a strong rise and even golden-brown crust in breads and bagels. The active enzymes in diastatic malt improve the yeast's efficiency, allowing it to grow for the duration of the fermentation period and improving oven-spring and texture. A little goes a long way (about 1 tsp. per 3 cups flour), so if you decide to invest in some, purchase a small amount to ensure freshness. I use the Hoosier Hill Farm brand, but other brands package it in smaller quantities. However, it is not required for any of the recipes.

Espresso powder is a dried powder made from brewed coffee made with specially selected beans (note that it is NOT ground coffee, nor is it instant coffee, although instant coffee may be used as a substitute). The powder is very fine, so it dissolves easily, enhancing the flavor of chocolate in a recipe (much like adding vanilla extract). When used in moderation (typically under 2 tsps.), it does not add any coffee flavor of its own. If you want the added coffee flavor, add it in small increments above the recommended amount. Espresso powder is always listed as optional, but is invaluable as a way to intensify chocolate and/or add coffee flavor. I use the espresso powder from King Arthur Flour or Java and Co., both available on Amazon.

MIXING

I indicate using a stand mixer whenever mixing and kneading is involved in a recipe, but it is not necessary. I used the standard paddle or flex beater (which eliminates the need to scrape down the bowl as often) on my Kitchenaid 6 qt. stand mixer for mixing (unless noted). Any recipe indicating the use of a stand mixer can be mixed with a hand mixer or by hand. Mixing times are important and are detailed in each recipe. Overmixing in certain baked goods such as quick breads will result in overdeveloped gluten and sometimes create unwanted air pockets. In contrast, some recipes that require more developed gluten will also require kneading (see the note below) in addition to mixing. In general, ingredients should be as close to the same temperature as possible before mixing.

A pastry blender (a tool with several narrow strips of stainless steel, joined at a handle) is useful for blending butter or solid shortening into dry ingredients. A food processor can also accomplish this, although it is not necessary. I use a 14-cup Cuisinart for some large jobs like mixing dough for pastry crusts, and a 3-cup "mini-processor" for small tasks like finely chopping nuts. If you choose to use a food processor, use the pulse button to prevent over-mixing.

A bench scraper is an invaluable tool for gathering and mixing dough on a board or work surface. It's also handy for transferring individual items intact (like donuts or Danish pastry) before they are cooked. Although it's not essential, a bench scraper is one kitchen item I'd recommend you purchase (under $10) to make your baking life easier.

KNEADING

Kneading helps develop the gluten in bread and some pastry doughs. Developing gluten is especially important for bread, because it will hold the gasses that the yeast produces, which in turn helps the bread to rise. Gluten will develop naturally to a certain extent, but kneading accelerates the process. There are recommended kneading times in those recipes that require gluten development, but because there are so many variables involved, you may need to adjust the amount of time. I suggest hand-kneading even after using the dough hook on the mixer to ensure the dough is the proper texture.

So how do you know how long to knead? Even if you use a stand mixer to knead, you will need to evaluate the gluten development using your own senses. The first way is to judge the appearance and texture of the dough. When dough has been kneaded adequately, it will have a soft, silky texture and will spring back when poked with a finger. In addition, you will want to use the standard method to test the dough, called the windowpane test. Simply pull off a small piece of dough and stretch it in each direction. If it forms a thin, translucent membrane (like a windowpane), your dough has been kneaded enough. If it breaks or cracks, you should continue kneading.

GREASING THE PAN VS USING LINERS

I typically use parchment paper for ease of cleanup and its easy release, but it is not necessary. If you do not have parchment, greasing the pan is the easiest alternative. A Silpat or other silicone liner may also be substituted on baking sheets. For baked goods that might be hard to remove from the pan, lining the pan with foil and greasing it will substitute for parchment. I often use muffin liners to reduce the amount of cleanup (there are also stand-alone silicone liners available for these). I sometimes use stand-alone paper molds for individual muffins and monkey breads (I like the mini-panettone molds—mainly for presentation), but again, they are not necessary. Flouring a pan after buttering or greasing is important for quick breads so that they rise evenly. It also creates a barrier between the butter and the batter to prevent the butter from melting into the batter. If you're making a chocolate bread or muffin where the flour might affect the appearance, you can use cocoa powder instead of flour for coating the pan.

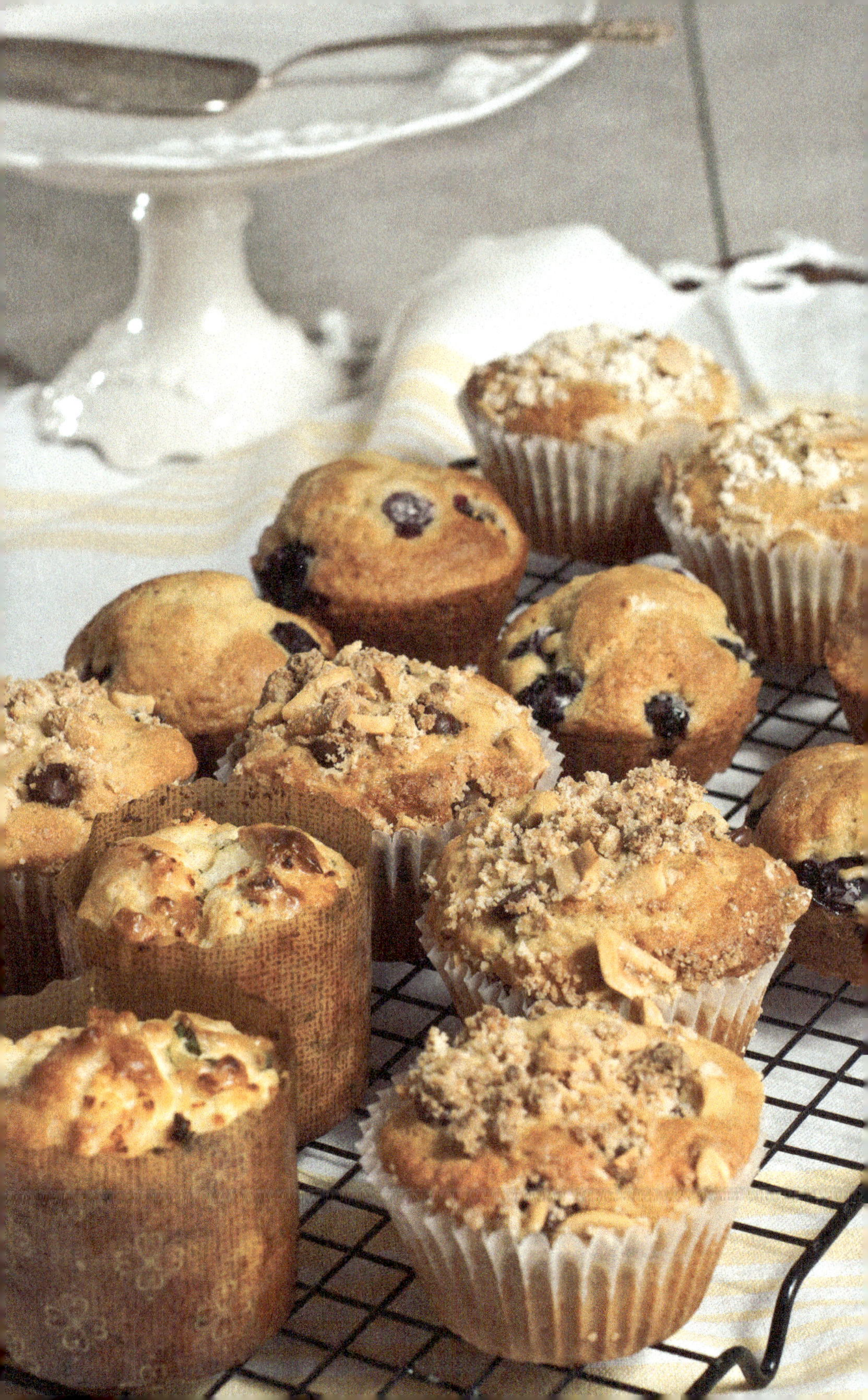

CHAPTER ONE

Muffins, Scones and Quick Breads

- Apricot Muffins with Almond Streusel
- Strawberry Buttermilk Muffins
- Apple Crumb Muffins
- Coconut Muffins with Pineapple Glaze
- Peanut Crumb Chocolate Chip Muffins
- Oatmeal White Chocolate Muffins
- Blueberry Muffins with Cinnamon Sugar
- Pumpkin Coconut Streusel Muffins
- Citrus Yogurt Muffins
- Honey Raisin Bran Muffins
- Coffee Chocolate Pecan Popovers
- Goat Cheese Herb Muffins
- Sweet Corn, Bacon and Jalapeno Muffins
- Lemon Currant Scones
- Cranberry Ginger Cream Scones
- Blueberry Scones
- Cherry Crumb Scones
- Irish Raisin Scones

- Pecan Chocolate Chip Scones
- Pumpkin Ginger Scones
- Ham and Cheese Scones
- Orange Poppy Seed Bread
- Chocolate Cherry Hazelnut Bread
- Blueberry Streusel Bread
- Cranberry Pecan Bread
- Pumpkin Bread with Walnut Streusel
- Walnut Bread
- Strawberry Balsamic Bread
- Raspberry Almond Bread

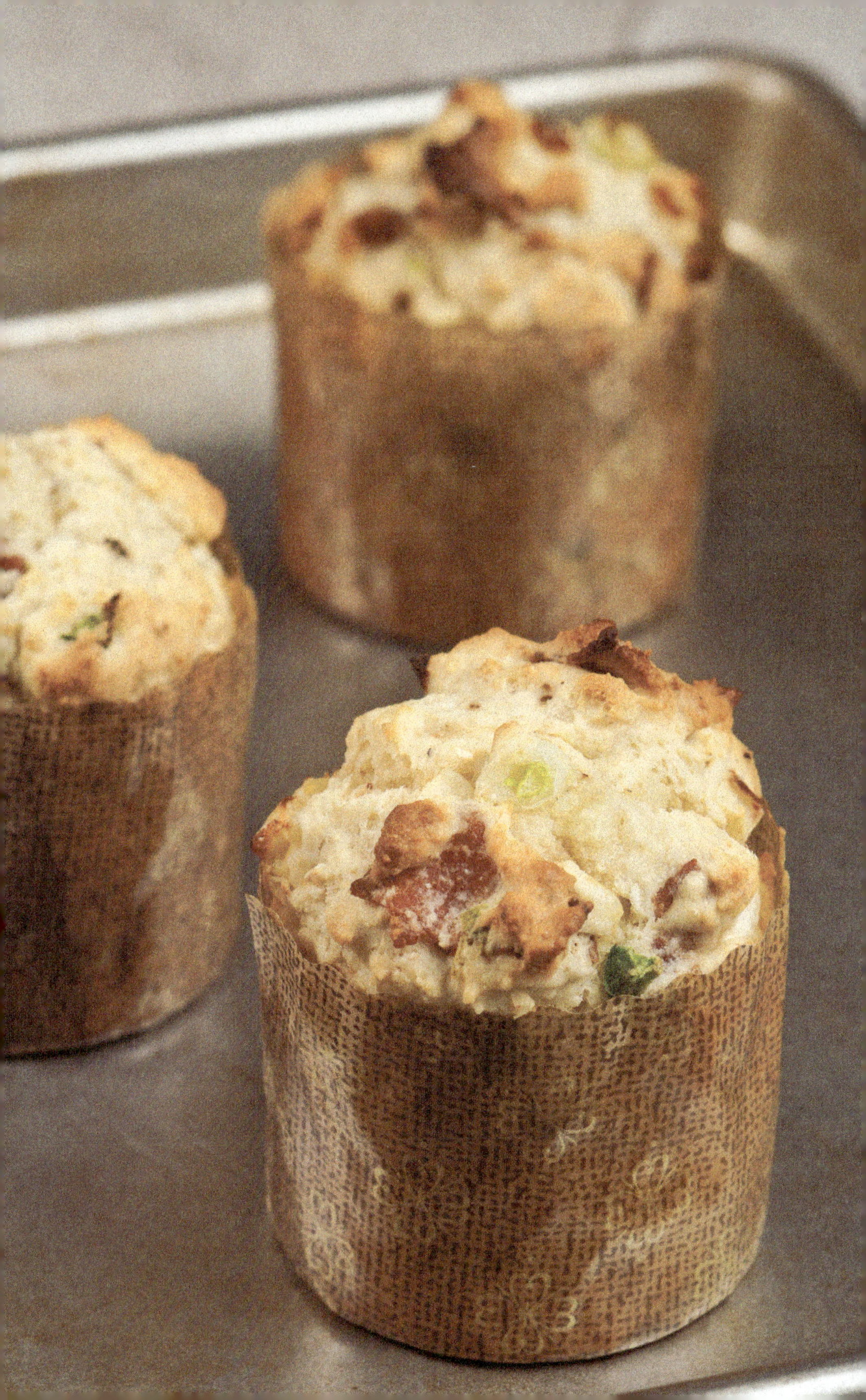

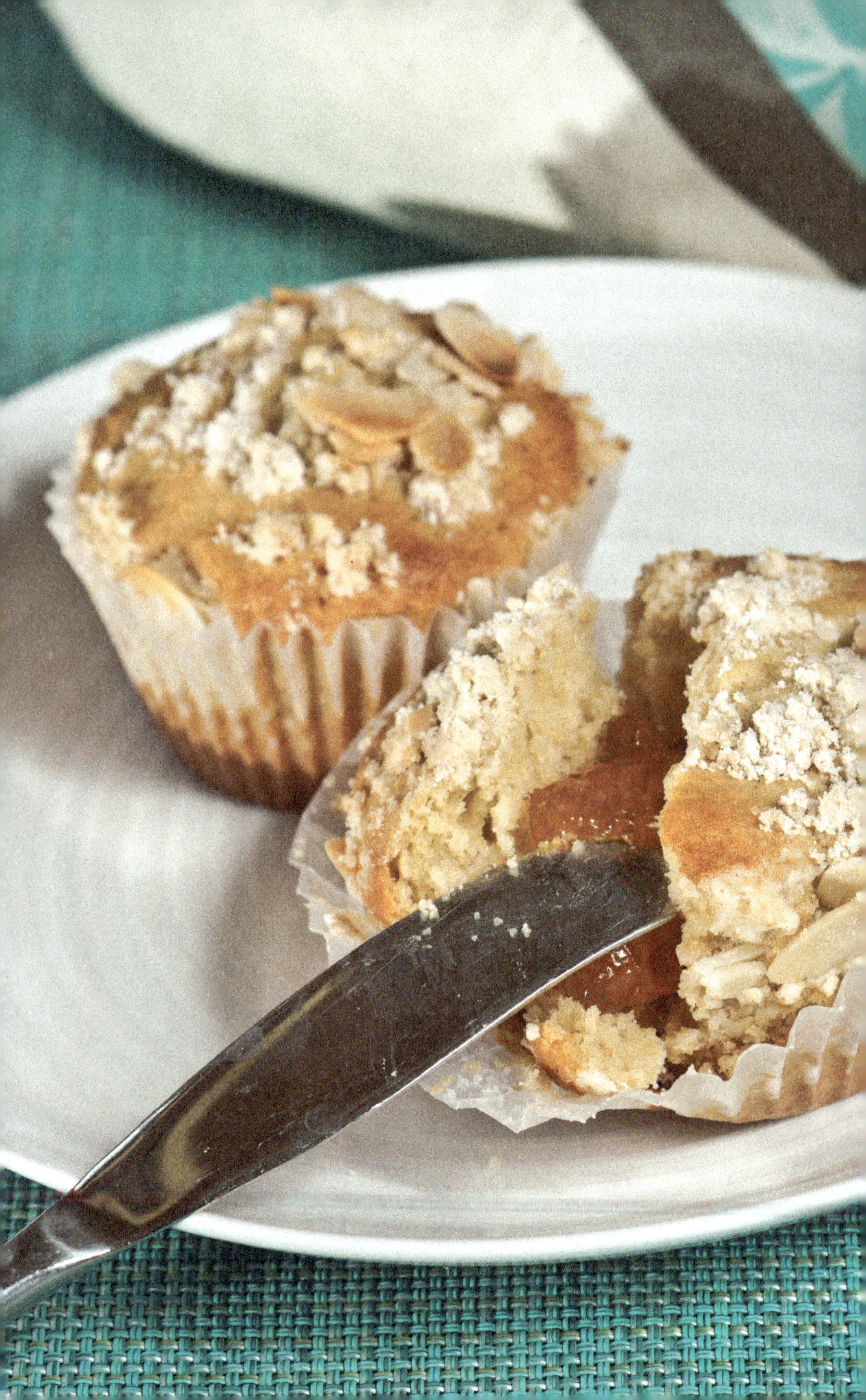

Apricot Muffins with Almond Streusel

I like the flavor combination of apricot and almond, but any flavor jam would work in these fruit-filled muffins.

MAKES 12 MUFFINS

- 2 ¼ cups (10 oz.) all-purpose flour
- 2 tbsps. light brown sugar
- 8 tbsps. unsalted butter, softened
- ½ cup (1.9 oz.) sliced almonds
- 1 tbsp. baking powder
- ½ tsp. baking soda
- ½ tsp. salt
- ⅔ cup (4.7 oz.) granulated sugar
- 2 large eggs
- 1 tsp. almond extract
- 1 cup (8.1 oz.) sour cream
- ½ cup (5.6 oz.) apricot fruit spread (see recipe p. 305)

Preheat the oven to 375 degrees F. Grease 12 standard muffin tins or line with paper liners.

In a small bowl, combine ¼ cup (1.1 oz.) flour and brown sugar. Cut 2 tbsps. butter into the mixture with a pastry blender until crumbly. Stir in the almonds and set aside.

Combine the remaining 2 cups flour, baking powder, baking soda and salt in a medium bowl. In a separate medium bowl, beat the remaining 6 tbsps. butter and granulated sugar until light and lemony. Beat in the eggs, almond extract and sour cream until smooth. Stir the wet ingredients into the flour mixture until just combined.

Spoon half the batter evenly among the muffin tins. Drop a heaping teaspoon of apricot fruit spread into the center of each muffin. Top with the remaining batter, covering the fruit. Divide the almond mixture evenly among the muffins.

Bake for 20–25 minutes, until the tops are golden and springy to the touch (and a toothpick inserted into the center comes out clean). Cool for 5 minutes before serving.

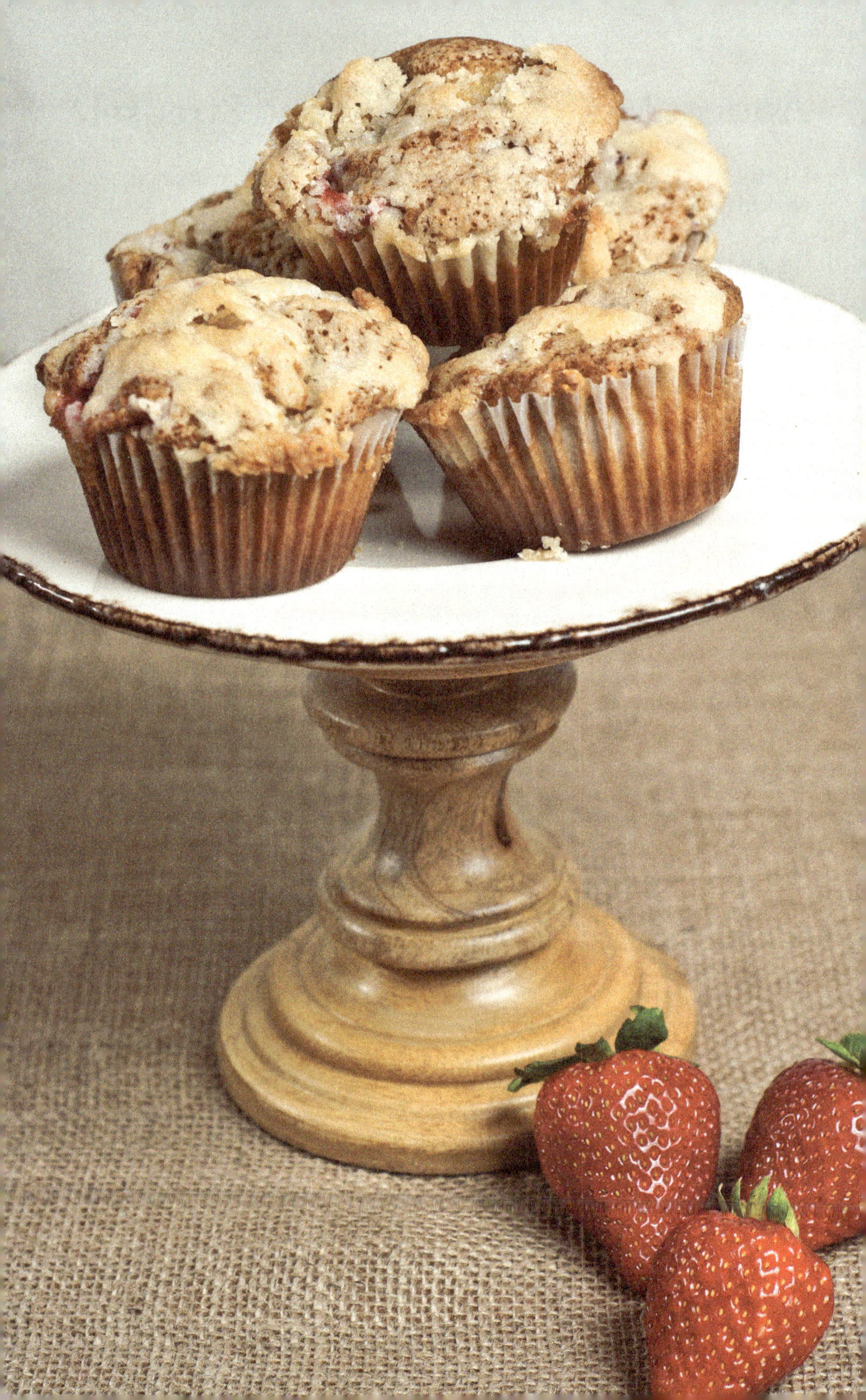

Strawberry Buttermilk Muffins

When strawberries are abundant in season, baking them into these muffins topped with a crisp butter-sugar topping is a great way to enjoy the surplus.

MAKES 12 MUFFINS

- 1 cup (7 oz.) granulated sugar
- 2 ½ cups (11 oz.) plus 3 tbsps. all-purpose flour
- 7 tbsps. unsalted butter, melted
- 1 tsp. baking powder
- ½ tsp. baking soda
- ¼ tsp. salt
- 1 cup (8 fl. oz.) buttermilk
- 1 ¼ tsps. vanilla extract
- 1 large egg
- 2 cups (11 oz.) fresh strawberries, hulled and coarsely chopped

Preheat the oven to 350 degrees F. Grease 12 standard muffin cups or use paper liners and set aside.

To make the topping, combine ⅓ cup (2.3 oz.) sugar and 3 tbsps. flour in a small bowl. Stir in 2 tbsps. melted butter. Set aside.

Combine the remaining 2 ½ cups flour, remaining ⅔ cup (4.7 oz.) sugar, baking powder, baking soda and salt in a large bowl. Whisk the buttermilk, vanilla, egg and remaining 5 tbsps. butter in a separate medium bowl. Make a well in the center of the dry ingredients and pour in the buttermilk mixture. Stir until just combined. Fold in the strawberries.

Divide the batter among the 12 muffin cups. Spoon the topping evenly over the muffins.

Bake for 25–30 minutes, until the tops are golden and springy to the touch (and a toothpick inserted into the center comes out clean).

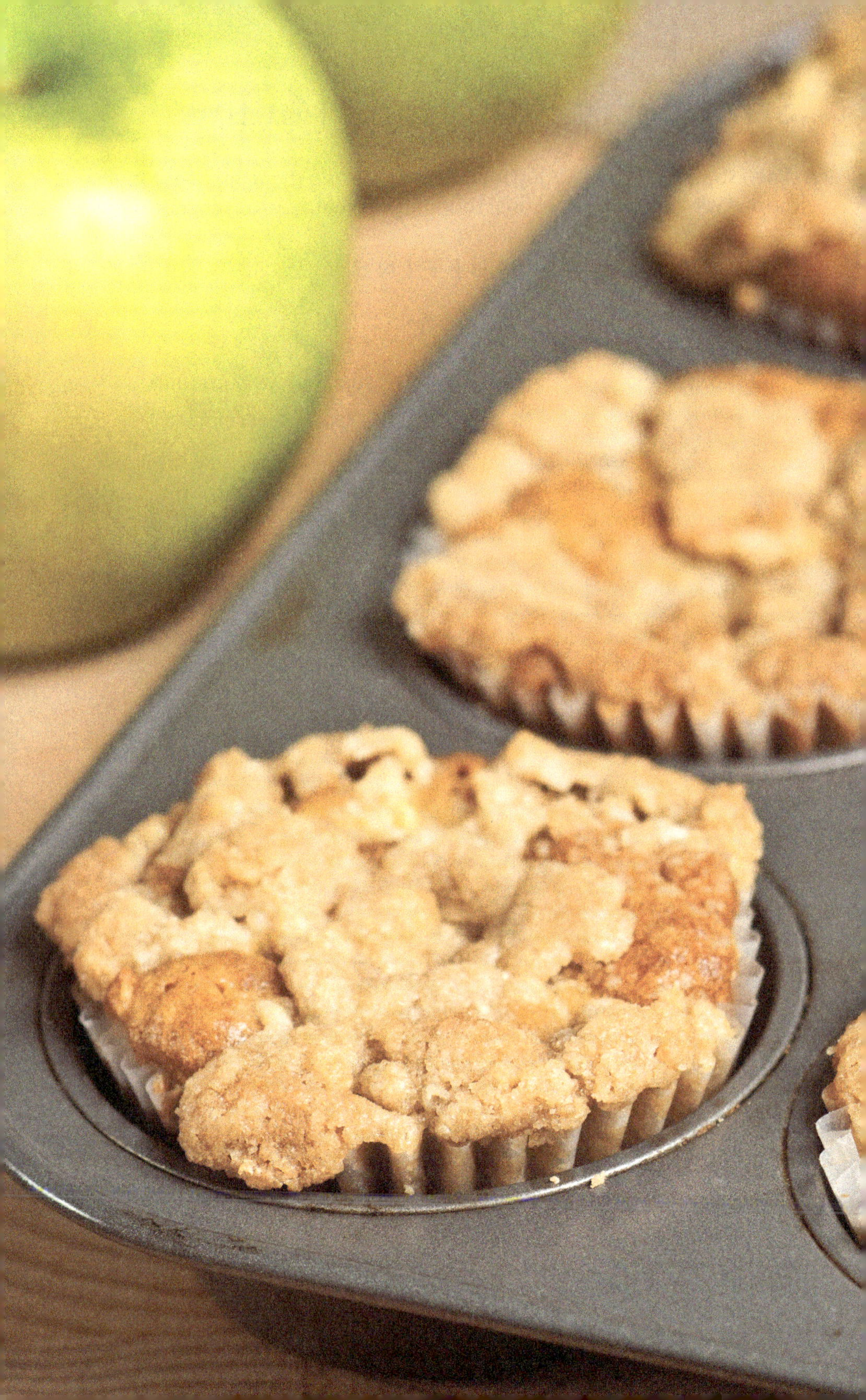

Apple Crumb Muffins

These simple-to-make muffins are moistened with sour cream and diced apples, and finished with a crumb topping.

MAKES 12 MUFFINS

- 2 ¼ cups (10 oz.) all-purpose flour
- ¼ cup (2 oz.) light brown sugar
- ½ tsp. ground cinnamon
- 1 ½ tsps. salt
- 8 tbsps. unsalted butter, cut into bits
- ½ cup (3.5 oz.) granulated sugar
- 1 tsp. baking powder
- ½ tsp. baking soda
- 1 ½ tsps. ground cinnamon
- ½ cup (4 oz.) sour cream
- 1 large egg
- 1 tsp. vanilla extract
- 2 large baking apples, peeled, cored and finely diced

Preheat the oven to 350 degrees F. Lightly grease 12 standard muffin tins or use paper liners and set aside.

Make the crumb topping by combining ½ cup (2.2 oz.) flour, brown sugar, ½ tsp. cinnamon and salt in a medium bowl. Cut 3 tbsps. butter pieces into the mixture with a pastry blender until mixture is crumbly.

Combine the remaining 1 ¾ cups (7.7 oz.) flour, granulated sugar, remaining 1 tsp. salt, baking powder, baking soda and remaining 1 tsp. cinnamon in a large bowl. Add the remaining 5 tbsps. butter pieces and combine with a pastry blender until mixture is crumbly. Whisk the sour cream, egg and vanilla together in a measuring cup. Add the sour cream mixture to the flour mixture and mix until just smooth. Fold in the diced apple.

Evenly divide the batter among the muffin cups. Sprinkle topping evenly over the muffins. Bake the muffins for 20–25 minutes, until tops are golden and springy to the touch (and a toothpick inserted into the center comes out clean). Cool slightly before serving.

Coconut Muffins with Pineapple Glaze

These coconut-filled muffins have a moist texture. The pineapple glaze adds a tropical flair, but they are also delicious with a simple dusting of confectioners' sugar.

MAKES 12 MUFFINS

- 1 ½ cups (6.6 oz.) all-purpose flour
- 1 tsp. baking powder
- ¼ tsp. salt
- 6 tbsps. unsalted butter, softened
- ¾ cup (5.3 oz.) granulated sugar
- 2 large eggs
- ½ cup (4 fl. oz.) whole milk
- ¼ tsp. coconut extract (optional)
- 1 ⅓ cups (4.4 oz.) sweetened shredded coconut
- 1 ½ cups (6.4 oz.) confectioners' sugar
- ½ cup (4.3 oz.) crushed pineapple

Preheat the oven to 350 degrees F. Grease 12 standard muffin tins or use paper liners and set aside.

Combine the flour, baking powder and salt in a large bowl. In a separate bowl, beat 4 tbsps. butter and granulated sugar until fluffy, about 3–4 minutes. Whisk the eggs, milk and extract (if using) together and pour them into the flour mixture. Mix until just combined. Stir in the coconut.

Divide the batter evenly among the muffin cups. Bake for 20–25 minutes, until tops are golden and springy to the touch (and a toothpick inserted into the center comes out clean).

To make the glaze, combine the remaining 2 tbsps. butter, confectioners' sugar, 1 tbsp. water and pineapple until smooth. After the muffins have cooled for 5 minutes, spoon the glaze evenly over the muffins. Allow the glaze to set for 5 minutes before serving.

Peanut Crumb Chocolate Chip Muffins

Peanut butter and chocolate chips come together in these not overly sweet muffins. The crunchy peanut topping is a treat, but the chocolate chip muffins are also delicious plain.

MAKES 12 MUFFINS

- 9 tbsps. unsalted butter
- 2 ½ cups (11 oz.) all-purpose flour
- ¼ cup (2 oz.) plus 2 tbsps. light brown sugar
- 2 tbsps. peanut butter
- ⅓ cup (1.7 oz.) peanuts, coarsely chopped
- ½ cup (3.5 oz.) granulated sugar
- 2 tsps. baking powder
- ½ tsp. baking soda
- ¼ tsp. salt
- ⅔ cup (5.3 fl. oz.) buttermilk
- 2 large eggs
- 1 tsp. vanilla extract
- 1 ½ cups (7 oz.) semi-sweet chocolate chips

Preheat the oven to 350 degrees F. Grease 12 standard muffin tins or use paper liners and set aside.

Melt 8 tbsps. butter and allow to cool slightly. Set aside.

Combine ½ cup (2.2 oz.) flour and 2 tbsps. brown sugar in a medium bowl. Cut the remaining 1 tbsp. butter into the flour mixture. Use a fork to cut the peanut butter into the flour until mixture is crumbly. Stir in the peanuts and set aside.

Combine the remaining 2 cups (8.75 oz.) flour, ¼ cup (2 oz.) brown sugar, granulated sugar, baking powder, baking soda and salt in a large bowl. In a separate bowl, whisk together the melted butter, buttermilk, eggs and vanilla. Make a well in the center of the dry ingredients and pour in the butter mixture. Mix until just combined. Fold in the chocolate chips.

Divide the batter evenly among the muffin cups. Divide the peanut topping evenly over the muffins. Bake for 20–25 minutes, until the tops are golden and springy to the touch (and a toothpick inserted into the center comes out clean). Cool slightly before serving.

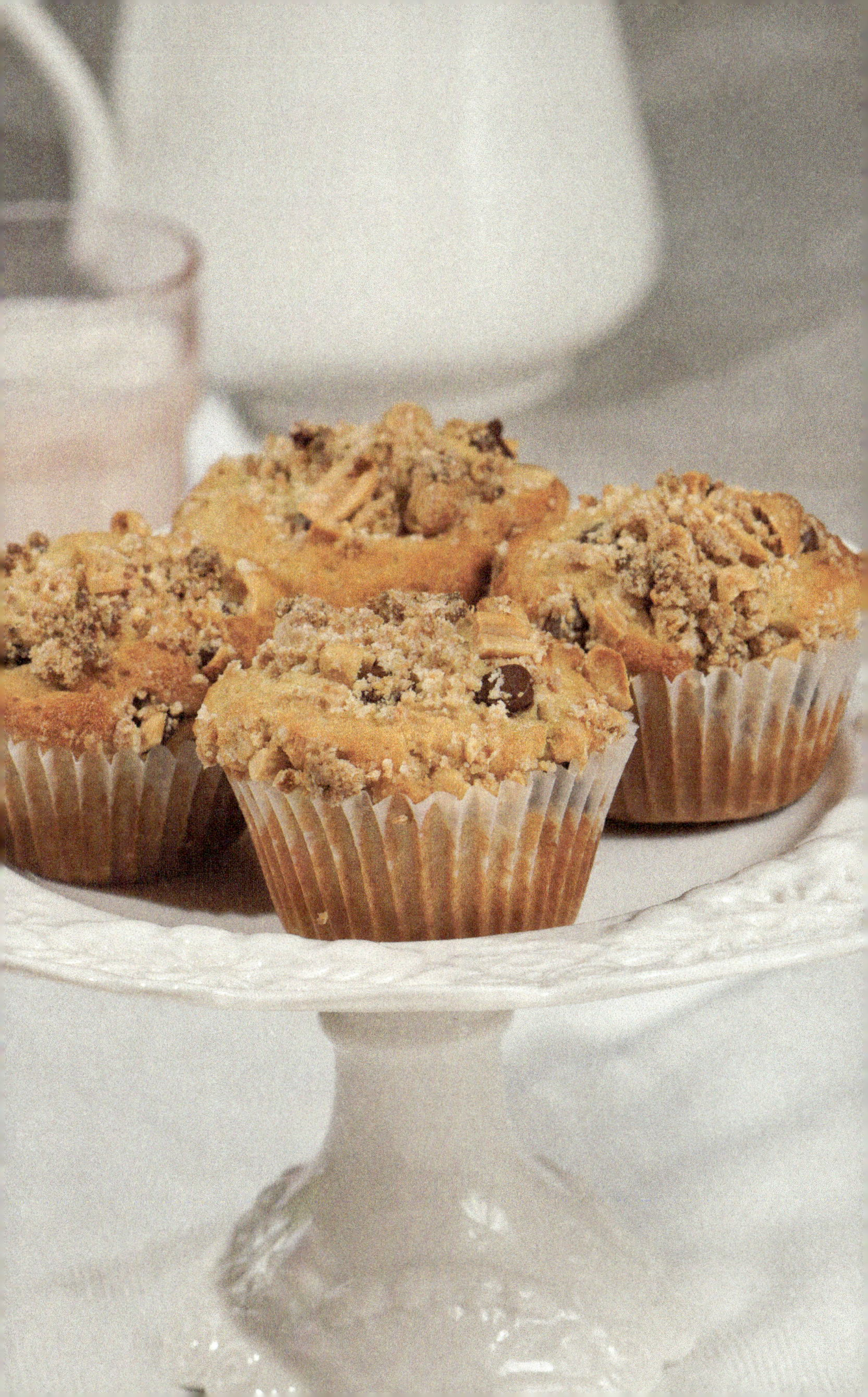

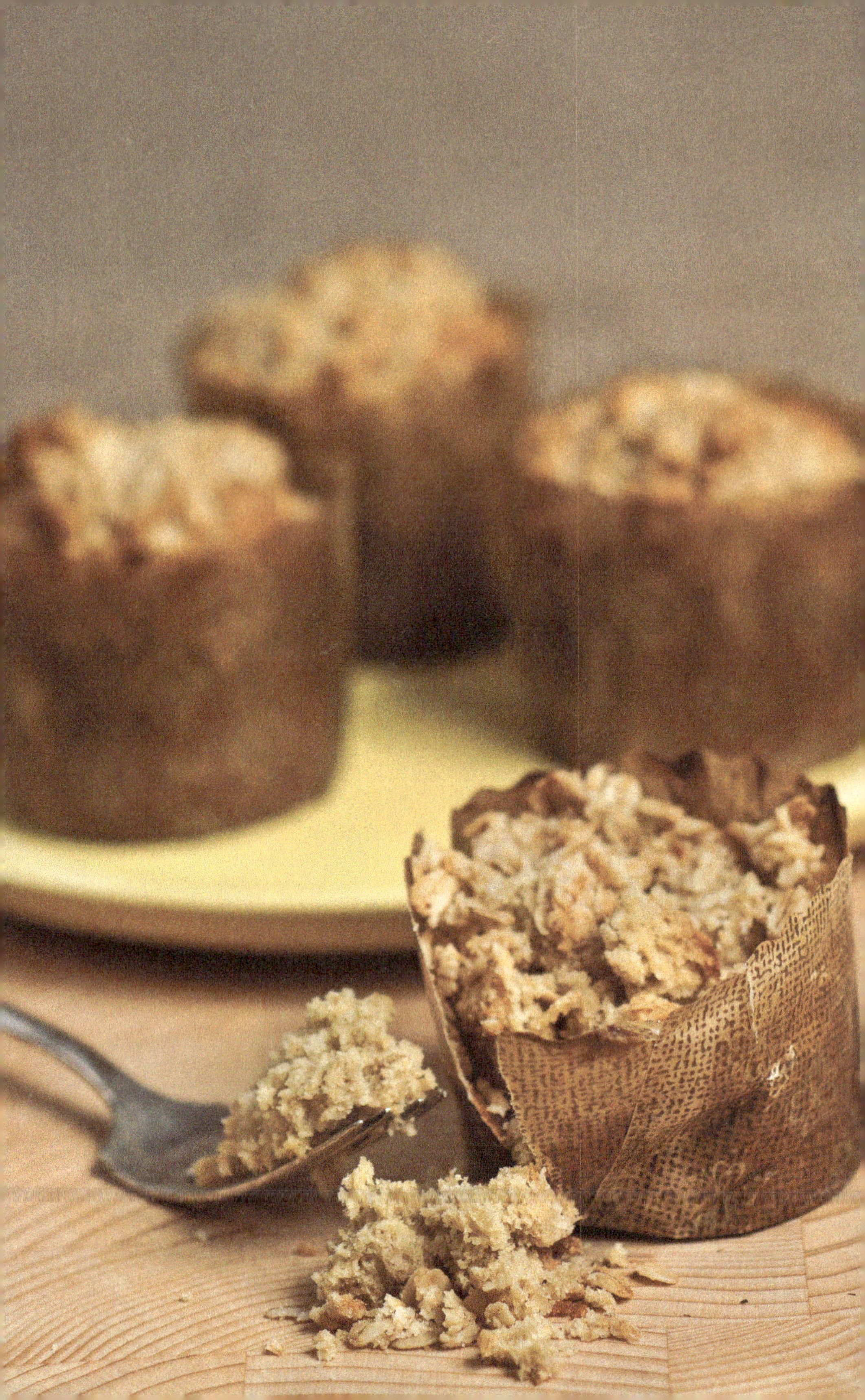

Oatmeal White Chocolate Muffins

White chocolate adds a subtle vanilla-scented sweetness to these oatmeal-filled muffins.

MAKES 12 MUFFINS

- 5 tbsps. unsalted butter
- 2 cups (6.7 oz.) old-fashioned oats
- ½ cup (4 oz.) plus 2 tbsps. light brown sugar
- 1 ¼ cups (5.5 oz.) all-purpose flour
- 1 tsp. baking powder
- ½ tsp. baking soda
- ¼ tsp. salt
- 1 tsp. ground ginger
- 1 ¼ tsps. ground cinnamon
- ½ tsp. ground nutmeg
- 1 large egg
- 1 cup (8.6 oz.) applesauce (see recipe p. 309)
- ½ cup (4 fl. oz.) whole milk
- 1 cup (5 oz.) white chocolate chips
- 3 tbsps. granulated sugar

Preheat the oven to 350 degrees F. Line 12 standard muffin tins with paper liners.

Melt 2 tbsps. butter. Combine ½ cup (0.9 oz.) oats and 2 tbsps. brown sugar in a small bowl. Add the melted butter and use a fork to combine. Set aside.

Whisk the remaining 1 ½ cups (2.7 oz.) oats, flour, baking powder, baking soda, salt, ginger, cinnamon and nutmeg together in a medium bowl. Combine the remaining 3 tbsps. butter and remaining ½ cup (4 oz.) brown sugar in the bowl of a stand mixer. Cream until light and fluffy. Add the egg and beat to combine. Add half the flour mixture and mix to combine. Stir in the applesauce and milk. Mix in the remaining flour mixture until just combined. Stir in the white chocolate.

Divide the batter among the 12 muffin tins. Sprinkle the reserved oat mixture evenly over the muffins.

Bake for 25–30 minutes, until the tops are golden and springy to the touch (and a toothpick inserted into the center comes out clean). Cool slightly before serving.

Blueberry Muffins with Cinnamon Sugar

I prefer to use frozen Maine blueberries which are smaller and often more flavorful than cultivated berries in these muffins to prevent the blueberries from streaking the batter. Substitute local seasonal berries if available.

MAKES 12 MUFFINS

- 2 cups (8.75 oz.) plus 2 tbsps. all-purpose flour
- 2 tsps. baking powder
- ½ tsp. salt
- 12 tbsps. unsalted butter, softened
- 1 ⅓ cup (9.4 oz.) granulated sugar
- 2 large eggs
- 1 cup (8 fl. oz.) whole milk
- 1 ½ cups (7.8 oz.) blueberries
- 1 tbsp. cinnamon

Preheat the oven to 375 degrees F. Grease 12 standard muffin tins or use paper liners and set aside.

Combine 2 cups (8.75 oz.) flour, baking powder and salt in a medium bowl and set aside.

Combine 8 tbsps. butter and ⅔ cup (4.7 oz.) granulated sugar in the bowl of a stand mixer until fluffy. Add the eggs one at a time and beat to combine. Add half the flour mixture and mix to combine. Add the buttermilk and mix to combine. Mix in the remaining flour mixture until just combined. Toss the blueberries with the remaining 2 tbsps. flour. Fold the blueberries into the batter.

Divide the batter among the 12 muffin tins. Bake for 20–25 minutes, until the tops are golden and springy to the touch (and a toothpick inserted into the center comes out clean).

Combine the remaining ⅔ cup (4.7 oz.) sugar and cinnamon in a small bowl. Melt the remaining 4 tbsps. butter and brush it evenly over the tops of the warm muffins. Sprinkle the cinnamon sugar evenly over the muffin tops to coat. Allow the muffins to cool for 5 minutes before serving.

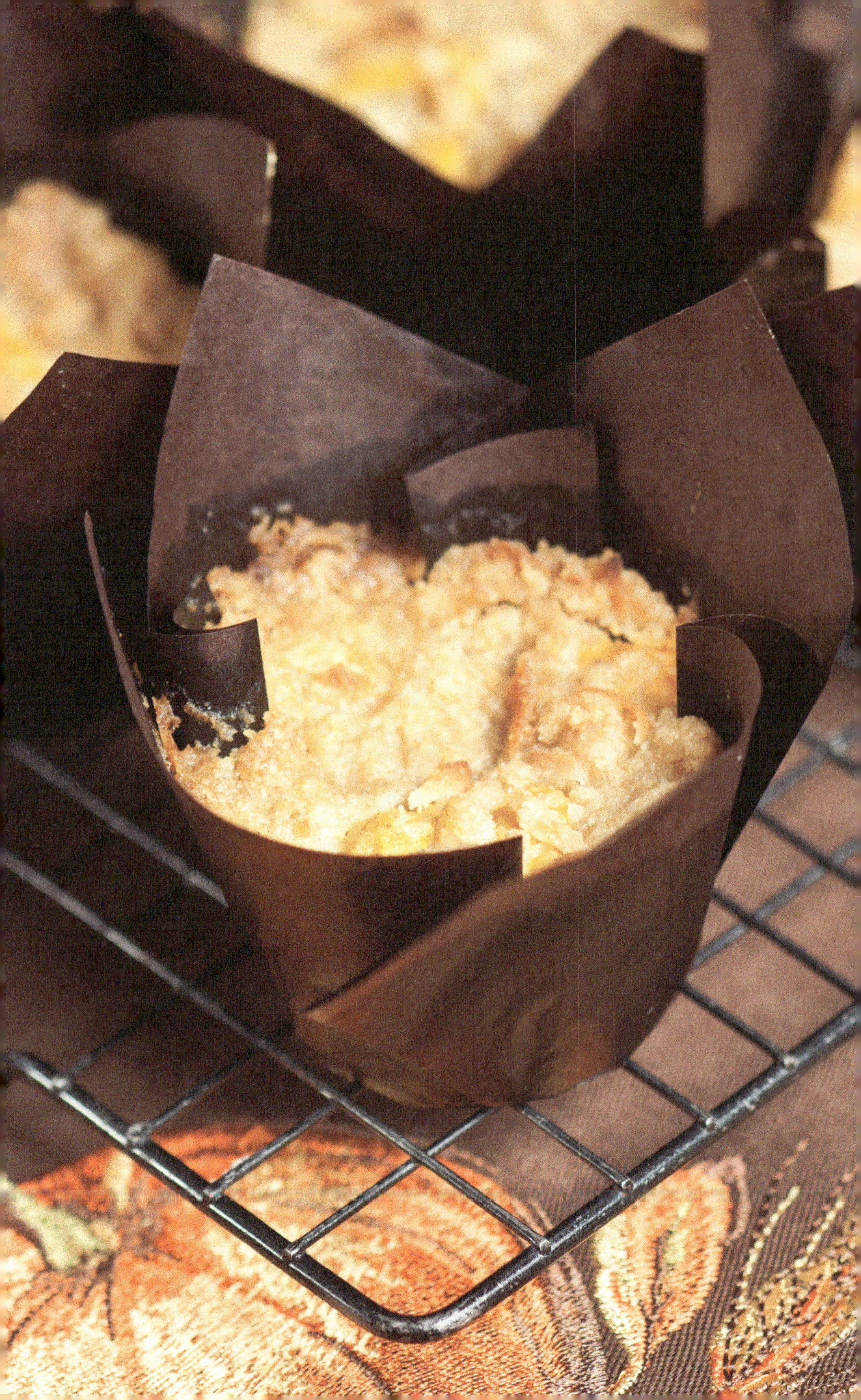

Pumpkin Coconut Streusel Muffins

Pumpkin and coconut are a complementary pairing in this moist streusel-topped muffin.

MAKES 12 MUFFINS

- 2 ½ cups (11 oz.) all-purpose flour
- ¼ cup (2 oz.) plus 3 tbsps. light brown sugar
- 8 tbsps. unsalted butter, softened
- ¼ cup (0.8 oz.) sweetened flake coconut
- 1 tsp. baking powder
- ½ tsp. baking soda
- ¼ tsp. salt
- 1 tsp. ground cinnamon
- ½ tsp. ground ginger
- ½ tsp. ground nutmeg
- ¼ tsp. ground cloves
- ½ cup (3.5 oz.) granulated sugar
- 1 cup (8.6 oz.) pumpkin puree
- 2 large eggs
- ½ cup (4 fl. oz.) buttermilk

Preheat oven to 350 degrees F. Grease 12 standard muffin tins or use paper liners and set aside.

Make the streusel topping by combining ½ cup (2.2 oz.) flour and 3 tbsps. brown sugar in a medium bowl. Cut 3 tbsps. butter into bits. Cut the butter pieces into the mixture with a pastry blender until mixture is crumbly. Fold in the coconut and set aside.

In a medium bowl, sift together the remaining 2 cups (8.75 oz.) flour, baking powder, baking soda, salt, cinnamon, ginger, nutmeg and cloves.

Combine the remaining 5 tbsps. butter, remaining ¼ cup (2 oz.) brown sugar and granulated sugar in the bowl of a stand mixer. Beat until fluffy. Add the pumpkin and eggs and beat until smooth. Stir in half of the flour mixture and beat until smooth. Mix in the buttermilk. Mix in the remaining flour mixture until just combined. Evenly divide the batter among the muffin cups. Sprinkle the streusel topping evenly over the muffins.

Bake for 20–25 minutes, until tops are golden and springy to the touch (and a toothpick inserted into the center comes out clean). Cool slightly before serving.

Citrus Yogurt Muffins

Orange and lemon balance the tang of yogurt in these moist muffins, flavored with poppy seeds.

MAKES 12 MUFFINS

- 2 cups (8.75 oz.) all-purpose flour
- 1 tsp. baking powder
- ½ tsp. baking soda
- ½ tsp. salt
- 8 tbsps. unsalted butter, softened
- ¾ cup (5.3 oz.) granulated sugar
- 2 large eggs
- 1 cup (8.6 oz.) plain yogurt
- 1 tsp. lemon zest
- 1 tsp. orange zest
- 1 cup (4.23 oz.) confectioners' sugar
- 1 tsp. lemon juice
- 2 tsps. orange juice
- 2 tsps. poppy seeds

Preheat the oven to 350 degrees F. Grease 12 standard muffin tins or use paper liners and set aside.

Whisk the flour, baking powder, baking soda and salt together in a medium bowl and set aside. Combine the butter and sugar in the bowl of a stand mixer. Cream until light and fluffy. Add the eggs one at a time and beat to combine. Add half the flour mixture and mix to combine. Add the yogurt and mix to combine. Mix in the remaining flour mixture until just combined. Stir in ½ tsp. lemon zest and ½ tsp. orange zest.

Divide the batter among the 12 muffin tins. Bake for 20–25 minutes, until the tops are golden and springy to the touch (and a toothpick inserted into the center comes out clean).

Whisk together the confectioners' sugar, lemon juice and orange juice until smooth. Stir the remaining ½ tsp. lemon zest, orange zest and poppy seeds.

Allow the muffins to cool for 5 minutes. Transfer the muffins to a rack. Divide the glaze evenly among the warm muffins. Allow the glaze to set up for 5 minutes before serving.

Honey Raisin Bran Muffins

The dense, moist texture of these flavorful muffins is similar to a sticky pudding.

MAKES 12 MUFFINS

- 2 cups (11.6 oz.) dark raisins
- 10 tbsps. unsalted butter, softened
- 1/2 cup (3.5 oz.) granulated sugar
- 1/2 cup (4 oz.) light brown sugar
- 2 tbsps. molasses
- 1 1/4 cups (5.5 oz.) all-purpose flour
- 3/4 cup (2.7 oz.) wheat bran

- 1 1/2 tsps. baking soda
- 1/2 tsp. salt
- 1 tsp. finely grated orange zest
- 1/3 cup (4 oz.) honey
- 2 large eggs
- 1/2 cup (4 fl. oz.) buttermilk
- 2 tsps. vanilla extract

Soak the raisins for 10 minutes in boiling water. Drain the water and puree the raisins in a food processor (or mince by hand) and set aside.

Preheat the oven to 350 degrees F.

Combine 4 tbsps. butter, granulated sugar and brown sugar and beat until fluffy. Add the molasses and 1 tbsp. warm water. Brush the insides of 12 standard muffin tins with the butter mixture, reserving the rest. Set aside.

Combine the flour, bran, baking soda, salt and orange zest in a large bowl. Melt the remaining 6 tbsps. butter and whisk in the honey until smooth. In a separate bowl, whisk together the eggs, buttermilk and vanilla until combined. Stir in the butter-honey mixture and pureed raisins until combined.

Make a well in the center of the dry ingredients and pour in the raisin mixture. Mix until just combined.

Divide the batter among the 12 muffin tins. Bake for 15 minutes. Brush any remaining glaze over the tops of the muffins and bake for

5-8 minutes longer, until a toothpick inserted into the center comes out clean. Allow the muffins to cool in the pan for 3 minutes. Transfer the muffins to a rack to finish cooling before serving.

Coffee Chocolate Pecan Popovers

While these are not muffins, they are so good for breakfast that I had to fit them in here. The key to great popovers is getting the pan very hot before adding the batter and then not opening the oven door except to rotate the pan.

MAKES 6 LARGE POPOVERS

- 2 tbsps. unsalted butter, melted
- 3 large eggs
- 1 ½ cups (12 oz.) whole milk, warmed (about 110–115 degrees F)
- 1 tsp. espresso powder (or substitute 1 tsp. instant coffee)
- ¼ cup (1 oz.) finely ground pecans
- 1 cup (4.4 oz.) all-purpose flour
- ¼ tsp. salt
- ¼ cup (1.2 oz.) bittersweet chocolate shavings

Preheat the oven to 400 degrees F.

Whisk together 1 tbsp. butter, eggs and milk in a large bowl. Add the espresso powder, pecans and flour and beat until smooth, then set aside.

Grease 6 popover tins (or use muffin tins) with the remaining 1 tbsp. melted butter and place the pan in the oven for 3–4 minutes.

Remove the pan from the oven and fill the cups about ¾ full with batter. Divide the chocolate evenly among the tins and top with the remaining batter. Bake for 15 minutes. Rotate the pan 180 degrees and bake for 30 minutes longer without opening the oven. The popovers should be puffed and golden on top. Remove from the oven and serve immediately.

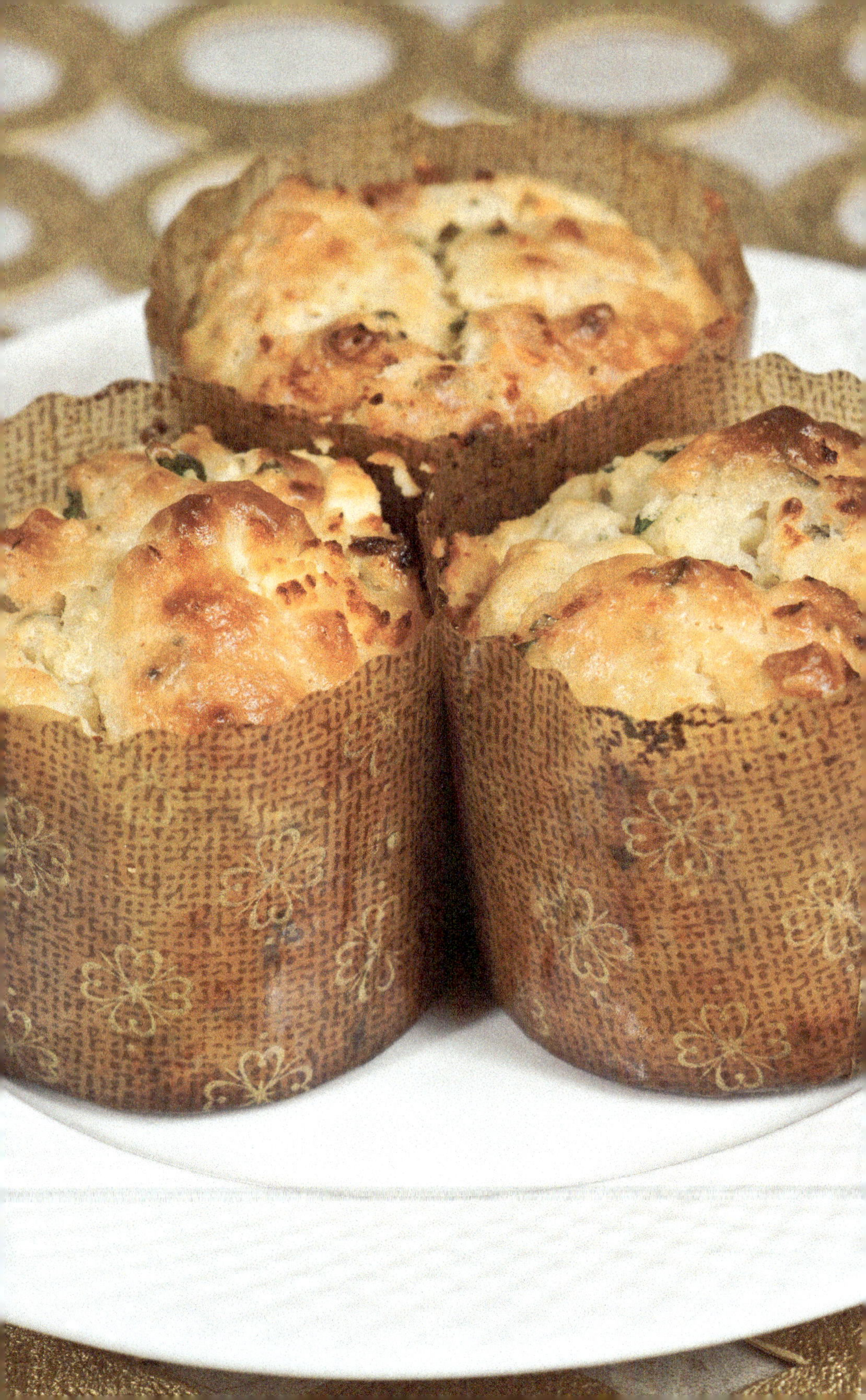

Goat Cheese Herb Muffins

Savory muffins flavored with goat cheese and herbs are reminiscent of the flavors of the south of France. Add chopped Kalamata olives, sun-dried tomatoes or roasted red peppers for interesting variations.

MAKES 12 MUFFINS

- 2 cups (8.75 oz.) all-purpose flour
- 1 tsp. granulated sugar
- 1 tbsp. baking powder
- ½ tsp. baking soda
- ½ tsp. salt
- 1 tsp. chopped fresh thyme
- ¼ tsp. chopped fresh sage
- 1 tsp. herbs de Provence (or substitute dried sage)
- 8 tbsps. unsalted butter, softened
- 2 large eggs
- 1 tsp. Dijon mustard
- 1 cup (8.6 oz.) plain full fat yogurt
- ½ cup (2 oz.) crumbled fresh goat cheese

Preheat the oven to 375 degrees F. Grease 12 standard muffin tins or use paper liners and set aside.

Combine the flour, sugar, baking powder, baking soda, salt, thyme, sage and herbs de Provence in a large bowl. Cut in the butter with a pastry blender until crumbly. Whisk together the eggs, mustard and yogurt in a measuring cup. Make a well in the center of the dry ingredients and pour in the yogurt mixture. Stir until just combined. Fold in the crumbled goat cheese. Divide the mixture evenly among the 12 muffin tins.

Bake for 20–25 minutes, until the tops are golden and firm to the touch. Cool for 5 minutes before serving.

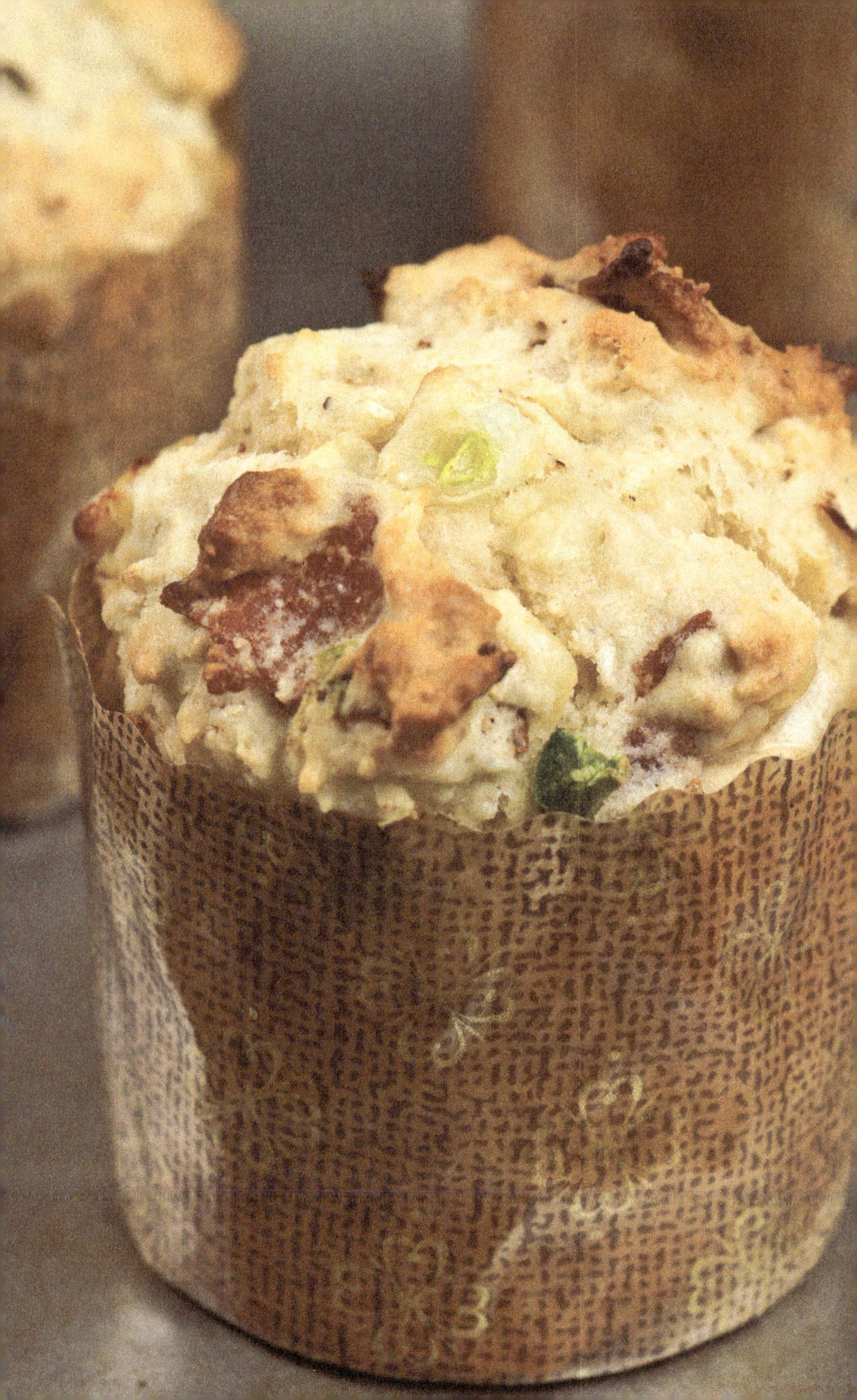

Sweet Corn, Bacon and Jalapeno Muffins

These cornmeal muffins with a Southwest twist make a delicious accompaniment to eggs. Slice them in half and serve them toasted, topped with poached eggs, for a special breakfast treat.

MAKES 12 MUFFINS

- 6 slices bacon
- 1 cup (4.4 oz.) all-purpose flour
- 1 cup (5.6 oz.) cornmeal, white or yellow
- 1 tbsp. baking powder
- ½ tsp. salt
- 1 tsp. crushed red pepper
- ⅔ cup (5.4 oz.) sour cream
- ¾ cup (6 fl. oz.) whole milk
- 4 tbsps. unsalted butter, melted
- 1 large egg
- 2 tsps. minced jalapeno
- 3 scallions, trimmed and minced
- ½ cup (2.9 oz.) cooked corn
- 2 tsps. chopped cilantro (optional)

Preheat the oven to 375 degrees. Grease 12 standard muffin tins or line with paper liners.

Place the bacon in a large skillet. Cook over medium-low heat until crisp, draining off excess fat as necessary, about 4–5 minutes per side. Drain on paper towels and allow to cool. Crumble the bacon into a small bowl and set aside.

Combine the flour, cornmeal, baking powder, salt and red pepper in a large bowl. In a separate medium bowl, whisk together the sour cream, milk, butter and egg. Make a well in the center of the dry ingredients and pour in the sour cream mixture. Stir until just combined. Fold in the crumbled bacon, jalapeno, scallions, corn and cilantro (if using). Divide the mixture evenly among the 12 muffin tins.

Bake for 20–25 minutes, until the tops are golden and firm to the touch. Cool for 5 minutes before serving.

Lemon Currant Scones

Lemon-scented scones studded with currants are a wonderful breakfast treat. The dough should be just moist, so be careful not to overmix it after adding the liquid. These scones (along with some of the recipes to follow) are cut into larger wedges, but can be made into smaller scones according to taste (see the Chef's Tip). Scone dough may also be shaped and then frozen prior to baking, making it easy to bake off a few warm-from-the-oven scones at a time.

MAKES 10–12 SCONES

- 2 cups (8.75 oz.) all-purpose flour
- ¼ cup (1.8 oz.) granulated sugar
- 2 ½ tsps. baking powder
- ½ tsp. baking soda
- ½ tsp. salt
- 1 tbsp. finely grated lemon zest
- 6 tbsps. unsalted butter, cut into bits

- ½ cup (2.9 oz.) currants (reconstituted in warm water if desired)
- 1 large egg
- ⅔ cup (5.3 oz.) buttermilk
- 1 cup (4.2 oz.) confectioners' sugar
- 2 tbsps. lemon juice

Preheat the oven to 375 degrees F. Line a baking sheet with parchment paper or lightly grease.

Combine the flour, sugar, baking powder, baking soda, salt and lemon zest in a large bowl. Cut the butter into the flour mixture with a pastry blender to form a coarse mixture. Stir in the currants. Whisk the egg and buttermilk together in a measuring cup and pour it into the flour butter mixture. Stir until just combined.

Turn the dough onto a lightly floured surface and press it into an 8" disk about ½" thick. Cut the dough in half. Cut each half into 5–6 even triangles and place them on the baking sheet at least 1" apart. Bake 12–15 minutes, until the tops are golden brown. Transfer the scones to a rack to cool slightly.

Whisk together the confectioners' sugar and lemon juice to form a glaze. Drizzle the glaze evenly over the scones. Allow the glaze to set up to 5 minutes before serving.

Chef's Tip: To make 20–24 smaller scones, divide the dough in half. Form each half into a disk about 4" in diameter and cut each disk in half. Cut each half into 5–6 even triangles and proceed with baking.

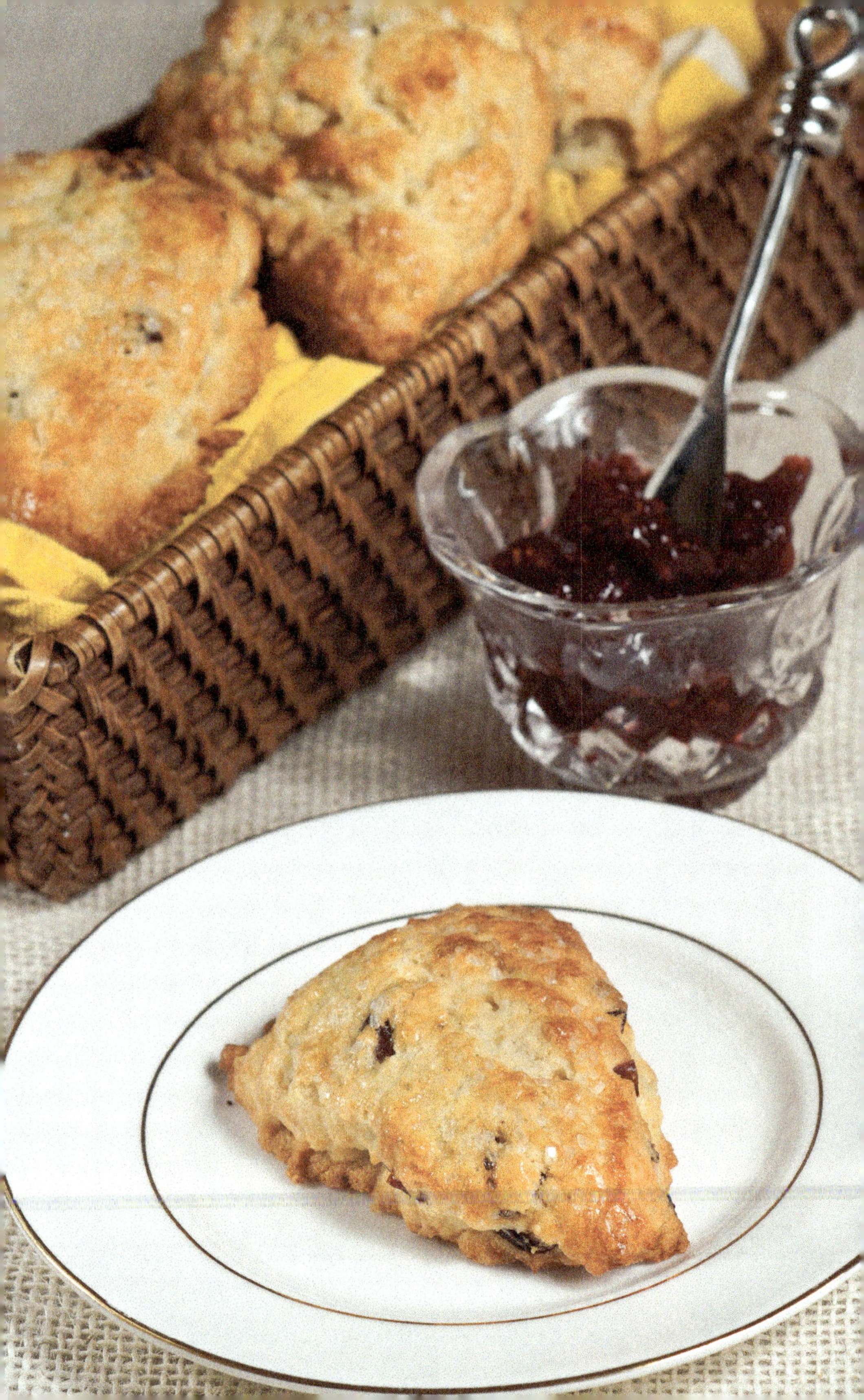

Cranberry Ginger Cream Scones

Cream scones have a tender, cake-like crumb with flaky layers. Here they are formed into the traditional triangle scones. Because the dough is so tender, these may also be cut out with a round cookie cutter or other shape, gathering and reshaping the scraps as necessary without toughening the scones.

MAKES 10-12 SCONES

- 1 ⅔ (7.3 oz.) cups all-purpose flour
- ⅓ cup (1.9 oz.) white cornmeal
- ⅓ cup (2.3 oz.) granulated sugar
- 2 tsps. baking powder
- ¼ tsp. salt
- 5 tbsps. unsalted butter, cut into bits
- ¾ cup (6 fl. oz.) heavy cream
- ¾ cup (4.4 oz.) dried cranberries
- ¼ cup (1.5 oz.) diced candied ginger
- 1 large egg
- 2 tsps. sanding sugar

Preheat the oven to 375 degrees F. Line a baking sheet with parchment paper.

Combine the flour, cornmeal, sugar, baking powder and salt in a large bowl. Cut the butter in with a pastry blender until crumbly. Form a well in the center of the flour mixture and pour in the cream. Stir the mixture until just combined. Stir in the cranberries and ginger. Form the dough into a ball and transfer it to a lightly floured work surface. Knead the dough for 1 minute.

Press the dough into a 10" x 15" rectangle about ¼" thick. Using the long side, roll the dough up as if making a jellyroll. Flatten the dough and fold it up in half. Press the dough into an 8" disk about ½" thick. Cut the dough in half. Cut each half into 5-6 even triangles and place them on the baking sheet at least 1" apart. Whisk the egg with a pinch of salt in a small bowl. Brush the tops of the scones with egg and sprinkle the sanding sugar evenly over top.

Bake for 15-18 minutes, until golden brown. Cool for 5 minutes on a rack before serving. Store completely cooled scones in an airtight container for up to 3 days.

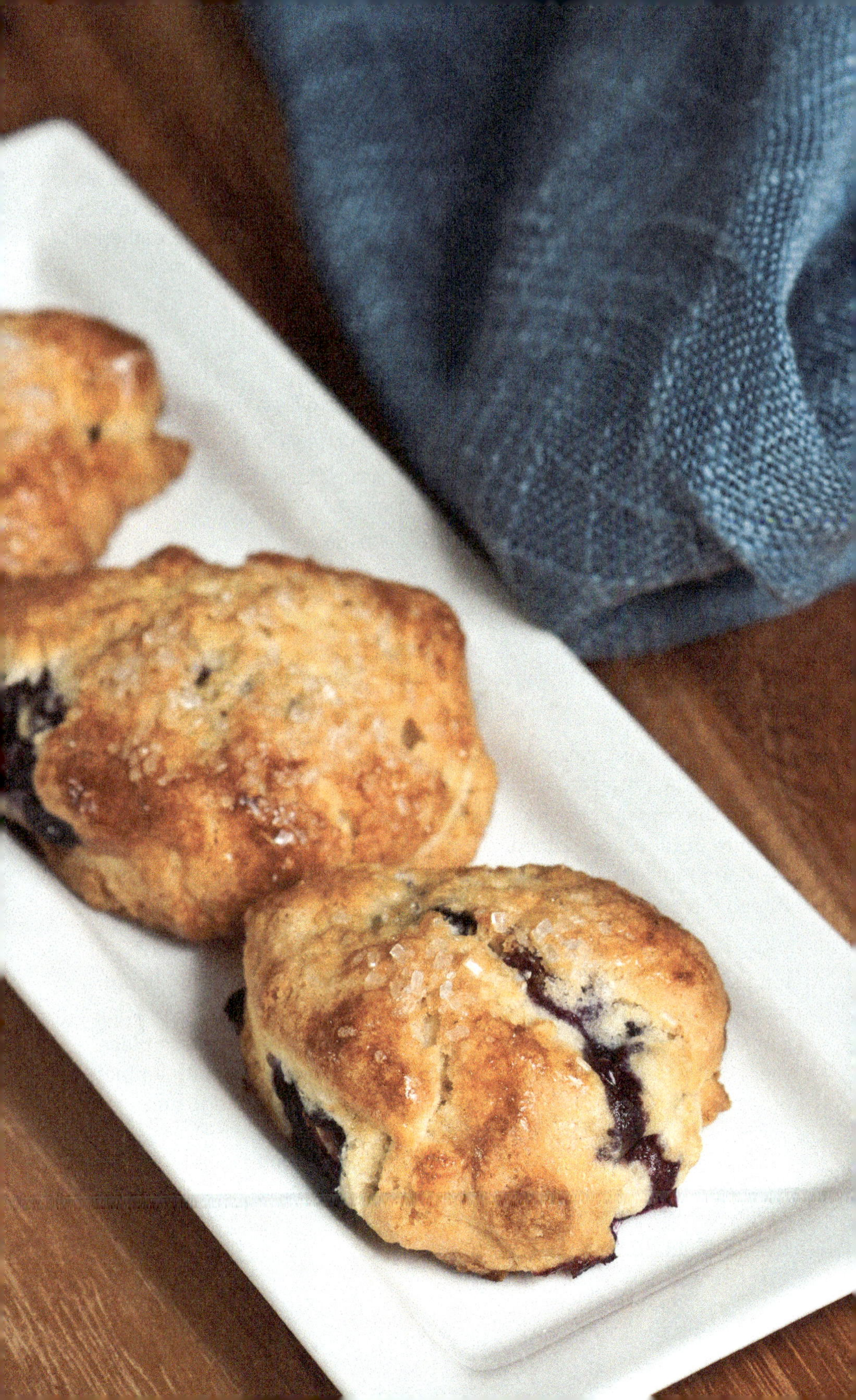

Blueberry Scones

These scones hold their shape better after freezing, so they are a natural for making ahead. Keep a stash in your freezer (as we did at the inn) for a quickly baked breakfast treat.

MAKES 10–12 SCONES

- 3 cups (13.2 oz.) all-purpose flour
- ½ cup (3.5 oz.) granulated sugar
- 1 tbsp. baking powder
- 1 tsp. baking soda
- ½ tsp. salt

- 8 tbsps. unsalted butter, cut into bits
- ¾ cup (6 fl. oz.) buttermilk
- 1 cup (5.2 oz.) blueberries, frozen
- 2 tbsps. heavy cream
- 1 tsp. sanding sugar

Combine the flour, sugar, baking powder, baking soda and salt in a large bowl. Cut in the butter with a pastry blender until the mixture is crumbly. Stir in the buttermilk. Fold in the blueberries. Form the dough into a ball with lightly floured hands. Divide the dough in half and press each half into a 4" disk. Wrap the dough in plastic wrap and freeze for at least 30 minutes or up to 3 days.

Preheat the oven to 375 degrees F. Line a baking sheet with parchment paper.

Press 1 piece of the dough into an 8" circle. Cut the dough in half. Cut each half into 5–6 even triangles and place them on the baking sheet at least 1" apart. Brush the tops of the scones with cream and sprinkle the sugar evenly over the tops.

Bake for 18–20 minutes, until golden brown. Cool for 5 minutes before serving. Store completely cooled scones in an airtight container for up to 3 days.

Cherry Crumb Scones

BAKING FOR BREAKFAST

Cherry Crumb Scones

These round scones are flavored with orange zest and dried cherries, and baked with a crunchy crumb topping.

MAKES 8 LARGE ROUND SCONES

- 3 cups (13.2 oz.) all-purpose flour
- 3 tbsps. light brown sugar
- ¼ tsp. ground cinnamon
- 11 tbsps. unsalted butter, cut into bits
- ¼ cup (1.8 oz.) granulated sugar
- 2 ½ tsps. baking powder
- ½ tsp. salt
- 1 tsp. finely grated orange zest
- ½ cup (2.9 oz.) dried tart cherries
- ¾ cup (6 fl. oz.) buttermilk
- 1 large egg

Preheat oven to 375 degrees F. Line a baking sheet with parchment.

In a small bowl, combine ½ cup (2.2 oz.) flour, brown sugar and cinnamon. Cut 3 tbsps. butter into the mixture with a pastry blender until crumbly. Set aside.

Combine the remaining 2 ½ cups flour (11 oz.), granulated sugar, baking powder, salt and orange zest in a large bowl. Cut the remaining 8 tbsps. butter into the flour mixture with a pastry blender until crumbly. Whisk the egg and buttermilk together in a measuring cup. Stir the wet ingredients into the flour mixture until just combined.

Form the dough into a ball and transfer it to a lightly floured work surface. Knead the dough for 1 minute. Press the dough into a 9" disk about 1" thick. Using a floured 3" biscuit cutter, cut the dough into rounds. Fold the excess dough together, reshape and continue to cut circles until 8 are formed. Place them on the baking sheet at least 2" apart. Divide the topping evenly among the round scones, pressing it down lightly.

Bake for 18–20 minutes, until golden brown on top. Cool for 5 minutes before serving.

Irish Raisin Scones

This is my recollection of what a scone was as a kid: lightly sweetened buttery dough, shaped like a biscuit, studded with raisins and the perfect foil for creamy Irish butter and jam. These scones are more muffin-like than the denser scones that have become popular in America. Adding cornstarch softens the dough for a lighter crumb.

MAKES 8 LARGE ROUND SCONES

- 1 ¾ cups (7.7 oz.) all-purpose flour
- ¼ cup (1.8 oz.) granulated sugar
- 2 tsps. baking powder
- ½ tsp. salt
- 2 tbsps. cornstarch, optional (see Chef's Tip)
- 5 tbsps. unsalted butter, cut into bits
- ½ cup (2.9 oz.) raisins
- ½ cup (4 fl. oz.) whole milk
- 1 large egg
- 2 tbsps. heavy cream
- 2 tbsps. sanding sugar

Preheat the oven to 425 degrees F. Line a baking sheet with parchment.

Combine the flour, sugar, baking powder and salt in a large bowl. Cut the butter in with a pastry blender until crumbly. Stir in the raisins. In a measuring cup, whisk the milk and egg together. Make a well in the center of the dry ingredients and pour in the buttermilk mixture. Mix just until a soft dough forms.

Turn the dough onto a light floured work surface. Pat the dough into a circle about 1 ½" thick. Cut the dough into rounds with a floured 3" biscuit cutter, placing them 1 ½" apart on the baking sheet. Reform the dough and continue until 8 scones are formed. Place the baking sheet in the refrigerator for 15 minutes.

Brush the tops of the scones with cream and sprinkle the sanding sugar evenly over top.

Bake until tops are golden brown, about 15–18 minutes, rotating pan halfway through baking. Transfer the scones to a baking rack to cook for 5 minutes before serving.

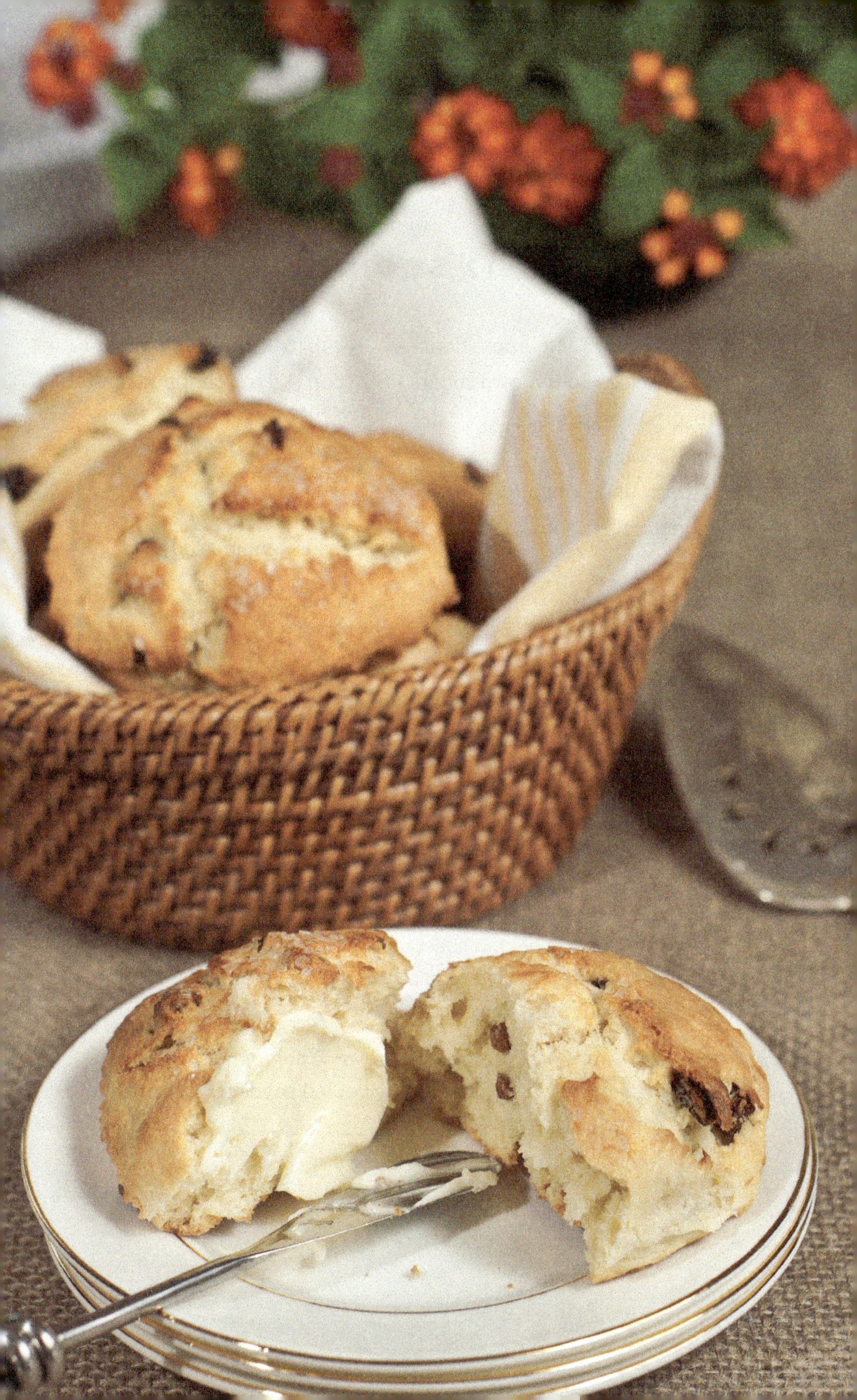

Pecan Chocolate Chip Scones

I love the combination of melted chocolate and toasted pecans in this cookie-like scone.

MAKES 10-12 SCONES

- 2 cups (8.75 oz.) all-purpose flour
- ⅓ cup (2.6 oz.) light brown sugar
- 1 tbsp. baking powder
- ½ teaspoon salt
- ½ tsp. ground cinnamon
- ½ cup unsalted butter, cut into bits
- ¾ cup (6 fl. oz.) heavy cream
- ½ cup (1.9 oz.) chopped toasted pecans
- ½ cup (2.3 oz.) semi-sweet chocolate chips
- 1 large egg
- 2 tbsps. sanding sugar

Preheat the oven to 375 degrees F. Line a baking sheet with parchment paper.

Combine the flour, brown sugar, baking powder, salt and cinnamon in a large bowl. Cut the butter in with a pastry blender until crumbly. Form a well in the center of the flour mixture and pour in the cream.

Stir the mixture until just combined. Stir in the pecans and chocolate chips. Form the dough into a ball and transfer it to a lightly floured work surface. Knead the dough for 1 minute. Press the dough into an 8" disk about ½" thick. Cut the dough in half. Cut each half into 5-6 even pieces and place them on the baking sheet at least 1" apart. Whisk the egg with a pinch of salt in a small bowl. Brush the tops of the scones with egg and sprinkle the sanding sugar evenly over top.

Bake for 15-18 minutes, until golden brown. Cool for 5 minutes on a rack before serving. Store completely cooled scones in an airtight container for up to 3 days.

Pumpkin Ginger Scones

Fresh-from-the-oven spice-scented scones are topped with white chocolate glaze for a sweet treat.

MAKES 10–12 SCONES

- 2 cups (8.75 oz.) all-purpose flour
- ⅓ cup (2.6 oz.) light brown sugar
- 2 tsps. baking powder
- ½ tsp. baking soda
- ¼ tsp. salt
- 1 tsp. ground cinnamon
- ¼ tsp. ground cloves
- ½ tsp. ground ginger
- ½ tsp. ground nutmeg
- 8 tbsps. unsalted butter, cut into bits
- ½ cup (4.3 oz.) pumpkin puree
- 3 tbsps. whole milk
- 1 large egg
- 2 teaspoons vanilla extract
- ¼ cup (1.5 oz.) crystallized ginger, finely chopped
- 1 cup (5 oz.) chopped white chocolate
- 3 tbsps. heavy cream
- ¼ cup confectioners' sugar

Combine the flour, brown sugar, baking powder, salt, cinnamon, cloves, ground ginger and nutmeg in a large bowl. Cut the butter in with a pastry blender until crumbly. Whisk the pumpkin, milk, egg and vanilla together in a small bowl. Form a well in the center of the flour mixture and stir in the pumpkin mixture until just combined. Fold in the crystallized ginger.

Form the dough into a ball and transfer it to a lightly floured work surface. Knead the dough for 1 minute. Press the dough into an 8" disk about ½" thick. Cover and refrigerate the dough for at least 30 minutes.

When ready to bake, preheat the oven to 400 degrees F. Line a baking sheet with parchment paper.

Cut the dough in half. Cut each half into 5–6 even triangles and place them on the baking sheet at least 1" apart.

Bake for 15–18 minutes, until golden brown.

In the meantime, combine the white chocolate and heavy cream in a bowl set over simmering water (or use a double boiler). Stir until chocolate is melted. Remove from the heat and whisk in the confectioners' sugar until smooth.

Cool the scones for 5 minutes on a rack. Drizzle the glaze evenly over the scones. Allow the glaze to set for 5 minutes before serving. These scones are best eaten the day they are made.

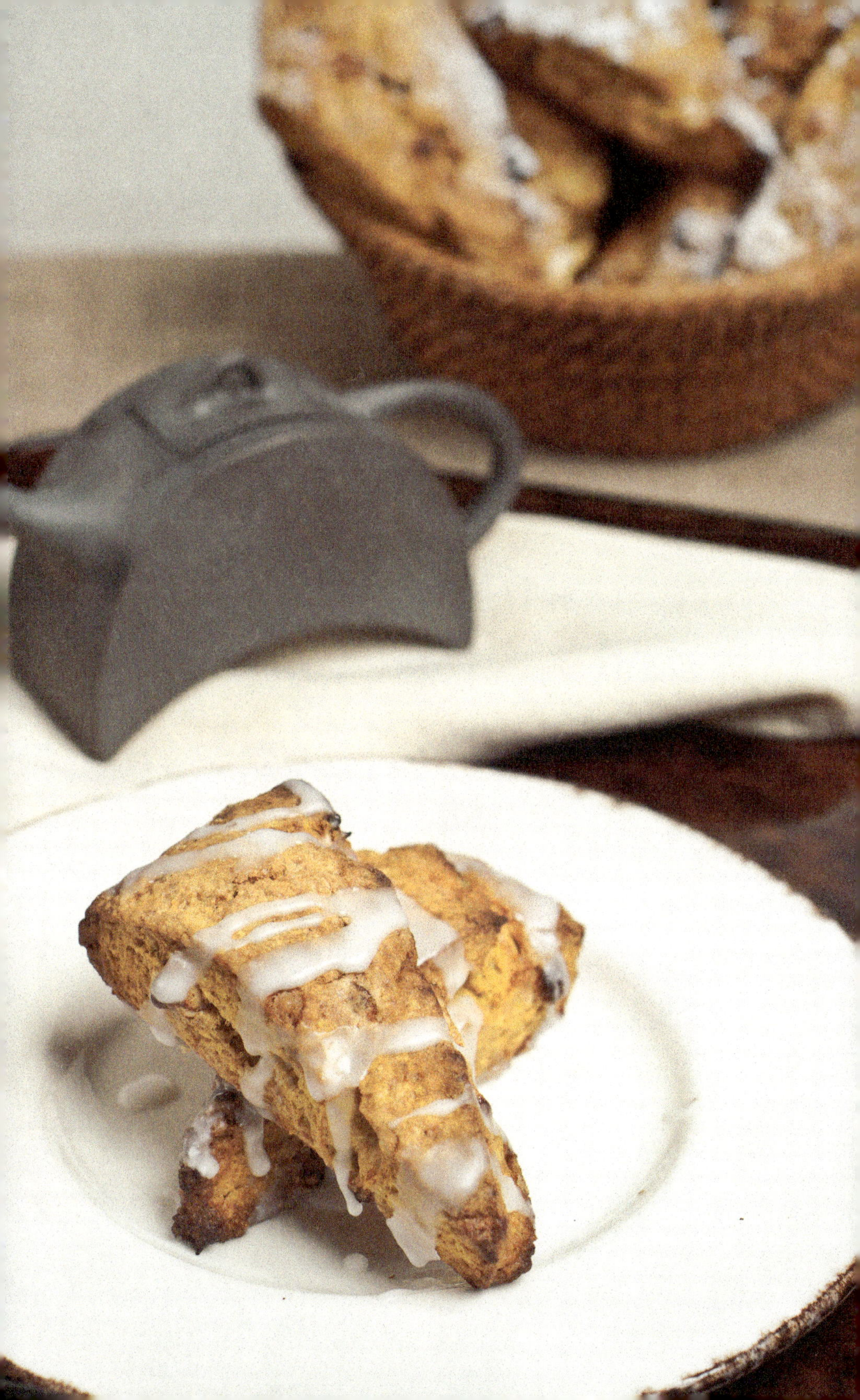

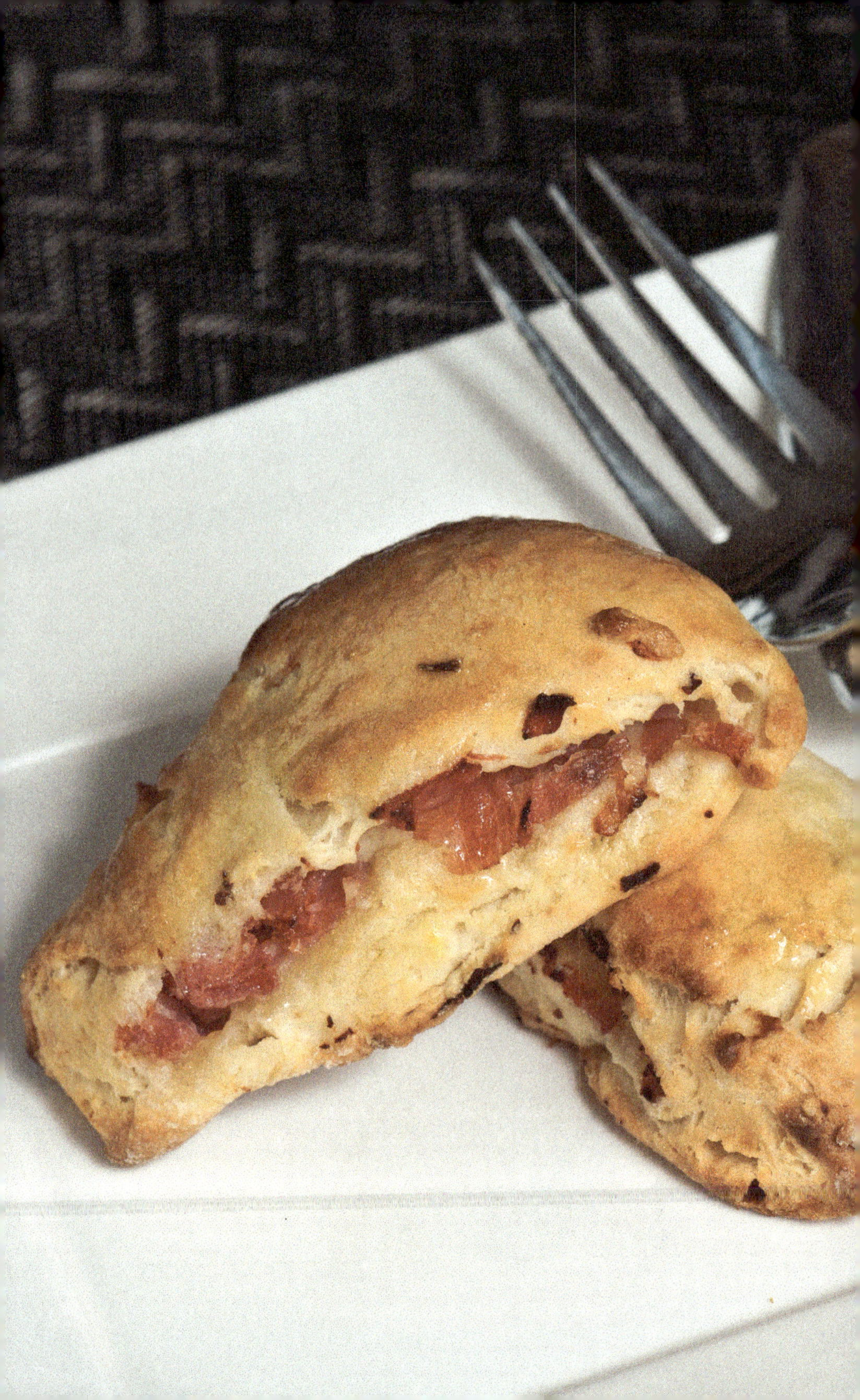

Ham and Cheese Scones

This is an all-purpose recipe for a savory scone, able to be adapted according to taste. Some interesting combinations include serrano ham with Manchego, cooked bacon with cheddar and prosciutto with fontina. The addition of different herbs and spices would also make interesting variations.

MAKES 10–12 SCONES

- 2 cups (8.75 oz.) all-purpose flour
- 1 tbsp. baking powder
- 1 tsp. granulated sugar
- ½ tsp. salt
- 4 tbsps. unsalted butter, cut into bits
- 6 thin slices ham, coarsely chopped (about 3 oz.)
- 1 cup (4 oz.) grated Gruyere cheese
- 1 cup (8 fl. oz.) heavy cream
- 1 large egg

Preheat the oven to 400 degrees F. Lightly grease a baking sheet or line it with parchment.

Whisk together the flour, baking powder, sugar and salt in a large bowl. Cut the butter into the flour mixture with a pastry blender until crumbly. Fold in the ham and cheese until evenly distributed. Stir in the cream. Form the mixture into a ball and transfer it to a lightly floured work surface.

With lightly floured hands, pat the dough into an 8" disk about ½" thick. Cut the dough in half. Cut each half into 5–6 even triangles and place them on the baking sheet at least 1" apart. Whisk the egg with a pinch of salt in a small bowl. Brush the tops of the scones with the egg wash.

Bake for 20–25 minutes, until golden brown. Allow the scones to cool for 5 minutes before serving.

Orange Poppy Seed Bread

This is one of my favorite breakfast treats because it is so moist, unlike many quick breads. It's simple to assemble and stays fresh and delicious for several days after baking. Thin slices of this bread layered with cream cheese make a delicious tea-time sandwich.

MAKES 1 LOAF

- 12 tbsps. unsalted butter, softened
- ¾ cup (5.3 oz.) granulated sugar
- 2 large eggs
- 2 cups (8.75 oz.) all-purpose flour
- 2 tsps. baking powder
- ½ tsp. salt
- 4 tsps. finely grated orange zest
- 3 tbsps. poppy seeds
- ½ cup (4 oz.) sour cream
- 1 tsp. orange extract
- ¼ cup (1.5 oz.) candied orange peel, finely chopped (optional— see Chef's Tip)
- 2 tbsps. orange juice
- 1 cup (4.23 oz.) confectioners' sugar

Preheat oven to 350 degrees F. Grease and flour a large (9" x 5" x 3") loaf pan (or grease the pan, line with parchment, grease again and dust with flour).

Combine the butter and sugar in the bowl of a stand mixer until fluffy. Add the eggs one at a time and mix to combine. Combine the flour, baking powder, salt, 3 tsps. orange zest and poppy seeds in a medium bowl. Add half the flour mixture to the butter mixture and mix until just combined. Add the sour cream and orange extract and mix until just combined. Fold in the candied orange peel. Spoon the batter into the loaf pan.

Bake until golden brown and a toothpick inserted into the center comes out clean, about 55–60 minutes. Cool 5 minutes in the loaf pan.

In the meantime, combine the remaining 1 tsp. orange zest, orange juice and confectioners' sugar in a medium bowl. Transfer the bread to a cooling rack. Use a fork to prick the top of the bread all over about 1" deep. Pour the glaze evenly and slowly over the bread, allowing the top to absorb it. Cool for at least 15 minutes, until glaze is set.

Chef's Tip: How to Make Candied Orange Peel—Slice the ends off the orange (or lemon for lemon peel), then score the peel from one end to the other into 4 vertical segments. Remove each segment (including white pith) in 1 piece. Cut into ¼"-wide strips. Cook in large pot of boiling water for 15 minutes; drain, rinse and drain again. Remove the peels in large sections. Slice the peels into thin ¼"-wide strips. Bring 3 inches water to a boil in a medium saucepan. Place the peels into the boiling water and blanch them for 5 minutes. Drain the peels and repeat. Drain the peels again. In a medium saucepan, combine 1 cup granulated sugar with 1 cup water. Bring to a simmer and cook for 8–9 minutes, until temperature reaches 230–235 degrees F. Add the peels and reduce the heat to retain a simmer. Cook until the peels become translucent, about 45 minutes. If using the peels in bread, simply drain them and allow them to dry completely. If using for snacking or dipping in chocolate, drain them, then roll them in granulated sugar and allow them to cool.

Chocolate Cherry Hazelnut Bread

Chocolate and cherries have a natural affinity for each other, and are especially tasty in this rich bread topped with a hazelnut crumb mixture.

MAKES 1 LOAF

- ½ cup (4 oz.) light brown sugar
- 2 cups (8.75 oz.) plus 2 tbsps. all-purpose flour
- 2 tbsps. unsalted butter, cut into bits
- ¼ cup (1 oz.) hazelnuts, peeled and chopped (see Chef's Tip)
- 1 tsp. baking soda
- ½ tsp. salt
- ½ tsp. espresso powder (optional)
- ⅓ cup (2.6 fl. oz.) canola or coconut oil
- ½ cup (3.5 oz.) granulated sugar
- 1 large egg
- 1 cup (8 fl. oz.) buttermilk
- 1 tsp. vanilla extract
- ½ cup (2.9 oz.) dried tart cherries
- 1 cup (4.6 oz.) mini bittersweet chocolate chips (or finely chopped bittersweet chocolate)

Preheat the oven to 350 degrees F. Grease and flour a large (9" x 5" x 3") loaf pan (or grease the pan, line with parchment, grease again and dust with flour) and set aside.

Combine ¼ cup (2 oz.) brown sugar, 1 tbsp. flour and butter with a pastry blender or fork in a medium bowl. Stir in the hazelnuts and set aside.

Combine the remaining 2 cups (8.75 oz.) flour, baking soda, salt and espresso powder (if using) in a medium bowl. Combine the oil, remaining ¼ cup (2 oz.) brown sugar and granulated sugar in the bowl of a stand mixer. Beat in the egg. Add half the flour mixture to the oil mixture and mix until just combined. Add the buttermilk and vanilla and mix until just combined. Add the remaining flour mixture and mix until just combined. Toss the cherries and chocolate chips with the remaining 1 tbsp. flour to coat. Stir the coated cherries and chips into the batter. Spoon the batter into the loaf pan. Sprinkle the hazelnut topping evenly over top.

Bake until golden brown and a toothpick inserted into the center comes out clean, about 55–60 minutes. Cool for 5 minutes in the loaf pan, then remove to a rack to finish cooling.

Chef's Tip: To peel the hazelnuts, preheat the oven to 350 degrees F. Spread the nuts in a single layer on a baking sheet and toast until the skins are mostly split, about 8–10 minutes. Rub the nuts with double paper towels until skins are removed.

Blueberry Streusel Bread

One of our favorite summer outings when we had our Maine B & B was to wander the barren hillsides, looking for secret patches of wild blueberries to collect and serve at breakfast. Often the extra bounty became part of our breakfast baking, as in this delicious quick bread.

MAKES 1 LOAF

- 2 ¼ cups (10 oz.) all-purpose flour
- ¾ cup (5.3 oz.) granulated sugar
- ¼ cup (2 oz.) light brown sugar
- 2 tsps. ground cinnamon
- 6 tbsps. unsalted butter, softened
- 2 large eggs
- 2 tsps. baking powder
- ¼ tsp. salt
- 2 tsps. finely grated lemon zest
- ⅓ cup (2.7 fl. oz.) whole milk
- 1 tsp. vanilla extract
- 1 cup (5.2 oz.) fresh or frozen wild blueberries (or substitute cultivated berries)

Preheat the oven to 350 degrees F. Grease and flour a large (9" x 5" x 3") loaf pan (or grease the pan, line with parchment, grease again and dust with flour) and set aside.

Combine ¼ cup (1.25 oz.) flour, ¼ cup (1.8 oz.) granulated sugar, brown sugar and cinnamon in a medium bowl. Cut in 2 tbsps. butter with a pastry blender until crumbly. Set aside.

In the bowl of a stand mixer, combine the remaining 4 tbsps. butter and ½ cup (3.5 oz.) granulated sugar until light and fluffy. Add the eggs one at a time until combined. Combine the remaining 2 cups (8.75 oz.) flour, baking powder, salt and lemon zest in a medium bowl. Add half the flour mixture to the butter mixture and mix until just combined. Add the milk and vanilla and mix until just combined. Add the remaining flour mixture and mix until just combined. Fold in the blueberries and set aside.

Spoon half of the batter into the pan. Sprinkle half of the cinnamon sugar mixture over top. With a butter knife, swirl the cinnamon sugar mixture into the batter about 1" deep. Spoon the remaining batter on top. Sprinkle on the remaining cinnamon sugar mixture.

Bake until golden brown and a toothpick inserted into the center comes out clean, about 55–60 minutes. Cover the top with foil for the last 10–15 minutes if necessary to prevent over-browning. Cool 5 minutes in the loaf pan, then remove to a rack to finish cooling.

Cranberry Pecan Bread

The flavor of dried cranberries is enhanced by orange zest and cardamom in this deliciously moist bread.

MAKES 1 LOAF

- 2 cups (8.75 oz.) all-purpose flour
- 2 tsps. baking powder
- ½ tsp. baking soda
- ½ tsp. salt
- ¼ tsp. ground cardamom
- 1 tsp. finely grated orange zest
- 8 tbsps. unsalted butter, softened
- 1 cup (7 oz.) granulated sugar
- 3 oz. cream cheese, softened
- 2 large eggs
- ½ cup (4 fl. oz.) buttermilk
- 1 tsp. vanilla extract
- 1 cup (5.8 oz.) dried cranberries
- ½ cup (1.9 oz.) finely chopped pecans
- 1 tbsp. sanding sugar

Preheat the oven to 350 degrees F. Grease and flour a large (9" x 5" x 3") loaf pan (or grease the pan, line with parchment, grease again and dust with flour) and set aside .

Combine the flour, baking powder, baking soda, salt, cardamom and orange zest in a medium bowl and set aside.

Combine the butter, sugar and cream cheese in the bowl of a stand mixer. Beat until fluffy. Add the eggs one at a time until combined. Add half of the flour mixture and beat until just combined. Add the buttermilk and vanilla and mix until just combined. Add the remaining flour mixture and beat until just combined. Stir in the cranberries and pecans. Sprinkle the sanding sugar evenly over the top of the loaf.

Bake for 50–60 minutes, until top is golden and a toothpick inserted into the center comes out clean. Cool in the pan for 5 minutes. Remove from the pan and transfer the loaf to a rack to cool completely.

Pumpkin Bread with Walnut Streusel

The smell of this spice-scented pumpkin bread baking is a sure sign that autumn has arrived. The simple walnut streusel topping adds texture and a little sophistication.

MAKES 1 LOAF

- 2 ½ cups (11 oz.) all-purpose flour
- 1 cup (7.76 oz.) light brown sugar
- 5 tbsps. unsalted butter, cut into bits
- ½ cup (2 oz.) chopped walnuts
- ¾ cup (5.3 oz.) granulated sugar
- ½ cup canola or coconut oil
- ½ cup (4.3 oz.) applesauce (see recipe p. 309)
- 2 large eggs
- ¾ cup (6.5 oz.) pumpkin puree
- 1 tsp. baking soda
- ½ tsp. salt
- 1 tsp. ground all-spice
- ¼ tsp. ground cloves
- 1 tsp. ground nutmeg

Preheat the oven to 350 degrees F. Grease and flour a large (9" x 5" x 3") loaf pan (or grease the pan, line with parchment, grease again and dust with flour) and set aside.

Combine ½ cup (2.2 oz.) flour and ½ cup (4 oz.) brown sugar in a medium bowl. Cut the butter in with a pastry blender until crumbly. Stir in the chopped walnuts and set aside.

Combine the remaining ½ (4 oz.) brown sugar, granulated sugar, canola oil and applesauce in a medium bowl. Whisk in the eggs until combined. Whisk in the pumpkin puree. Combine the remaining 2 cups (8.75 oz.) flour, baking powder, salt, all-spice, cloves and nutmeg in a separate large bowl. Stir the wet ingredients into the flour mixture until just combined. Spoon the batter into the loaf pan. Sprinkle the streusel evenly over top.

Bake until golden brown and a toothpick inserted into the center comes out clean, about 55–60 minutes. Cover the top with foil for the last 10–15 minutes if necessary to prevent over-browning. Cool 5 minutes in the loaf pan, then remove to a rack to finish cooling.

Walnut Bread

This delicious bread is just slightly sweet, so it can be served with a variety of breakfast entrees. I often make this recipe in mini loaf pans for gifting over the holidays.

MAKES 1 LOAF

- 2 cups (8.75 oz.) all-purpose flour
- ¾ cup (5.3 oz.) granulated sugar
- 1 tbsp. baking powder
- 1 tsp. salt
- 1 large egg
- 6 tbsps. unsalted butter, melted
- 1 cup (8 fl. oz.) whole milk
- 1 tsp. vanilla extract
- 1 cup (4.1 oz.) chopped walnuts

Preheat the oven to 350 degrees F. Grease and flour a large (9" x 5" x 3") loaf pan (or grease the pan, line with parchment, grease again and dust with flour) and set aside.

Combine the flour, sugar, baking powder and salt in a large bowl. In a separate bowl, whisk together the egg, melted butter, milk and vanilla extract until combined. Make a well in the center of the dry ingredients and pour in the wet ingredients. Mix until just combined. Fold in the walnuts. Spoon the batter into the loaf pan.

Bake until golden brown and a toothpick inserted into the center comes out clean, about 55–60 minutes. Cover the top with foil for the last 10–15 minutes if necessary to prevent over-browning. Cool 5 minutes in the loaf pan, then remove to a rack to finish cooling.

Strawberry Balsamic Bread

Balsamic vinegar enhances the sweetness of strawberries and brightens their flavor. The top of this bread will sink as it cools, but don't let it scare you—it simply becomes more firm and decadent in the process.

MAKES 1 LOAF

- 2 cups (10.7 oz.) strawberries, hulled and chopped
- 1 ¼ cups (8.8 oz.) granulated sugar
- 1 tsp. lemon juice
- 1 tbsp. balsamic vinegar
- 2 cups (8.75 oz.) all-purpose flour
- ½ tsp. baking powder
- 1 tsp. ground cinnamon
- ½ tsp. salt
- ⅔ cup (5.2 fl. oz.) canola oil
- 2 large eggs
- ¼ cup (2 fl. oz.) buttermilk
- 1 tsp. vanilla extract

Combine ½ cup (2.7 oz.) strawberries, ½ cup sugar (3.5 oz.) and lemon juice in a small saucepan. Bring the mixture to a boil over medium-high heat. Simmer until thickened, about 6–8 minutes (until it reaches a temperature of 220 degrees F). Allow to cool completely.

In the meantime, combine the remaining 1 ½ cups (8 oz.) strawberries and balsamic vinegar in a small bowl. Allow the mixture to macerate for 20 minutes. Drain off the excess balsamic vinegar.

Preheat the oven to 350 degrees F. Grease and flour a large (9" x 5" x 3") loaf pan (or grease the pan, line with parchment, grease again and dust with flour) and set aside.

Whisk the flour, baking powder, cinnamon and salt in a large bowl. In a separate bowl, whisk the remaining ¾ cup (5.3 oz.) sugar, oil, eggs, buttermilk and vanilla. Pour the wet ingredients into the dry ingredients and stir until just combined. Fold in the remaining 1 ½ cups (8 oz.) strawberries. Spread the batter into the pan. Spoon the cooled strawberry mixture over the top and swirl into the batter about 1" deep. Bake for 1 ¼-1 ½ hours until firm and a toothpick inserted in the middle comes out clean. Cool in the pan for 5 minutes. Transfer to a rack to cool completely before serving.

Raspberry Almond Bread

While the fresh raspberry preserves are best made ahead, feel free to use whatever jam or preserve you have on hand in this easy-to-make bread.

MAKES 1 LOAF

- 2 ¼ (10 oz.) cups all-purpose flour
- ¼ cup (2 oz.) light brown sugar
- ¾ cup (5.3 oz.) granulated sugar
- ¼ cup (.80 oz.) old-fashioned oats
- 2 tsps. ground cinnamon
- 8 tbsps. unsalted butter, softened
- ½ cup (2 oz.) sliced almonds

- 2 large eggs
- 2 tsps. baking powder
- ¼ tsp. salt
- 2 tsps. finely grated lemon zest
- ⅓ cup (2.6 fl. oz.) whole milk
- 1 tsp. almond extract
- 1 cup (11.3 oz.) raspberry jam (see recipe p. 307)

Preheat the oven to 350 degrees F. Grease and flour a large (9" x 5" x 3") loaf pan (or grease the pan, line with parchment, grease again and dust with flour) and set aside.

Combine ¼ cup (1.25 oz.) flour, brown sugar, ¼ cup (1.8 oz.) granulated sugar, oats and cinnamon in a medium bowl. Cut in 4 tbsps. butter with a pastry blender until crumbly. Stir in the almonds and set aside.

In the bowl of a stand mixer, combine the remaining 4 tbsps. butter and ½ cup (3.5 oz.) granulated sugar until light and fluffy. Add the eggs one at a time until combined. Combine the remaining 2 cups (8.75 oz.) flour, baking powder, salt and lemon zest in a medium bowl. Add half the flour mixture to the butter mixture and mix until just combined. Add the milk and almond extract and mix until just combined. Add the remaining flour mixture and mix until just combined.

Spoon half of the batter into the pan. Divide the preserves in half. Drop teaspoons of half the preserves over top. Spoon the remaining batter on top. Drop teaspoons of the remaining preserves on top. With a butter knife, swirl the cinnamon sugar mixture into the batter about 1" deep. Sprinkle on the almond mixture.

Bake until golden brown and a toothpick inserted into the center comes out clean, about 55–60 minutes. Cover the top with foil for the last 10–15 minutes if necessary to prevent over-browning. Cool 5 minutes in the loaf pan, then remove to a rack to finish cooling completely.

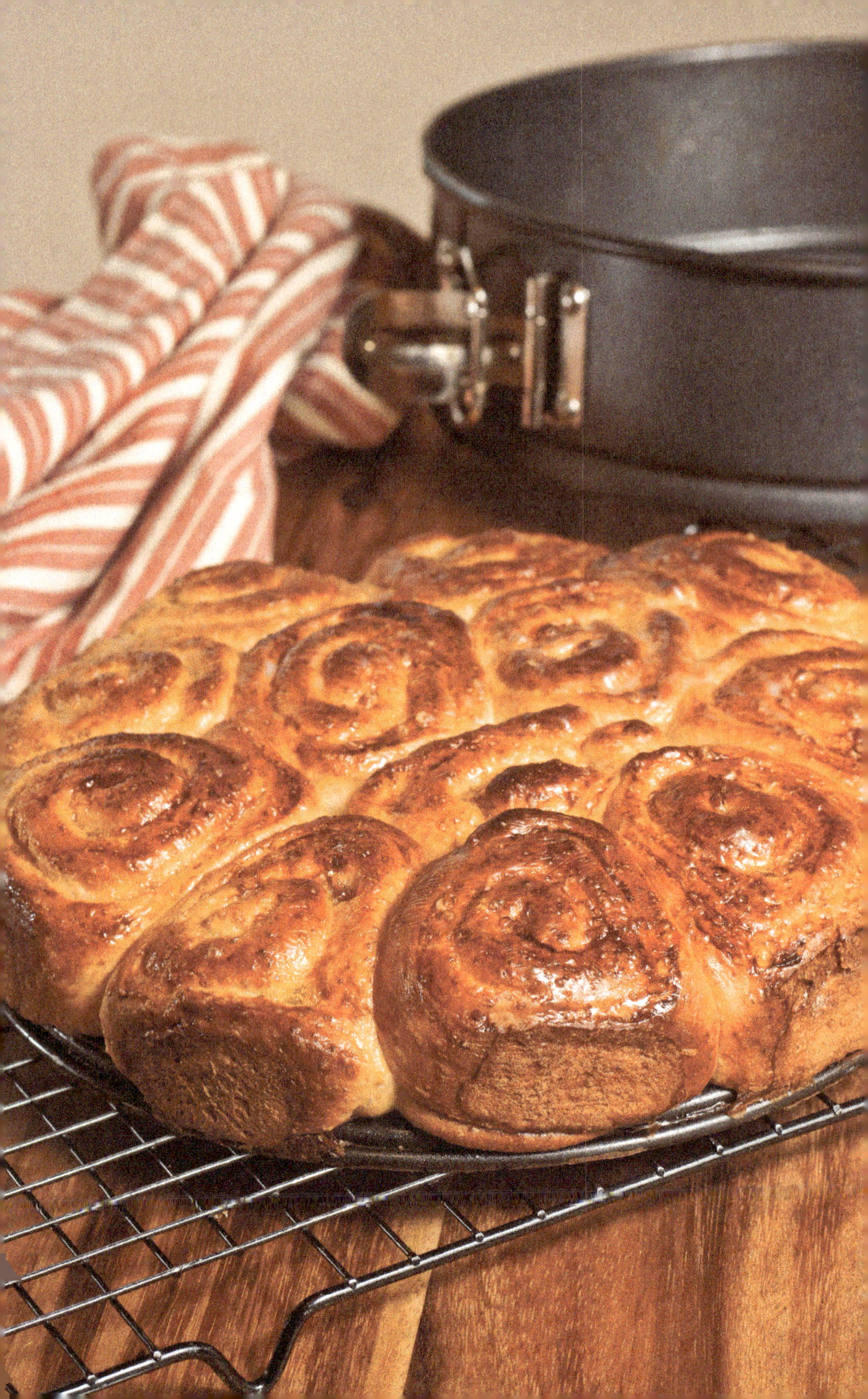

CHAPTER TWO
Coffeecakes, Sweet Rolls and Danish

- Raspberry Cream Coffeecake
- Crumb Coffeecake
- Peach Streusel Coffeecake
- Apple Crumb Sour Cream Coffeecake
- Almond Fig Coffeecake
- Blueberry Butter Coffeecake
- Ricotta and Chocolate Coffeecake
- Apple Walnut Streusel Coffeecake
- Plum Sour Cream Coffeecake
- Spice Coffeecake
- Honey Pecan Monkey Bread
- Monkey Bread with Caramel Glaze
- Pecan Sticky Buns
- Maple Caramel Sticky Buns
- Croissant Cinnamon Rolls
- Almond Croissant Rolls
- Raisin Cream Croissant Rolls

- Apricot Orange Sweet Rolls
- Honey Almond Crescents
- Cheese Danish
- Coconut Almond Bear Claw Danish
- Mixed Berry Braid
- Cherry Strudel
- Apricot Cheese Pastry Ring
- Cinnamon Pecan Pastry Ring
- Crescents with Pecans and Coconut

Raspberry Cream Coffeecake

This is one of my favorite foolproof coffeecakes, featuring an almond cream center and tender crumb topping.

SERVES 8-10

- 8 oz. cream cheese
- 1 cup (8 oz.) sour cream
- 2 large eggs
- ¾ cup (5.3 oz.) granulated sugar
- 2 tsps. almond extract
- 2 ½ cups (10 oz.) all-purpose flour

- 12 tbsps. unsalted butter, cut into bits
- 1 tsp. baking powder
- ½ tsp. salt
- 4 tbsps. heavy cream
- 1 cup (11.3 oz.) raspberry jam (see recipe p. 307)

Preheat the oven to 350 degrees F. Grease a 9–10" spring form pan and set it on a rimmed baking sheet.

Combine the cream cheese and ¼ cup (2 oz.) sour cream in the bowl of a stand mixer until smooth. Add 1 egg and mix until combined. Mix in ¼ cup (1.8 oz.) sugar and 1 tsp. almond extract until combined. Spoon the mixture into a small bowl and set aside.

Combine the flour, remaining ½ cup (3.5 oz.) sugar, baking powder and salt in a large bowl. Cut the butter into the mixture with a pastry blender until crumbly. Reserve 1 cup (5 oz.) of this mixture for the topping.

In a separate medium bowl, whisk together the remaining ½ cup (4 oz.) sour cream, remaining egg, 1 tsp. almond extract and heavy cream. Stir the sour cream mixture into the remaining flour-butter mixture until combined.

Spread the batter evenly in the prepared pan. Spread the almond cream over the batter. Spoon the raspberry jam evenly over the cream layer. Sprinkle the reserved flour-butter mixture over top.

Bake for 40–45 minutes, until firm and lightly browned. Allow to cool for 5 minutes. Remove the coffeecake from the spring form and transfer to a rack. Cool 15–20 minutes longer before serving.

Make Ahead Tip: Mix the crust, topping and cream filling the night before and refrigerate for easy assembly and baking in the morning.

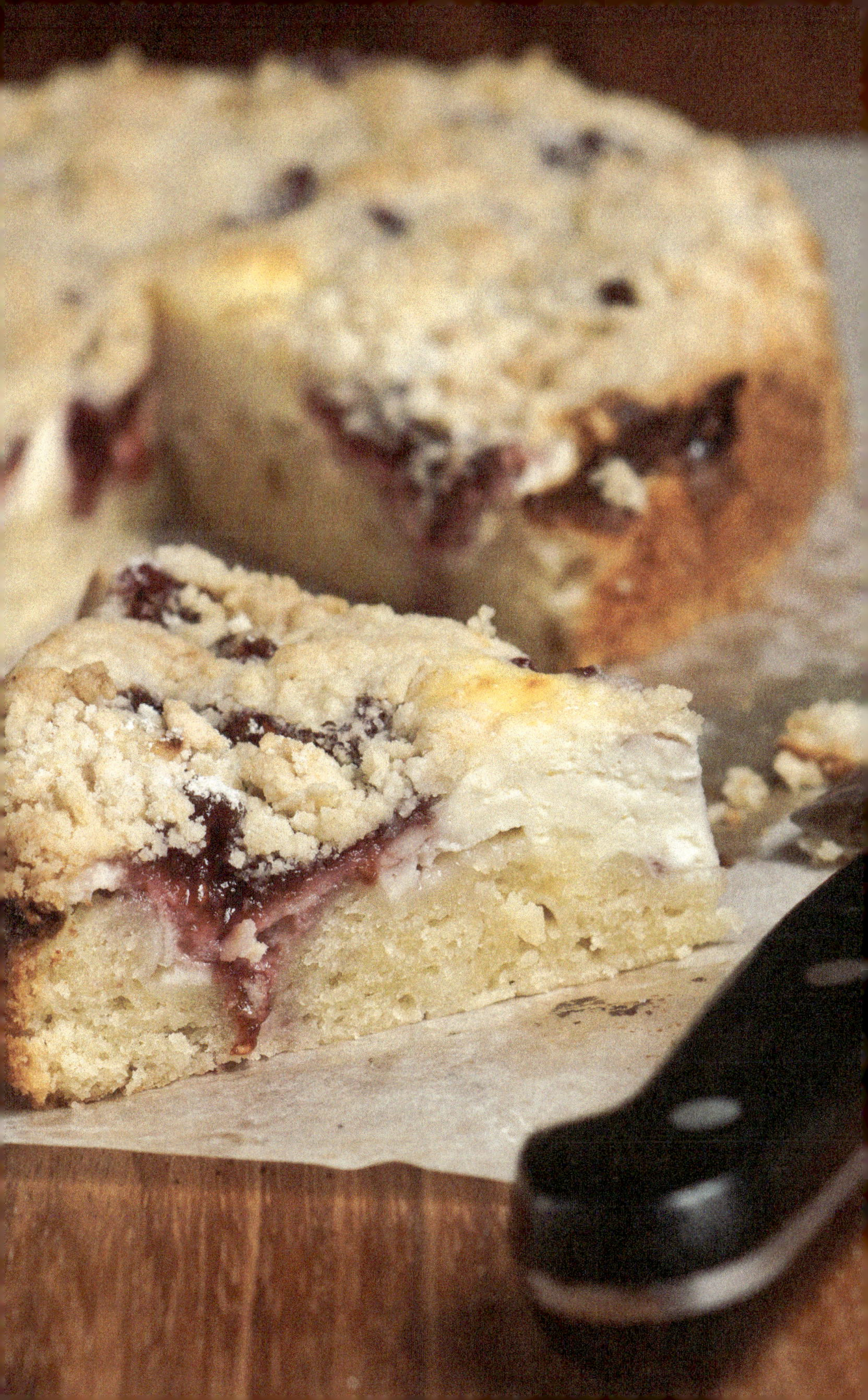

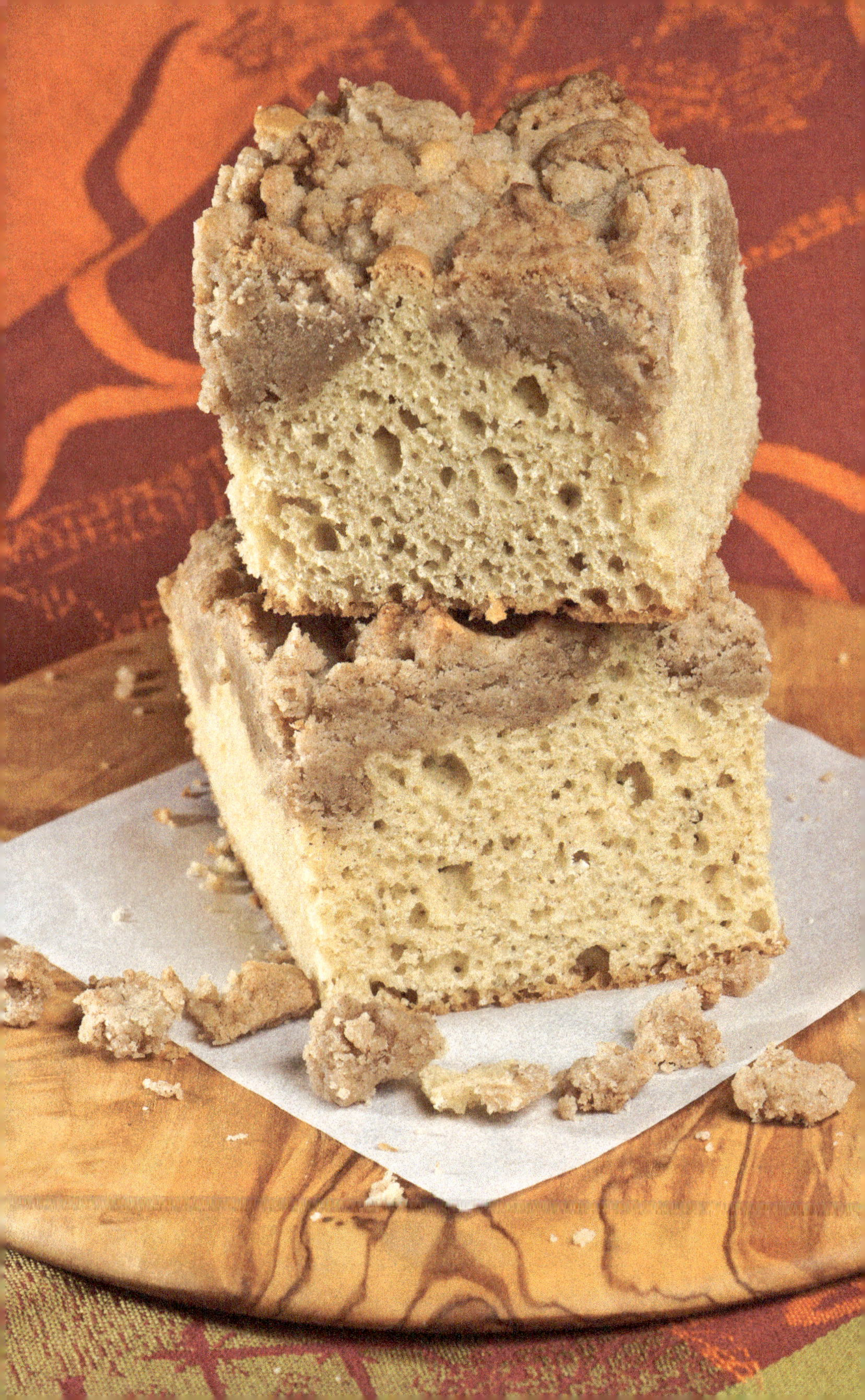

Crumb Coffeecake

This New York-style coffeecake (code for heavy on the crumb topping!) is delicious warm from the oven, but can also be made several days before serving.

SERVES 8-10

- 5 ½ cups (24.2 oz.) all-purpose flour
- 1 cup (7 oz.) granulated sugar
- 5 tsp. baking powder
- 1 tsp. salt
- 2 large eggs
- 1 cup (8 fl. oz.) whole milk
- 2 tbsps. canola oil
- 4 tsps. vanilla extract
- 1 cup (7.76 oz.) light brown sugar
- 2 tsps. cinnamon
- 16 tbsps. butter, melted and cooled

Place the rack in the center of the oven and preheat the oven to 325 degrees F. Lightly grease a 9" x 13" baking pan, dust with flour and set aside.

In a medium bowl, sift together 3 cups (13.2 oz.) flour, the granulated sugar, baking powder and salt. In a second bowl, whisk together the egg, milk, oil and vanilla. Pour the wet ingredients into the dry and mix until just combined. Spread the batter evenly into the prepared pan.

In a medium bowl, combine the remaining 2 ½ cups (11 oz.) flour, brown sugar and cinnamon. Pour the melted butter over the dry ingredients and toss with a fork to combine. Press the mixture together to form large crumbs. Sprinkle the crumbs evenly over the batter.

Place pan in the oven and bake 30–35 minutes, until a toothpick inserted into the center comes out clean. Allow to cool on a baking rack, then cut into 3" squares. Store in an airtight container for up to 3 days.

Make Ahead Tip: Make the coffeecake up to 3 days before for serving. Freeze whatever cake is not consumed to enjoy over the next few weeks.

Peach Streusel Coffeecake

We were fortunate to have an amazing peach orchard nearby at our inn, so I had many opportunities to create delicious breakfast treats with fresh peaches. This versatile peach coffeecake is best served warm from the oven. If your peaches are not sweet and ripe, toss them with 1–2 tbsps. granulated sugar before assembling the tart. This recipe may also be made in 4 individual tart pans.

SERVES 8–10

- 3 large peaches, peeled, pitted and thinly sliced (about 2 cups)
- 2 tsps. lemon juice
- 1 ⅔ (7.3 oz.) cups all-purpose flour
- 2 tbsps. light brown sugar
- ½ tsp. ground cinnamon
- 6 tbsps. unsalted butter, softened
- ¼ cup (1.8 oz.) granulated sugar
- 1 ½ tsps. baking powder
- ½ tsp. salt
- ¼ cup (2 fl. oz.) whole milk
- 1 large egg
- 1 tsp. vanilla extract

Preheat the oven to 400 degrees F. Grease and flour a 9–10" spring form pan and set on a rimmed baking sheet.

Toss the peaches with the lemon juice in a medium bowl and set aside.

Combine ⅓ cup (1.5 oz.) flour, brown sugar and cinnamon in a small bowl. Cut in 2 tbsps. butter with a pastry blender until crumbly. Set aside.

Combine the remaining 1 ⅓ cups (5.8 oz.) flour, granulated sugar, baking powder and salt in a large bowl. Cut in the remaining 4 tbsps. butter with a pastry blender until crumbly. Whisk the milk, egg and vanilla together in a measuring cup. Stir the milk mixture into the flour-butter mixture until just combined.

Spread the batter in the prepared pan. Arrange the peaches in an overlapping circular pattern. Sprinkle the topping evenly over the peaches.

Bake for 35–40 minutes, until the peaches are tender and a toothpick inserted into the center comes out clean. Allow to cool for 5 minutes. Remove from the spring form and serve warm.

Make Ahead Tip: Cut fruit may be refrigerated overnight for up to 8 hours in a solution of Fruit Fresh, or other ascorbic acid fruit preserver. Make the streusel topping the night before and refrigerate until ready to finish the tart.

Apple Crumb Sour Cream Coffeecake

Delicious fresh from the oven, the addition of sour cream and chopped apples also keeps this coffeecake moist for several days after baking.

🧊 **SERVES 10–12**

- 3 large baking apples, peeled, cored and chopped (about 2 cups)
- 2 tsps. lemon juice
- 18 tbsps. unsalted butter
- 3 ½ cups (15.35 oz.) all-purpose flour
- ¼ cup (1.8 oz.) granulated sugar
- 1 ¼ cups (9.7 oz.) light brown sugar
- 2 tsps. ground cinnamon
- ¾ tsp. baking powder
- 1 tsp. baking soda
- ½ tsp. salt
- 1 tsp. ground cinnamon
- 2 large eggs
- 1 cup (8 oz.) sour cream
- 1 tsp. vanilla extract

Preheat the oven to 350 degrees. Grease and flour a 9" x 13" baking pan.

Toss the apples and lemon juice in a medium bowl and set aside.

To make the crumb topping, melt 10 tbsps. butter and allow it to cool slightly. In a medium bowl, combine 1 ½ cups (6.6 oz.) flour, granulated sugar, ¼ cup (2 oz.) brown sugar and cinnamon. Pour the melted butter over the dry ingredients and toss with a fork until crumbs form. Set aside.

Combine the remaining 2 cups (8.75 oz.) flour, baking powder, baking soda, salt and cinnamon in a medium bowl and set aside. Mix the remaining 8 tbsps. butter and 1 cup (7.7 oz.) brown sugar in the bowl of a stand mixer until fluffy. Add the eggs, one at a time, and beat until smooth. Mix in the sour cream and vanilla. Add the dry ingredients and mix until just combined. Fold in the apples.

Spread the apple batter into the prepared baking pan. Sprinkle on the crumb topping.

Bake for 35–40 minutes, until golden brown and a toothpick inserted into the middle comes out clean. Cool for 15 minutes before serving.

Make Ahead Tip: Make the crumb topping the night before and refrigerate until ready to assemble. Cut fruit may be refrigerated overnight for up to 8 hours in a solution of Fruit Fresh, or other ascorbic acid fruit preserver.

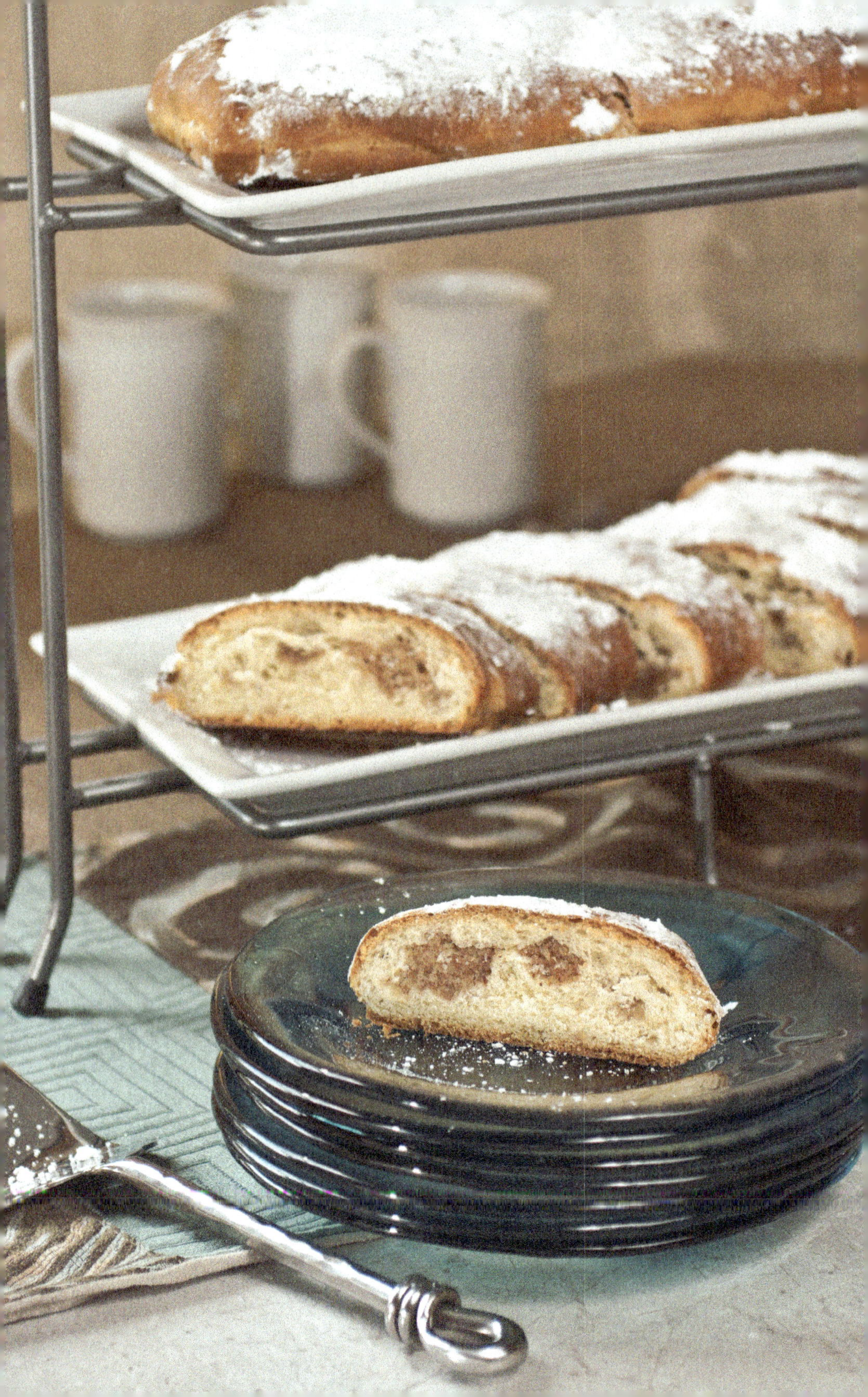

Almond Fig Coffeecake

This recipe produces two loaves filled with almond paste and chopped dried fruit. It reminds me of a less dense version of the traditional German Christmas cake known as stollen. Here the yeast is fermented before mixing the dough for added flavor.

MAKES 2 LOAVES

- ¾ cup (4 oz.) dried figs, coarsely chopped
- ¼ cup (1.5 oz.) golden raisins
- 3 cups (13.2 oz.) plus 3–5 tbsps. all-purpose flour
- ½ cup (4 fl. oz.) whole milk
- 3 tsps. instant yeast
- ¼ cup (1.8 oz.) granulated sugar
- 1 tsp. vanilla extract
- 1 large egg
- 1 large egg yolk

- 1 tsp. finely grated lemon zest
- ½ tsp. salt
- ½ tsp. ground all-spice
- 8 tbsps. unsalted butter, softened
- ½ cup (1.6 oz.) chopped almonds
- 2 logs almond paste, about 6 oz. (see recipe p. 304)
- ¼ cup (1.05 oz.) confectioners' sugar

Place the figs and raisins in a small bowl or measuring cup. Add warm water just to cover. Cover with plastic wrap or foil and allow the figs to soak for at least 30 minutes, or overnight.

Combine 1 cup (4.4 oz.) flour, milk, ¼ cup (2 fl. oz.) warm water and yeast in the bowl of a stand mixer and mix until smooth, about 3-4 minutes. Transfer the mixture to a medium bowl, cover and allow to rise and ferment for 1 hour at room temperature.

Drain the liquid from the dried figs and raisins and set aside.

Place the fermented mixture into the bowl of a stand mixer. Add 2 cups (8.75 oz.) flour, sugar, vanilla, egg, egg yolk, lemon zest, salt and all-spice. Mix at low speed until the dough pulls together, about 3-4 minutes. Add the butter 1 tbsp. at a time, fully incorporating each tablespoon before adding the next. Beat the mixture on medium-low speed for 2 minutes. Gradually add the remaining flour 1 tbsp. at a time until the dough begins to pull away from the sides of the bowl. Switch to the dough hook. Continue to add flour 1 tablespoon at a time until the dough just forms a ball. Knead 4–5 minutes on medium-low speed, until the dough is smooth and supple, but still sticky. Add the figs, raisins and almonds and knead until all are evenly incorporated into the dough. Place the dough into an oiled bowl and turn to coat. Cover with plastic wrap and let rise until doubled, about 1 ½–2 hours, or in the refrigerator overnight.

Turn the dough out onto a lightly floured piece of parchment and divide it in half. With lightly floured hands, press the dough into 2 (7" x 9") ovals. Crumble 1 almond log paste down the center of each loaf. Lightly press the crumbled almond paste into the dough. Fold one side of the dough over to cover it. Carefully lift the dough onto a parchment-lined baking sheet, placing the loaves at least 4" apart. Press lightly on the folded side to help the loaf keep its shape. Cover with plastic wrap and let rise until almost doubled in size, about 30–40 minutes.

In the meantime, preheat the oven to 350 degrees F.

Bake the loaves until golden brown, about 40–45 minutes (tent the loaves with foil if they brown too quickly). Remove from the oven and immediately sprinkle on half the confectioner's sugar. Place the loaves on a rack to cool slightly. Turn the loaves over and sprinkle with the remaining confectioners' sugar.

Make Ahead Tip: Allow the dough to ferment in the refrigerator overnight. Assemble the loaves with the filling and give them the final rise just before baking them off in the morning.

This recipe also freezes well for up to 1 month. If freezing it, do not sprinkle with confectioners' sugar. If you want to enjoy a few slices at a time, slice the loaf into quarters before freezing. To serve it, first thaw the bread. Preheat the oven to 375 degrees F and place the loaf on a parchment-lined baking sheet. Bake for 5 minutes until just heated through, then sprinkle with confectioners' sugar to serve.

Blueberry Butter Coffeecake

A trip to Brittany, France, inspired this thin butter coffeecake topped with blueberries. This easy-to-assemble recipe is quickly prepared while the oven is heating, and is best eaten warm. When local berries are unavailable, I use frozen wild Maine blueberries for their sweet blueberry flavor.

SERVES 6-8

- 8 tbsps. unsalted butter, softened
- 1 cup (7 oz.) plus 1 tbsp. granulated sugar
- 2 large eggs
- 1 cup (4.4 oz.) plus 1 tbsp. all-purpose flour
- 1 tsp. baking powder
- ¼ tsp. salt
- 1 cup (5.2 oz.) blueberries, fresh or frozen
- Confectioners' sugar for dusting

Preheat the oven to 350 degrees. Lightly grease a 9" or 10" spring form pan.

Beat the butter and 1 cup (7 oz.) sugar with a mixer until light and fluffy. Add the eggs 1 at a time and mix until combined. In a separate bowl, combine 1 cup (4.4 oz.) flour, baking powder and salt. Add the flour mixture and beat until just combined. Spread the batter in the prepared pan. Toss the blueberries with the remaining 1 tbsp. flour and 1 tbsp. sugar. Spread the blueberries evenly over the top of the batter. Bake until center is set and golden, about 35-45 minutes, until golden and toothpick inserted into the center comes out clean. Cool slightly, then remove from pan. Sprinkle with confectioners' sugar to serve.

Ricotta and Chocolate Coffeecake

This combination of ricotta and chocolate is reminiscent of Italian cannoli. The crumb topping adds a sweet finishing touch.

SERVES 10-12

- 3 cups (13.2 oz.) all-purpose flour
- ⅔ cup (5.2 oz.) light brown sugar
- ¼ tsp. salt
- 12 tbsps. unsalted butter, cut into bits
- 2 tsps. finely grated orange zest
- 2 tsps. baking powder
- 3 large eggs
- ¾ cup (6 fl. oz.) whole milk
- 2 tsps. vanilla extract
- 1 ½ cups (12 oz.) whole milk ricotta
- 3 tbsps. granulated sugar
- ¼ cup (1.2 oz.) coarsely chopped bittersweet chocolate

Preheat the oven to 350 degrees F. Grease a 9" x 13" baking pan.

Combine the flour, brown sugar and salt in a large bowl. Cut the butter into the flour mixture with a pastry blender until crumbly. Reserve 1 cup (5 oz.) of the mixture for the topping. Stir 1 tsp. orange zest and baking powder into the remaining flour mixture. Whisk two eggs, milk and vanilla together in a measuring cup and stir into the flour mixture. Set aside.

Whisk the ricotta, granulated sugar, remaining egg and remaining 1 tsp. orange zest in a medium bowl. Fold in the chocolate.

Spread the batter in the bottom of the pan. Spoon the ricotta mixture evenly over top. Spoon the reserved crumb mixture evenly over top.

Bake for 40-45 minutes, until golden and a toothpick inserted into the center comes out clean. Allow the coffeecake to cool for 10 minutes before cutting into squares to serve.

Make Ahead Tip: The cream filling and crumb topping may be made and refrigerated the night before assembling the coffeecake.

Apple Walnut Streusel Coffeecake

This delicious coffeecake, filled with apples and scented with cinnamon, is best made at least one day before serving, making it perfect for entertaining.

SERVES 8-10

- 3 large baking apples, peeled, cored and thinly sliced
- 2 tsps. lemon juice
- 2 cups (14.1 oz.) granulated sugar
- ¼ cup (2 oz.) light brown sugar
- 3 ½ (15.4 oz.) cups all-purpose flour
- 2 tsps. ground cinnamon
- 15 tbsps. unsalted butter, softened
- ½ cup (2 oz.) chopped walnuts
- 4 large eggs
- 2 tsps. vanilla extract
- ½ cup (4 fl. oz.) orange juice
- 1 tbsp. baking powder
- ½ tsp. salt

Preheat the oven to 350 degrees F. Grease and flour a 10" tube or coffeecake pan.

In a medium bowl, toss the apple slices with lemon juice and set aside.

To make the streusel, combine ½ cup (3.5 oz.) granulated sugar, brown sugar, ½ cup (2.2 oz.) flour and cinnamon in a medium bowl. Cut 3 tbsps. butter into the mixture with a pastry blender until crumbly. Fold in the walnuts and set aside.

Cream the remaining 12 tbsps. butter and 1 ½ cups (10.6 oz.) granulated sugar in the bowl of a stand mixer until fluffy, about 3–4 minutes. Add the eggs, one at a time, and mix until smooth. Add the vanilla and orange juice and mix until smooth.

In a separate bowl, combine the remaining 3 cups (13.2 oz.) flour, baking powder and salt. Add the flour mixture and mix until just combined.

Spoon half the batter into the pan. Sprinkle with half of the streusel. Layer the apples on evenly. Spoon the rest of the batter over the apples and sprinkle the remaining streusel on top. Bake for 1 ½ hours minutes, until firm and golden (a toothpick inserted into the center should come out clean). Cool for 5 minutes in the pan, then invert onto a rack to cool completely before serving.

Make Ahead Tip: Make this coffeecake up to 2 days ahead before serving.

Plum Sour Cream Coffeecake

Sweet plums add depth of flavor to this tender crumb cake.

SERVES 8–10

- 5 plums, peeled, pitted and thinly sliced
- 1 ½ cups (10.6 oz.) plus 2 tbsps. granulated sugar
- 1 tsp. lemon juice
- 3 ¼ cups (14.4 oz.) all-purpose flour
- 8 tbsps. unsalted butter, melted
- 2 tsps. baking powder
- ½ tsp. baking soda
- ¼ tsp. salt
- 3 large eggs
- 1 cup (8 oz.) sour cream
- 2 tsps. vanilla extract

Preheat the oven to 350 degrees F. Grease and flour a 9–10" spring form pan.

In a small bowl, combine the plums, 2 tbsps. sugar and lemon juice and toss to coat. Set aside.

In a small bowl, combine 1 cup (4.4 oz.) flour, ½ cup (3.5 oz.) sugar and the melted butter. Stir with a fork until the mixture forms crumbs. Set aside.

Combine the remaining 2 ¼ cups (10 oz.) flour, 1 cup (7 oz.) granulated sugar, baking powder, baking soda and salt in a large bowl. Whisk together the eggs, sour cream and vanilla in a measuring cup. Make a well in the center of the flour mixture and add the sour cream mixture. Beat for 2–3 minutes, until smooth.

Spoon the batter into the prepared pan and spread evenly. Spoon the plum slices on in a single layer. Sprinkle the crumb topping evenly over top.

Bake for 45–50 minutes, until the topping is golden brown and a toothpick inserted into the center of the cake comes out clean. Transfer the pan to a wire rack and let cool for 5 minutes. Remove the spring form ring and cool for 15 minutes longer before serving.

Make Ahead Tip: Cut fruit may be refrigerated overnight for up to 8 hours in a solution of Fruit Fresh, or other ascorbic acid fruit preserver. The crumb topping may be made and refrigerated the night before assembling the coffeecake.

Spice Coffeecake

Spice cake is one of my favorite autumn desserts. This crumb-topped coffeecake isn't too sweet, but packs a lot of flavor.

SERVES 8-10

- 2 ¼ cups (10 oz.) all-purpose flour
- ¾ cup (5.8 oz.) light brown sugar
- 1 tsp. finely grated orange zest
- 14 tbsps. unsalted butter, cut into bits
- ¾ cup (5.3 oz.) granulated sugar
- ½ tsp. cinnamon
- ½ tsp. freshly grated nutmeg
- ½ tsp. ground ginger
- ¼ tsp. ground cloves
- 2 tsps. baking powder
- ¼ tsp. salt
- ⅔ cup (5.3 fl. oz.) buttermilk
- 3 large egg whites

Preheat oven to 350 degrees F. Grease an 8" x 8" baking dish and set aside.

Combine ½ cup (2.2 oz.) flour, brown sugar and orange zest in a medium bowl. Cut in 6 tbsps. butter with a pastry blender until crumbly. Set aside.

Combine the remaining 8 tbsps. butter and granulated sugar in the bowl of a stand mixer. Mix until light and fluffy, about 3-4 minutes. Combine the remaining 1 ¾ cups (7.8 oz.) flour, cinnamon, nutmeg, ginger, clove, baking powder and salt in a separate large bowl. Add half the flour mixture to the butter mixture and mix to combine. Stir in the buttermilk. Add the remaining flour and mix until just combined. Whisk the egg whites to soft peaks in a separate bowl. Fold the egg whites into the batter.

Spread the batter into the baking dish. Sprinkle the topping evenly over the batter. Bake for 35-40 minutes, until golden brown and a toothpick inserted into the center comes out clean. Allow the cake to cool for 5 minutes before cutting into squares to serve.

Make Ahead Tip: Make the crumb topping the night before assembling the coffeecake.

Honey Pecan Monkey Bread

Monkey bread typically features balls of yeast dough dipped in melted butter, rolled in cinnamon-sugar and baked in a fluted pan or in individual molds (see instructions on p. 113) . This version uses sweet roll dough for added flavor.

SERVES 8-10

- 1 cup (7.7 oz.) light brown sugar
- 2 tsps. ground cinnamon
- 16 tbsps. unsalted butter
- ½ recipe Sweet Roll Dough (see p. 280), refrigerated
- ⅓ cup (4 oz.) honey
- ⅓ cup (2.35 oz.) granulated sugar
- 2 cups (7.7 oz.) chopped pecans

Grease and flour a 10- to 12-cup Bundt pan and set aside.

Combine the brown sugar and cinnamon in a shallow dish and set aside. Melt 8 tbsps. butter and pour it into a shallow bowl. Set aside.

Turn the dough out onto a lightly floured work surface and press it into a roughly 6" x 10" rectangle. Cut the dough into 1" squares, forming 60 pieces total. Roll each piece of dough into a ball with lightly floured hands, stretching and tucking the dough as necessary to make the balls as smooth as possible.

Dip the balls, one at a time, into melted butter, allowing excess butter to drip back into the dish. Roll the dipped dough ball in the brown sugar mixture and place it into the Bundt pan. Continue dipping and layering the balls until all coated balls are in the pan.

Cover the pan with plastic wrap and let the monkey bread rise until puffy and doubled in size, about 1-1 ½ hours.

In the meantime, combine the remaining 8 tbsps. butter, honey and sugar in a small saucepan. Bring the mixture to a boil over medium heat, stirring constantly. Stir in the pecans and remove the pan from the heat. Set aside.

Preheat the oven to 350 degrees F.

Bake for about 30–35 minutes, until the dough is cooked through. Cool the monkey bread in the pan for 5 minutes, then turn it out on a platter or large plate. Pour the pecan glaze evenly over the monkey bread. Allow the glaze to set for 4–5 minutes and serve warm.

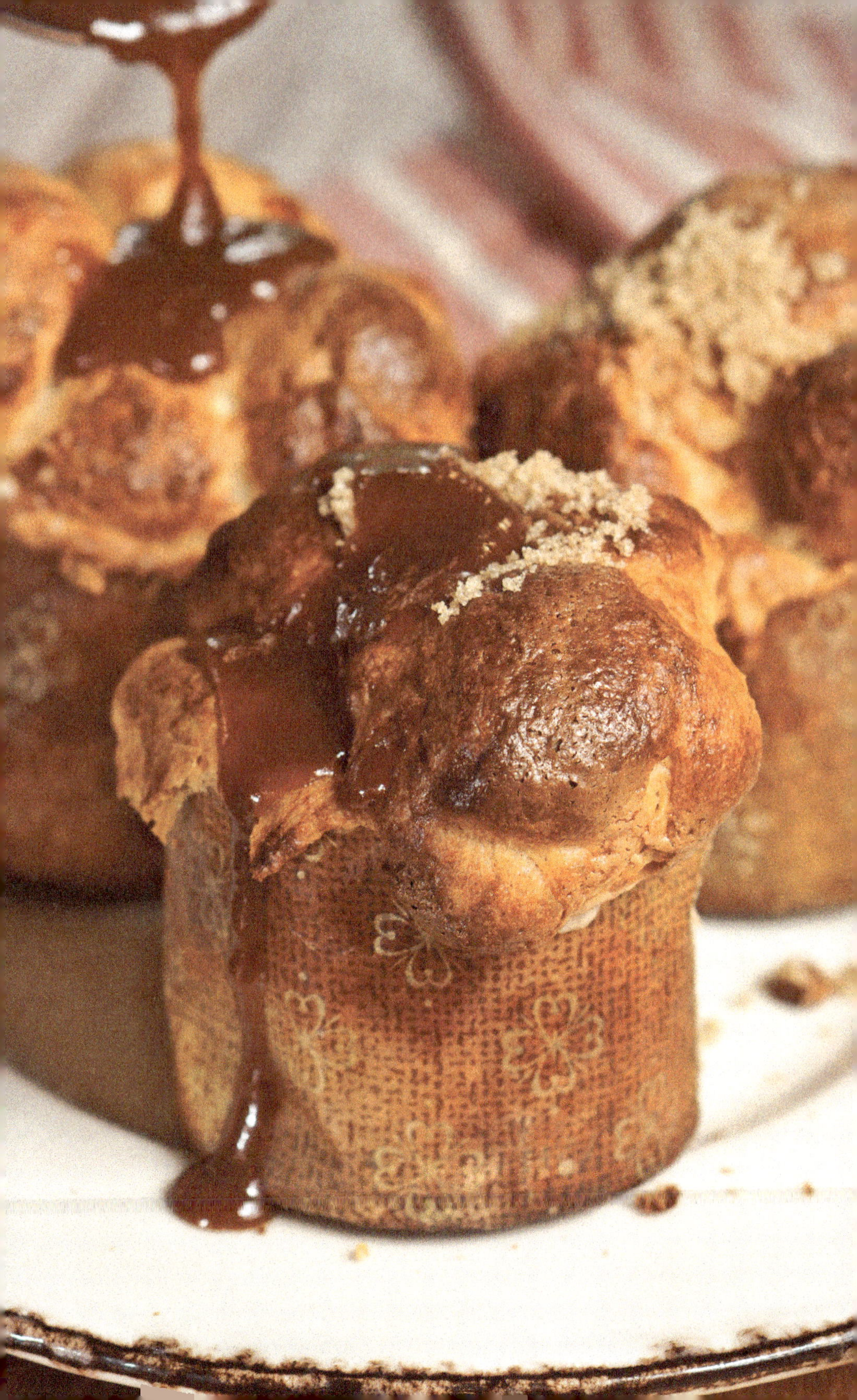

Monkey Bread with Caramel Glaze

This version of monkey bread is made in individual molds, perfect for entertaining or a buffet-style presentation. The recipe is easily divided in half if you need to serve less people. I like to use panettone paper molds for these to make individual servings. Please note that paper molds are not the same as paper liners—they are designed to replace pans and stand alone on a baking sheet. If you don't have the molds and still want to make individual breads, grease a standard muffin tin or line it with paper liners.

🍰 MAKES 12 INDIVIDUAL BREADS

- ½ recipe Traditional Brioche (see recipe p. 284) or 1 Recipe Simple Brioche (see recipe p. 288)
- 1 ¼ cups (9.7 oz.) light brown sugar
- ½ cup (3.6 oz.) granulated sugar

- 2 tsps. ground cinnamon
- ½ cup (4 oz.) crème fraiche
- 8 tbsps. unsalted butter
- 1 tsp. vanilla extract

Remove the brioche dough from the refrigerator (if it's frozen, defrost in the refrigerator overnight).

Line a baking sheet with parchment paper. Set 12 individual panettone or cupcake molds on the baking sheet and set aside.

Turn the dough out onto a lightly floured work surface and press it into a roughly 6" x 10" rectangle. Cut the dough into 1" squares, forming 60 pieces total. Roll each piece of dough into a ball with lightly floured hands, stretching and tucking the dough as necessary to make the balls as smooth as possible.

Whisk ¾ cup (5.7 oz.) brown sugar, ¼ cup (1.8 oz.) granulated sugar and cinnamon together in a medium bowl. Reserve 2 tbsps. of the mixture. Add the crème fraiche to the remaining cinnamon sugar and whisk to combine. Toss five pieces of dough in the crème fraiche mixture until the pieces are well coated and place them in one of the individual panettone molds. Continue until all 12 monkey breads are complete. Set the filled liners on the baking sheet. Cover with a tented, unscented plastic bag. Allow to rise at room temperature until the dough has almost doubled in size, about 1–1 ½ hours or in the refrigerator overnight.

Preheat the oven to 350 degrees F. Sprinkle the remaining cinnamon sugar evenly over the monkey breads. Bake for 20–25 minutes, until golden brown and slightly firm to the touch.

While the breads are baking, heat the butter in a medium saucepan over medium heat. Stir in the remaining ½ cup (4 oz.) brown sugar, ¼ cup (1.8 oz.) granulated sugar and vanilla. Bring the mixture just to a boil, whisking to melt the sugar. Spoon the warm sauce evenly over the monkey breads to serve.

Make Ahead Tip: Make the brioche ahead and keep it frozen until ready to make the monkey breads. Assemble the breads the night before you want to serve them and allow them to rise in the refrigerator overnight. Allow them to come to room temperature while preheating the oven.

Pecan Sticky Buns

These gooey sticky buns made with buttery brioche dough are best warm from the oven, but are also tasty the next day. However, because I don't use corn syrup in the glaze, the coating will crystallize slightly as the buns cool. To enjoy delicious buns the next day, simply reheat them briefly in the microwave or oven to melt the sugar crystals. You can also use the Sweet Roll Dough on p. 280 instead of the brioche.

MAKES 12 BUNS

- 1 ¼ cups (9.7 oz.) light brown sugar
- ½ cup (3.5 oz.) granulated sugar
- 2 tsps. ground cinnamon

- 1 cup (3.8 oz.) chopped pecans
- 8 tbsps. unsalted butter
- ½ recipe Traditional Brioche (see recipe p. 284) or 1 recipe Simple Brioche (p. 288)

Lightly grease 12 individual muffin tins or a 9" x 13" baking dish and set aside.

Combine the brown sugar, granulated sugar and cinnamon in a medium bowl. Place ½ cup of the mixture in a separate bowl and stir in half of the pecans. Set aside.

Melt the butter in a medium saucepan over medium heat. Reserve 2 tbsps. melted butter and set aside. Add the remaining brown sugar mixture to the saucepan, whisking until smooth and just bubbling. Divide the mixture evenly among the muffin cups (or pour evenly into the baking dish). Sprinkle the remaining chopped pecans evenly over the muffin cups (alternatively, you can place 3–4 pecan halves in a circular pattern in each cup).

Turn dough out onto a lightly floured surface and roll into a 16" x 12" rectangle (long side facing you). Brush the dough evenly with the reserved melted butter. Sprinkle on the brown sugar and pecan mixture, leaving a 1" border uncovered along the top. Starting at the long side close to you, tightly roll the dough up. Press on the seam to seal. Cut into 12 even pieces and place cut side down in the muffin tins. Cover and let rise for 1-1 ½ hours until almost doubled, or refrigerate overnight.

Preheat the oven to 350 degrees F.

Bake in preheated oven for 25–30 minutes, until golden brown. If necessary, tent the rolls with foil halfway through baking to prevent over-browning. Let cool in pan for 3 minutes, then invert onto a second baking sheet or serving platter. Scrape any remaining filling from the pan onto the rolls. Allow the rolls to cool slightly and the glaze to set up, about 10–15 minutes, before serving.

Make Ahead Tip: Assemble the buns and allow them to rise overnight in the refrigerator. Bring the buns to room temperature before baking off in the morning.

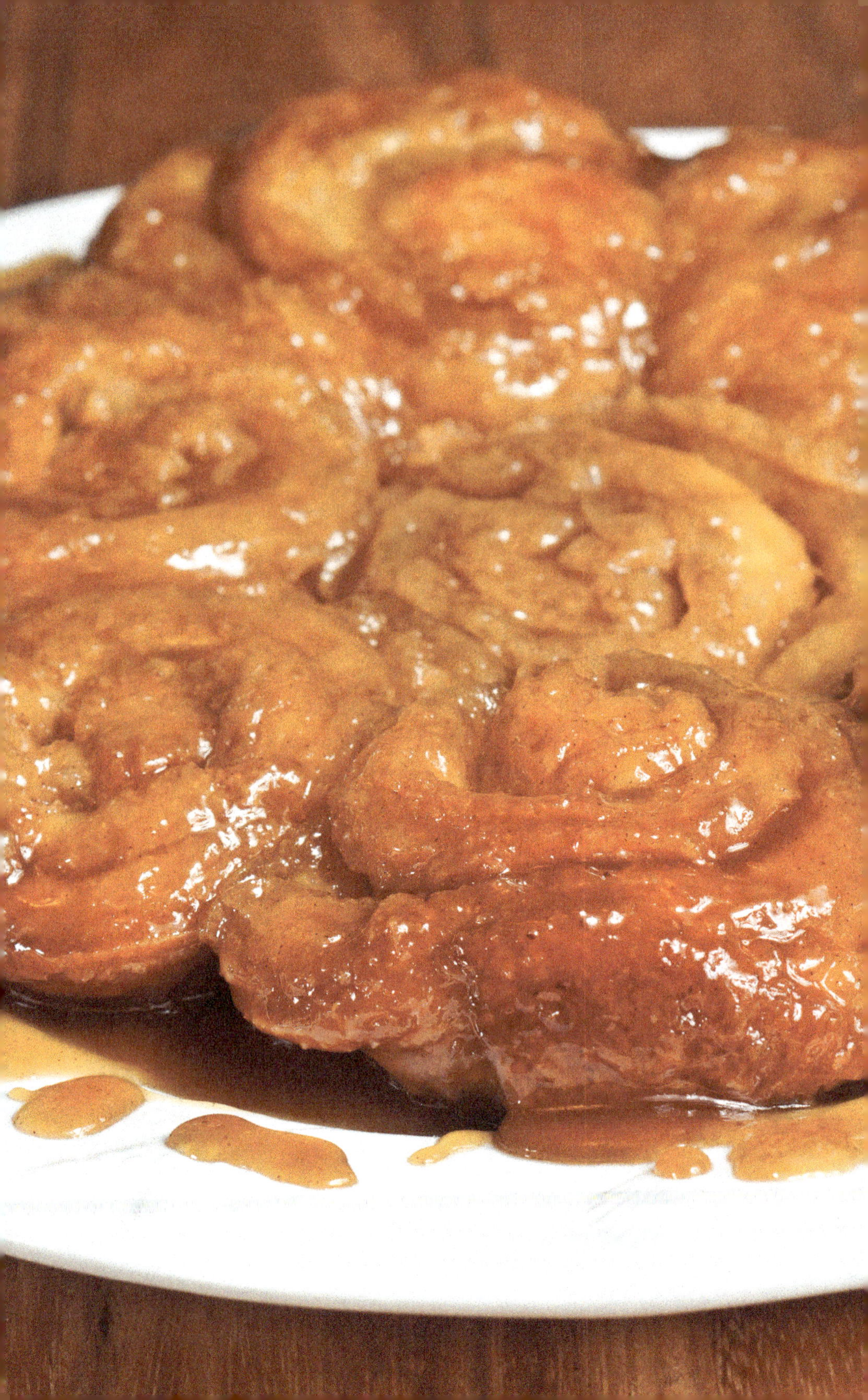

Maple Caramel Sticky Buns

Sweet roll dough coated with maple caramel glaze makes a delicious pull-apart sticky bun.

🍞 MAKES 8 BUNS

- ¼ cup (2.8 oz.) maple syrup
- 5 tbsps. unsalted butter, melted
- ⅓ cup (2.6 oz.) light brown sugar
- ⅓ cup (2.35 oz.) granulated sugar
- 2 tsps. ground cinnamon
- 1 tbsp. all-purpose flour
- ½ recipe Sweet Roll Dough (see recipe p. 280)

Grease a 9" cake pan and set aside.

Combine the maple syrup, 3 tbsps. melted butter and brown sugar in a small saucepan over medium heat. Stir until the sugar is melted, about 3-4 minutes. Pour the mixture into the bottom of the pan and cool completely to room temperature.

Combine the granulated sugar, cinnamon and flour in a small bowl or measuring cup.

Turn dough out onto a lightly floured surface and roll into a 12" x 12" square about ¼" thick. Brush the dough evenly with the remaining 2 tbsps. melted butter. Sprinkle on the cinnamon sugar mixture, leaving a 1" border uncovered along the top. Starting at the bottom, tightly roll the dough up. Press on the seam to seal. Cut into 8 even pieces. Place 7 pieces evenly around the outer edge of the pan, cut side down. Place the remaining piece in the center. Cover and let rise for 1-1 ½ hours or until doubled in volume and buns are touching.

Preheat the oven to 375 degrees F.

Bake for 25–30 minutes, until golden brown and dough is cooked through. If necessary, tent the rolls with foil halfway through baking to prevent over-browning.

Let cool in pan for 3 minutes, then invert onto a second baking sheet or serving platter. Scrape any remaining filling from the pan onto the buns (use caution, as the hot glaze can cause a serious burn). Allow the buns to cool slightly and the glaze to set up before serving, about 15–20 minutes.

Make Ahead Tip: Shape the buns and place them in the pan with the glaze the night before serving. Refrigerate overnight. Allow the buns to come to room temperature and rise until doubled before baking.

Croissant Cinnamon Rolls

The final rise of these rolls takes at least 2 hours, so if you want to serve them first thing in the morning, you will need to plan ahead. When we served these for breakfast at the inn, one of us would get over to the restaurant kitchen early and place the refrigerated buns in the oven with a pan of boiling water to jump-start the rise. You can also make mini-cinnamon rolls by rolling the dough into an 8" x 24" rectangle and dividing each roll into 20–24 pieces.

🔲 MAKES 12 ROLLS

- 1 cup (7.76 oz.) light brown sugar
- 2 tsps. ground cinnamon

- 1 recipe Traditional (p. 296) or Simple Croissant Dough (p. 300), refrigerated
- 1 large egg

Line 2 baking sheets with parchment. Mix the brown sugar and cinnamon together and set aside.

Remove the dough from the refrigerator and roll out to a rectangle about 10" x 15". Spread the cinnamon-sugar evenly over the dough, leaving a 1" border uncovered along the top. Starting at the side close to you, tightly roll the dough up. Press on the seam to seal. Trim off the ends. Wrap the log in plastic wrap and refrigerate for 30 minutes.

Line 2 baking sheets with parchment. Slice the dough into ¾" pieces. Place the pieces cut side down onto the baking sheet, leaving 2–3" between each. Tuck the end of each pastry underneath to prevent it from unravelling. Cover loosely and allow the buns to rise about 2–2 ½ hours until they are puffed and almost double in size (if you press on the dough, the imprint will remain).

Preheat the oven to 375 degrees F. Whisk the egg with a pinch of salt. Brush the buns all over with the egg wash. Bake the buns for 10 minutes. Sprinkle the remaining brown sugar mixture evenly over the tops of the buns and bake them for 5–8 minutes longer, until they are evenly browned. Allow the buns to cool 5 minutes, then transfer the rolls to a baking rack. Cool 5 minutes longer before serving.

Make Ahead Tip: Make the croissant dough and freeze it until 2 days before assembling the rolls. Defrost it overnight in the refrigerator before rolling out. The individual buns may be frozen on a baking sheet and placed in a Zip-lock bag to bake off at a later time. Defrost the frozen buns in the refrigerator overnight, then allow to rise as described above before baking.

Almond Croissant Rolls

This is a variation on the cinnamon rolls filled with almond cream, which has a thick consistency so it will not run out of the croissant rolls during baking. These rolls require at least 2 hours for the final rise, so plan accordingly if you want to serve them early in the morning.

🍞 **MAKES 12 ROLLS**

- 9 tbsps. unsalted butter, softened
- ½ cup (3.5 oz.) granulated sugar
- 1 cup (3.35 oz.) almond flour
- 1 large egg
- ¼ cup (1.1 oz.) all-purpose flour
- 1 recipe Simple (p. 300) or Traditional Croissant Dough (p. 296), refrigerated

Combine the butter, sugar and almond flour in the bowl of a stand mixer and beat until light and fluffy, about 5 minutes. Add the egg and mix until light and creamy, about 3-4 minutes. Add the all-purpose flour and beat on low until just incorporated, about 30 seconds. Set aside.

Remove the dough from the refrigerator and roll out to a rectangle about 10" x 15". Spread the almond filling evenly over the dough, leaving a 1" border uncovered along the top. Starting at the side close to you, tightly roll the dough up. Press on the seam to seal. Trim off the ends. Wrap the log in plastic wrap and refrigerate for 30 minutes.

Line 2 baking sheets with parchment. Slice the dough into ¾" pieces. Place the pieces cut side down onto the baking sheet, leaving 2-3" between each. Tuck the end of each pastry underneath to prevent it from unravelling. Cover loosely and allow the buns to rise about 2-2 ½ hours until they are puffed and almost double in size (if you press on the dough, the imprint will remain).

Preheat the oven to 375 degrees F.

Bake for 12-15 minutes, until golden brown. Allow the rolls to cool 5 minutes, then transfer them to a baking rack. Cool 5 minutes longer before serving.

Make Ahead Tip: Make the croissant dough and freeze it until 2 days before assembling the rolls. Defrost it overnight in the refrigerator before rolling out. The almond filling may be made up to 5 days in advance and refrigerated until ready to assemble the rolls.

Raisin Cream Croissant Rolls

A variation on traditional raisin croissants, these rolls require at least 2 hours for the final rise. As with the other croissant recipes, you will need to plan accordingly if you want to serve them first thing in the morning.

🧈 MAKES 12 ROLLS

- 2 ½ tbsps. all-purpose flour
- 1 tbsp. cornstarch
- 1 cup (8 fl. oz.) half and half
- 1 large egg, lightly beaten

- ¼ cup (1.8 oz.) granulated sugar
- ½ tsp. vanilla bean paste
- 1 recipe Simple (p. 300) or Traditional Croissant Dough (p. 296), refrigerated

Set a bowl over a second bowl filled with ice and water.

In a small mixing bowl, whisk the flour, cornstarch and ¼ cup (2 fl. oz.) half and half until smooth. Whisk in the egg and set aside.

Combine the remaining ¾ cup (6 fl. oz.) half and half, sugar and vanilla bean paste in a medium saucepan. Stir over medium heat until the sugar has dissolved and the mixture comes to a boil. Add the flour mixture and whisk vigorously. Whisk until mixture has thickened, about 2–3 minutes. Remove from the heat and transfer the custard to a bowl. Place plastic wrap directly on top of the custard to prevent a skin from forming. Let cool and refrigerate until needed.

Remove the dough from the refrigerator and roll out to a rectangle about 10" x 15" (long edge toward you). Spread the custard filling evenly over the dough, leaving a 1" border uncovered along the top. Sprinkle the raisins evenly over the custard. Starting at the side close to you, tightly roll the dough up. Press on the seam to seal. Trim off the ends. Wrap the log in plastic wrap and refrigerate for 30 minutes.

Line 2 baking sheets with parchment. Slice the dough into ¾" pieces. Place the pieces cut side down onto the baking sheet, leaving 2–3" between each. Tuck the end of each pastry underneath to prevent it from unravelling. Cover loosely and allow the buns to rise about 2–2 ½ hours until they are puffed and almost double in size (if you press on the dough, the imprint will remain).

Preheat the oven to 375 degrees F. Bake for 12–15 minutes, until golden brown.

Make Ahead Tip: Make the croissant dough and freeze it until 2 days before assembling the rolls. Defrost it overnight in the refrigerator before rolling out. The custard may be made the day before and refrigerated up to 24 hours.

Apricot Orange Sweet Rolls

I love the combination of apricot filling encased in sweet roll dough, finished with an orange-scented cream cheese glaze. You can also make this with the Simple Brioche Dough found on p. 288.

🧊 MAKES 12 ROLLS

- 1 cup (11.3 oz.) apricot fruit spread (see recipe p. 305) or preserves
- 3 tbsps. Grand Marnier or Cointreau (or substitute orange juice)
- 2 oz. cream cheese, softened
- 1 tbsp. unsalted butter, softened

- 2 tbsps. orange juice
- 1 tsp. vanilla extract
- 1 tsp. finely grated orange zest
- 1 cup (4.23 oz.) confectioner's sugar
- 1 recipe Sweet Roll Dough (see recipe p. 280)
- 1 large egg

In a small saucepan, combine the apricot spread with the Grand Marnier. Bring just to a boil over medium heat and stir for 1 minute. Remove from the heat and allow to cool completely.

Blend the cream cheese, butter, orange juice, vanilla, orange zest and confectioner's sugar in a medium bowl and whisk until smooth. Cover and set aside.

Lightly grease a 9" spring-form pan (or use a 3"-deep tart pan with a removable bottom) and place it on a baking sheet.

Turn the dough out onto a lightly floured surface and press it into a rectangle. Roll the dough out into a 15" x 9" rectangle. With the long side toward you, spread the apricot orange mixture evenly over the dough, leaving a 1" border at the top uncovered. Starting at the long side close to you, tightly roll the dough up. Press on the seam to seal. Cut into 12 even pieces. Place 9 pieces evenly around the outer edge of the pan, cut side down. Arrange the remaining 3 pieces in the center about 1" apart. Cover with plastic wrap and let rise for 1 ½–2 hours, until doubled in volume, or overnight in the refrigerator.

Preheat the oven to 350 degrees F. Remove the plastic wrap from the pan. Whisk together the egg with 1 tbsp. water. Brush the egg wash all over the rolls. Bake for 25–30 minutes until golden brown. Cover the pan loosely with foil for the last 10 minutes if necessary to prevent over-browning. Allow to cool for 5 minutes, then transfer the rolls to a baking rack.

Drizzle with the cream cheese glaze. Allow the glaze to set up for 5 minutes before serving.

Make Ahead Tip: Make the Sweet Roll Dough and glaze 2 days before and refrigerate until ready to assemble the rolls. The rolls may also be assembled the night before and allowed to rise in the refrigerator overnight.

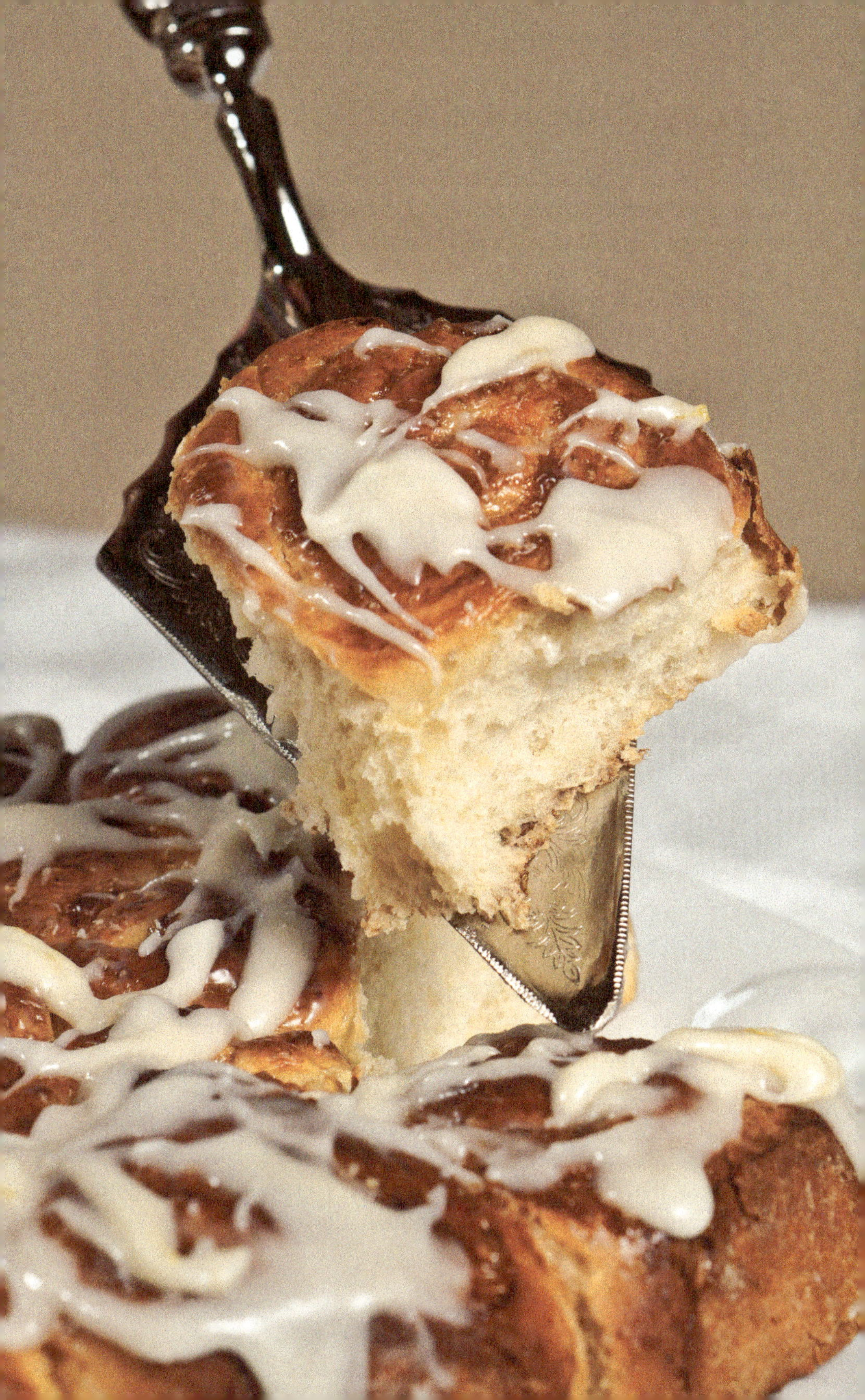

Honey Almond Crescents

These sweet crescents look similar to croissants, but without the extra time required to make the croissant dough. The honey cream cheese filling adds a rich flavor.

🧈 MAKES 8 LARGE CRESCENTS

- 6 tbsps. unsalted butter
- ¼ cup (3 oz.) plus 3 tbsps. honey
- ¼ cup (1.8 oz.) granulated sugar

- 4 oz. cream cheese, softened
- ½ cup (2 oz.) sliced almonds
- ½ recipe Sweet Roll Dough (see recipe p. 280)

Line a baking sheet with parchment and grease the parchment.

Combine the butter, ¼ cup (3 oz.) honey and granulated sugar in a medium saucepan. Bring to a boil over medium heat, stirring to dissolve the sugar. Pour the mixture into a heatproof measuring cup or bowl and cool completely. Refrigerate until ready to use.

Combine the cream cheese and remaining 3 tbsps. honey in a small bowl (or use an electric mixer). Stir in ¼ cup (1 oz.) almonds.

Turn the dough onto a lightly floured surface. Roll the dough into a 16" x 14" rectangle with the long edge facing you. Measure across the bottom edge and mark every 4". Cut the dough into 4 even rectangles, 4" x 14". Cut each rectangle in half diagonally, forming 2 even triangles (8 in total). Spread the cream cheese mixture evenly over the triangles.

Roll the dough up, lightly pressing outward as you roll so that the sides extend slightly. Place the rolled dough on a parchment-lined baking sheet, tucking the pointed tip underneath (you can tuck the pointed ends in together if you prefer a tighter crescent shape). Press down lightly to secure the tip underneath and flatten the bottom. Repeat with the remaining pieces of dough, placing eight finished rolls at least 2" apart on the baking sheet. Cover and let rise for 1–1 ½ hours, until almost doubled in volume, or overnight in the refrigerator.

Preheat the oven to 350 degrees F.

Bake for 20–25 minutes, until golden brown and the dough is firm and baked through. Transfer the crescents to a rack and allow them to cool slightly. Warm the glaze slightly and drizzle it evenly over the crescents. Sprinkle the remaining ¼ cup almonds over the glazed crescents. Allow the glaze to set up for 5 minutes before serving.

Make Ahead Tip: The filling may be combined and refrigerated the day before assembly. The rolled crescents may be refrigerated overnight and brought to room temperature before baking off.

Cheese Danish

🍰 MAKES 4 PASTRIES

This is a basic cheese Danish that's delicious as described, but can be enhanced with the addition of fruit spreads or even chocolate chips according to taste. This Danish is a simple folded pattern, but any variation may be used to enclose the filling. The recipe is easily converted for more servings.

- ¼ recipe Danish Pastry Dough recipe (see recipe p. 290)
- 4 oz. cream cheese, softened
- 3 tbsps. granulated sugar
- 1 large egg yolk
- ½ tsp. vanilla extract
- 1 tbsp. sour cream
- 1 tsp. finely grated lemon zest
- 1 large egg

Preheat the oven to 375 degrees F. Line a baking sheet with parchment and lightly grease the paper.

Roll out the pastry dough on a lightly floured surface to form a 16" x 16" square about ¼" thick. Divide the dough into 4 (4" x 4") squares.

Beat the cream cheese, sugar, egg yolk and vanilla by hand or with a mixer until smooth. Mix in the sour cream and lemon zest. Divide the filling evenly among the 4 squares. Whisk the egg with 1 tbsp. water and brush the mixture on the edges of the pastry. Fold in 2 opposite corners of each square to overlap in the center, pressing the 2 ends together. Brush the tops of the pastries with the remaining egg wash.

Place the Danish on the baking sheet and bake for 15–18 minutes, until the filling is firm and the pastries are golden brown. Cool the pastries on a baking rack until ready to serve.

Make Ahead Tip: Make the Danish Pastry Dough and freeze it until 2 days before assembling the rolls. Defrost it overnight in the refrigerator before rolling out. The cheese filling may be made the day before and refrigerated up to 24 hours.

Coconut Almond Bear Claw Danish

🍰 MAKES 6 DANISH

- 2 logs Almond Paste, about 6 oz. (see recipe p. 304)
- ¼ cup (0.82 oz.) sweetened shredded coconut
- 1 cup (3.8 oz.) vanilla cake crumbs (optional)—see Chef's Tip
- 1 large egg
- ½ recipe Danish Pastry Dough (see recipe p. 290)
- ¼ cup (1 oz.) sliced almonds

Divide the almond paste logs to form 6 (4") pieces, pressing the pieces together as necessary. Combine the coconut and cake crumbs (if using) on a plate or shallow dish and roll each log in the mixture, pressing to coat. Whisk the egg with 1 tbsp. water in a measuring cup or small bowl. Line a baking sheet with parchment paper.

Place the dough on a lightly floured work surface and roll out into a 10" x 15" rectangle. Cut the dough into 6 (5") squares. Place a log near the edge of 1 of the squares, leaving about a ½" edge. Lightly brush the edge with egg wash. Fold the dough over the filling, leaving about ⅓ of the dough still lying flat on the bottom. Make 3 (1" to 2") slashes evenly along the bottom edge of the remaining dough. Bend the filled end of the dough into a crescent to open the space up between the slashes. Place the pastry on the prepared baking sheet and continue until all 6 are formed. Refrigerate the remaining egg wash.

Cover the pan loosely with plastic wrap (or use an unscented plastic bag) and allow to rise at room temperature until the pastries are puffy, about 1 ½–2 hours.

Brush the tops of the pastries lightly with the egg wash and sprinkle on the sliced almonds.

Bake until golden brown, about 18–20 minutes, turning the pans halfway through baking. Transfer to a rack and cool for 10 minutes before serving

Chef's Tip: You can add cake crumbs to the filling to give it a little more body, but it's not necessary. If you do choose to add the crumbs, 2 unfrosted vanilla cupcakes will yield about 1 cup (4 oz.).

Make Ahead Tip: Make the Danish Pastry Dough and freeze it until 2 days before assembling the rolls. Defrost it overnight in the refrigerator before rolling out.

Mixed Berry Braid

Berries and cream cheese fill this lovely braided dough, which is actually quite easy to assemble. Make sure you place the dough on the parchment-lined sheet before filling, as it's difficult to move once filled.

SERVES 8-10

- 1 cup (4.3 oz.) blackberries
- 1 cup (4.3 oz.) raspberries
- ½ cup (3.5 oz.) plus 2 tbsps. granulated sugar
- 1 tbsp. lemon juice
- 4 oz. cream cheese, softened
- 1 tsp. lemon zest
- 1 large egg yolk
- 1 recipe Sweet Roll Dough (see recipe p. 280)
- 1 large egg
- 1 cup (4.23 oz.) confectioners' sugar
- 1 tsp. vanilla extract
- 2 tbsps. unsalted butter, softened

Combine the blackberries, raspberries, ½ cup (3.5 oz.) granulated sugar and lemon juice in a medium saucepan. Crush the berries with a potato masher to release their juices. Bring to a boil over medium-high heat, stirring to dissolve the sugar. Cook for 6–8 minutes, until the mixture is thickened (the temperature should reach 220 degrees F). Cool completely.

Combine the cream cheese, remaining 2 tbsps. granulated sugar and lemon zest in a medium bowl (or use an electric mixer). Beat in the egg yolk until just smooth. Set aside.

Roll the dough into a 12" x 12" square, about ¼" thick. Score the dough (without cutting through) into 3 even sections, 4" x 12" each.

Line a baking sheet with parchment and lightly grease the parchment. Place the squared dough onto the parchment. Slice the outer thirds of the dough into ¾" strips at a slight angle. (These thin strips will be folded over the filling to form the braid).

Spoon the cream cheese filling down the solid center of the pastry. Spread the berry filling evenly over top. Fold the left bottom strip up and over the filling at an angle. Repeat with the right bottom strip, slightly overlapping the first. Repeat with the remaining strips all the way up. Tuck the ends in to seal the filling. Cover the dough with plastic wrap and allow it to rest for 30 minutes.

In the meantime, preheat the oven to 375 degrees F. Whisk the egg with a pinch of salt. Brush it all over the braid. Bake for 15–20 minutes, until golden brown. Transfer the braid on the parchment to a rack to cool completely.

Combine the confectioners' sugar, vanilla and butter in a medium bowl. Whisk in 2 tbsps. water to form a glaze. Drizzle the glaze evenly over the braid. Allow the glaze to set up for 5 minutes before serving.

Make Ahead Tip: Make the Sweet Pastry Dough and fillings the night before and refrigerate. Assemble the braid in the morning before baking off.

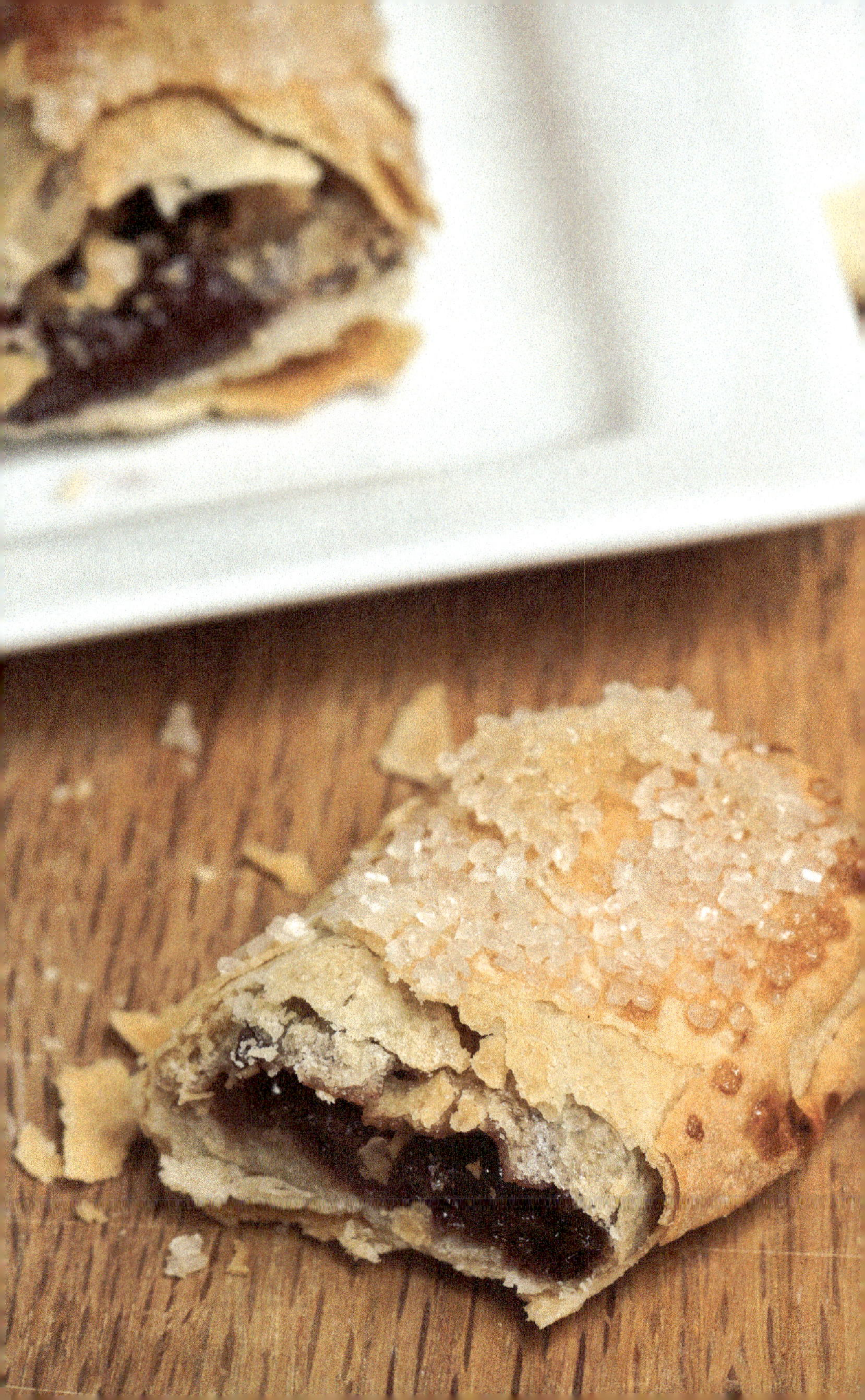

Cherry Strudel

Instead of the traditional strudel apple raisin filling, this sweet cherry filling makes this a seasonal summer treat. The addition of green tea brightens the flavor of the cherries. Making strudel involves stretching the dough till it's almost translucent. However, don't be intimidated—it's actually a very forgiving dough. Because this strudel is about half the size of a traditional one, it's more manageable to make in any size kitchen.

SERVES 6-8

- 2 cups (16 oz.) sweet cherries, stemmed and pitted
- ⅓ cup (2.35 oz.) granulated sugar
- 3 tbsps. brewed green tea
- 1 tsp. cornstarch
- 1 tsp. lemon juice

- 1 cup (4.4 oz.) all-purpose flour
- ¼ tsp. salt
- 1 ½ tbsps. canola oil
- 3 tbsps. unsalted butter, melted
- 1 tbsp. sanding sugar

Combine the cherries, sugar and green tea in a medium saucepan over medium heat. Stir until the sugar is completely dissolved. Bring the mixture to a boil and cook for 4-5 minutes, until slightly thickened. Whisk the cornstarch with 1 tbsp. water in a small bowl or measuring cup. Stir the cornstarch into the cherries and simmer, stirring constantly, until the mixture is thickened and the liquid is clear. Remove from the heat and stir in the lemon juice. Cool completely.

Combine the flour and salt in the bowl of a stand mixer. Stir the oil and ⅓ cup (2.6 fl. oz.) water into the flour. Mix on low until dough pulls away from the sides of the bowl. Switch to the dough hook and knead until smooth, about 5-6 minutes. Turn the dough onto a lightly floured work surface and knead for 2 minutes longer. Place the dough into a lightly greased bowl, cover and allow it to rest for 1 hour.

Preheat the oven to 400 degrees F. Line a baking sheet with parchment.

Lay a large (at least 12" x 18"), smooth kitchen towel on a work surface. Sprinkle the cloth with flour and place the dough in the center. Roll the dough out to a square 10" x 10", flipping the dough and adding flour as necessary so that it doesn't stick to the cloth.

Pick up the dough by an edge and allow the weight of the dough to stretch it. Place it on the towel and continue pulling and stretching from the center out to the edges, until the dough is tissue thin (the edges will be thicker) and measures about 12" x 18". Trim and discard the thicker edges of the dough.

Brush the dough with half the melted butter. Spoon the cherry filling onto the dough, leaving a 3" edge along 1 of the longer sides and 2" on the short ends, without filling. Use the towel to fold the 3" edge of the dough onto the filling. Continue to roll the strudel over, using the towel. About halfway through the rolling, tuck the ends under to seal them. Continue rolling until it forms a log. Transfer the strudel to the parchment seam side down. Brush the dough with the remaining melted butter and sprinkle on the sanding sugar.

Bake for 25–30 minutes, until deep golden brown. Slide the strudel and parchment onto a rack and cool for 30 minutes before serving.

Make Ahead Tip: The cherry filling may be made the day before and refrigerated until ready to assemble the strudel.

Apricot Cheese Pastry Ring

This tasty pastry round is similar to the recipe on p. 139, but without the added effort of braiding the dough.

🍰 SERVES 8-10

- 4 oz. cream cheese, softened
- 2 tbsps. granulated sugar
- 1 tsp. sour cream
- 2 tsps. vanilla extract
- 1 recipe Sweet Roll Dough (see recipe p. 280)

- 1 cup (11.3 oz.) apricot fruit spread (see recipe p. 305) or preserves
- 1 cup (4.23 oz.) confectioners' sugar
- 2 tbsps. whole milk

Line a baking sheet with parchment and lightly grease the parchment.

Combine the cream cheese and granulated sugar in a medium bowl (or use an electric mixer). Beat in the sour cream and 1 tsp. vanilla extract until just smooth. Set aside.

Roll the dough into a 10" x 16" rectangle, about ¼" thick. Position the long side toward you. Spread the cheese mixture evenly over the dough, leaving a 1" border at the top. Spoon the apricot spread evenly over the cheese. Starting with the long end at the bottom, roll the dough up into a log and press the edge to seal. Stretch the ends of the dough, curving them into a ring. Seal the ends together. Place the ring seam-side down on the parchment-lined sheet.

Cut ⅔ of the way through the loaf at about 1" intervals around the ring with kitchen shears. Twist the sections slightly to expose the cut sides. Cover the ring with plastic wrap and allow the dough to rise for 45 minutes.

Preheat the oven to 350 degrees F.

Bake the ring for 25–30 minutes, until the top is golden brown and the filling is beginning to bubble. Transfer the ring to a rack and cool completely.

Combine the confectioners' sugar, remaining 1 tsp. vanilla extract and milk in a medium bowl until smooth. Drizzle the glaze evenly over the ring. Allow the glaze to set up for 5 minutes before serving.

Make Ahead Tip: Make the sweet pastry dough and fillings the night before and refrigerate. Assemble the ring in the morning before baking off.

Cinnamon Pecan Pastry Ring

This pastry ring is delicious any time of the year, but is an especially lovely addition to a holiday breakfast menu.

SERVES 8–10

- ½ cup (4 oz.) light brown sugar
- 2 tsps. ground cinnamon
- 1 tbsp. all-purpose flour
- ½ cup (2 oz.) finely chopped pecans
- 1 recipe Sweet Roll Dough (see recipe p. 280)
- 2 tbsps. unsalted butter, melted
- 1 cup (4.23 oz.) confectioners' sugar
- 1 tsp. vanilla extract
- 2 tbsps. whole milk

Line a baking sheet with parchment and lightly grease the parchment.

Combine the brown sugar, cinnamon and flour in a medium bowl. Stir in the pecans and set aside.

Roll the dough into a 10" x 16" rectangle, about ¼" thick. Position the long side toward you. Brush the melted butter evenly over the dough. Sprinkle the cinnamon-sugar evenly over the dough, leaving a 1" border at the top. Starting with the long end at the bottom, tightly roll the dough up into a log and press the edge to seal. Stretch the ends of the dough, curving them into a ring. Seal the ends together. Place the ring seam-side down on the parchment-lined sheet.

Cover the ring with plastic wrap and allow the dough to rise for 45–60 minutes, until about double in size.

Preheat the oven to 350 degrees F.

Bake the ring for 25–30 minutes, until the top is golden brown. Transfer the ring to a rack and cool for 5 minutes.

Combine the confectioners' sugar, vanilla extract and milk in a medium bowl until smooth. Brush the glaze evenly over the braid. Allow the ring to cool before serving.

Make Ahead Tip: Make the Sweet Pastry Dough and filling the night before and refrigerate. Assemble the ring in the morning before baking off.

Crescents with Pecans and Coconut

These crescents use cream cheese dough and are similar to traditional rugelach. They are terrific for a breakfast buffet when guests want to try a variety of treats or for a coffee reception, since they are much smaller than a typical croissant. You can also use the Sour Cream Dough (p. 283) to make the crescents.

🍰 MAKES 24

- 2 tbsps. granulated sugar
- 2 tbsps. light brown sugar
- ½ tsp. ground cinnamon
- ½ cup (1.6 oz.) sweetened shredded coconut
- ¼ cup (1 oz.) pecans, finely chopped

- 1 recipe Cream Cheese Pastry Dough (see recipe p. 282), refrigerated
- 1 large egg
- 2 tbsps. sanding (decorating) sugar

To make the filling, combine the granulated sugar, brown sugar, cinnamon, coconut and pecans.

Line 2 baking sheets with parchment. On a lightly floured surface, roll 1 piece of the dough into a 10" to 11" circle. Sprinkle on half of the coconut pecan mixture. Gently press the filling into the dough with the back of a spoon.

Cut the circle into quarters, then each quarter into thirds to form 12 equal triangles. Starting at the base of each triangle, roll the dough up to form a crescent. Arrange the roll-ups on 1 baking sheet, tucking the points under the crescents, and refrigerate for at least 30 minutes. Repeat with the second packet of dough.

Preheat the oven to 350 degrees F.

Whisk the egg with 1 tbsp. water in a small bowl or measuring cup. Brush the egg wash over the crescents and sprinkle on the sanding sugar. Bake for 18–25 minutes, until puffed and golden brown. Transfer the crescents to a rack to cool.

Make Ahead Tip: The filling and dough may be made up to 2 days ahead before assembling the crescents. The unbaked crescents may be covered and refrigerated overnight or frozen for up to 2 months. The crescents may also be assembled and baked off up to 3 days before serving.

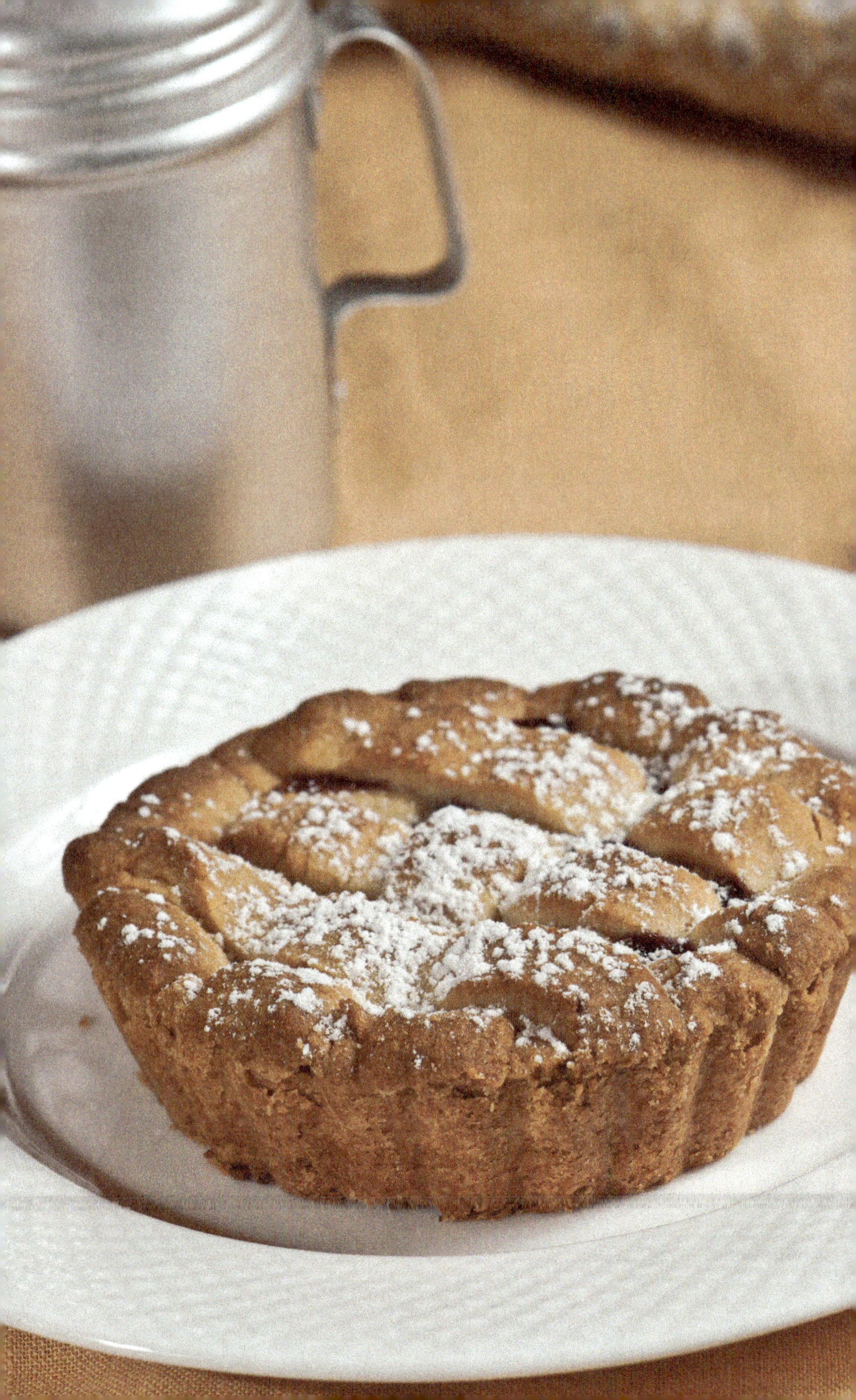

CHAPTER THREE
Cobblers, Crisps, Tarts and Turnovers

- Blueberry Peach Cobbler
- Cobblers, Crisps, Crumbles and Buckles: What's in a Name?
- Apple Buckle
- Apple Cranberry Crisp
- Peach Pecan Crumble
- Apricot Buckle
- Blackberry Cobbler
- Raspberry Lemon Buckle
- Strawberry Rhubarb Crumble
- Apricot Sour Cream Crumble
- Cherry Walnut Crumble
- Apple Raisin Sour Cream Crumble
- Pear Raisin Cobbler
- Mixed Berry Crisp
- Pear Cranberry Tart with Almond
- Blackberry Shortbread Tart
- Rustic Strawberry Ricotta Tart

- Raspberry Cream Tart
- Blueberry Lemon Tart
- Cranberry Raisin Tart
- Plum Custard Tart
- Apple Sour Cream Tart
- Pear Sour Cream Turnovers
- Mixed Berry Turnovers
- Cherry Cream Turnovers
- Apricot Raisin Turnovers

Blueberry Peach Cobbler

I can't even count how many times I've made this simply delicious cobbler at our Maine B & B, and later at our country inn. It's so easy to make and will delight your guests as much as it did mine.

SERVES 6

- ¼ cup (1.8 oz.) plus 2 tbsps. granulated sugar
- 1 ¼ cups (5.5 oz.) all-purpose flour
- 1 tsp. salt
- 2 cups (10.5 oz.) blueberries
- 3 large peaches, peeled, pitted and sliced (about 1 ½ cups)

- 2 tbsps. lemon juice
- 2 tsps. baking powder
- 4 tbsps. unsalted butter, cut into bits
- ⅓ cup (2.6 fl. oz.) whole milk
- 1 large egg
- 2 tbsps. confectioners' sugar

Preheat the oven to 400 degrees F. Grease a 9" x 9" baking dish (or grease 6 individual ramekins and place them on a baking sheet).

Mix ¼ cup (1.8 oz.) sugar, ¼ cup (1.1 oz.) flour and ½ tsp. salt in a medium bowl. Add the blueberries, peaches and lemon juice and toss the mixture to coat the fruit evenly. Spoon the mixture into the baking dish. Bake for 15–18 minutes, until fruit is hot and bubbling.

In the meantime, sift together the remaining 1 cup (4.4 oz.) flour, baking powder, 2 tbsps. sugar and ½ tsp. salt. Cut the butter into the dry ingredients with a pastry blender until the mixture resembles coarse meal. Whisk the milk and egg together in a measuring cup or small bowl. Pour the milk mixture into the flour mixture and stir with a fork until just blended. Remove the hot mixture from the oven. Drop the topping in heaping tablespoons onto the hot filling. Bake until the topping is golden brown, about 12–15 minutes longer.

Allow the cobbler to cool 5 minutes. Sprinkle on the confectioners' sugar to serve.

Cobblers, Crisps, Crumbles and Buckles:
What's in a Name?

Although often used interchangeably, these terms originally referred to a specific type of baked good.

- *Cobblers* are typically bubbling, lightly sugared fruit topped with individually dropped tablespoons of dough that form rounds. The biscuit-like appearance is thought to resemble cobblestones.

- *Crisps* are bubbling, lightly sugared fruit topped with a buttery streusel mixture containing oats.

- *Crumbles* are bubbling, lightly sugared fruit topped with a streusel mixture that does not contain oats.

- *Buckles*, which are actually quite different from the rest, typically begin with a base made of sweetened batter and are topped with the fresh fruit. As the fruit and cake cook, the cake rises, causing the fruit to sink to the bottom, or "buckle."

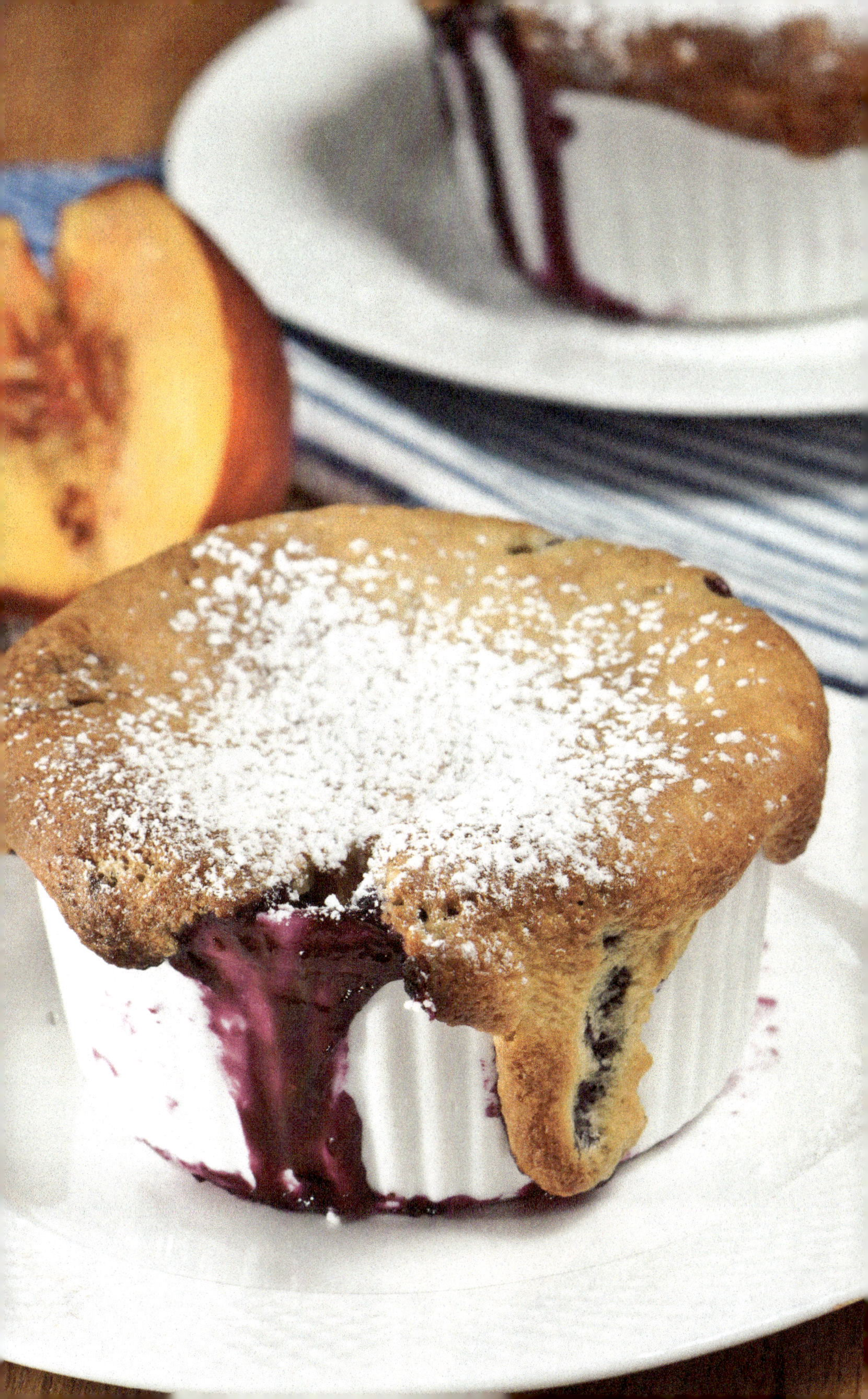

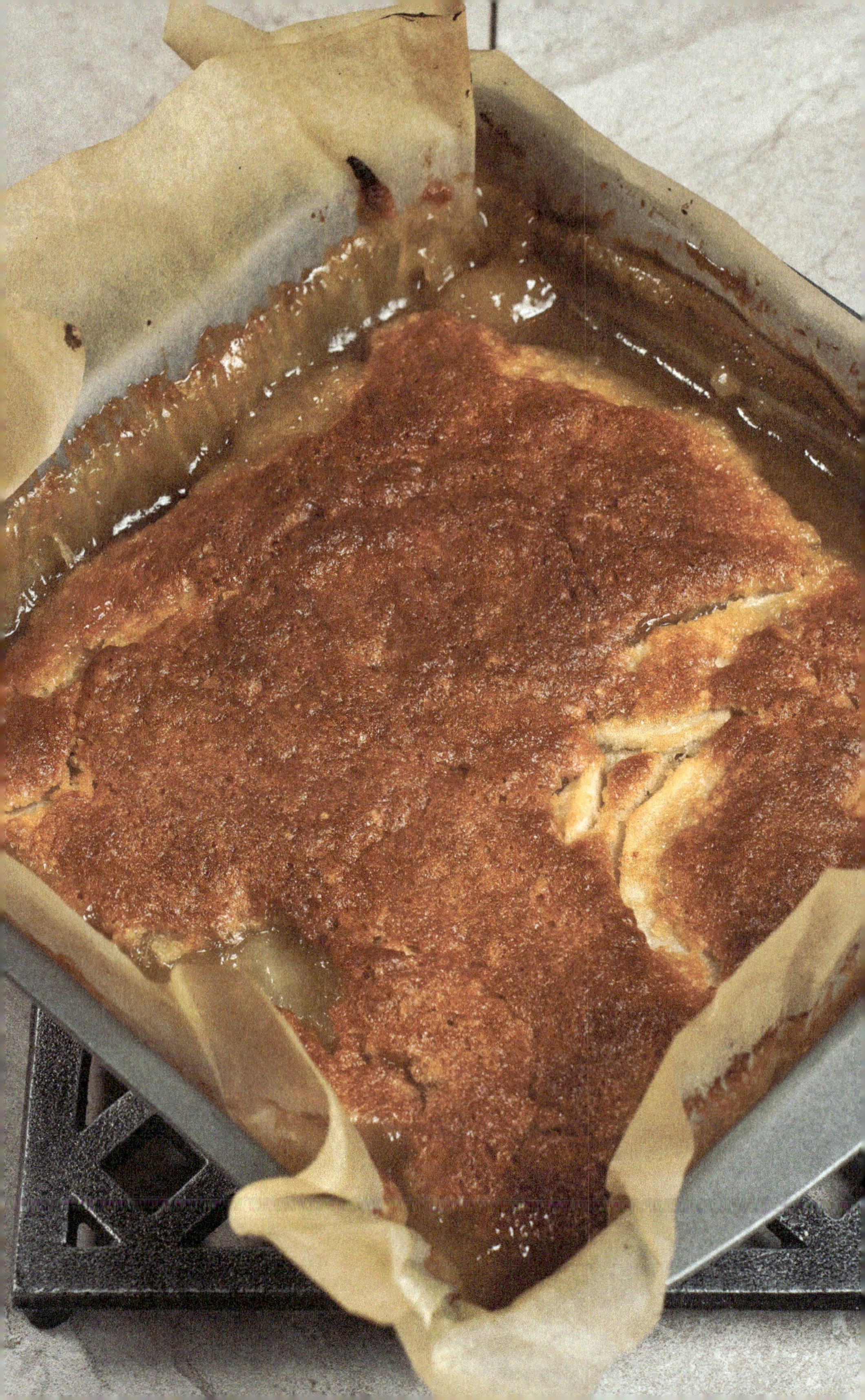

Apple Buckle

This buckle will challenge everything you think you know about baking. Here, some of the cake ingredients are folded in with the apples, and hot sugar syrup is poured over top. The result is a sweet, baked apple casserole with a crisp topping that's great for family-style or buffet service.

SERVES 6

- 1 cup (4.4 oz.) all-purpose flour
- 1 cup (7 oz.) granulated sugar
- 2 tsps. baking powder
- ½ tsp. salt
- ½ tsp. ground nutmeg
- ½ cup (4 fl. oz.) whole milk
- 1 tsp. vanilla extract
- 3 large apples, peeled, seeded and thinly sliced (about 3 cups)
- ½ cup (4 oz.) light brown sugar
- 2 tbsps. unsalted butter

Preheat the oven to 400 degrees F. Grease an 8" x 8" baking dish.

Combine the flour, ½ cup (3.5 oz.) granulated sugar, baking powder, salt and nutmeg. Stir in the milk and vanilla extract until just combined. Fold in the apples. Spread the mixture in the baking dish and set aside.

Combine 1 ½ cups (12 fl. oz.) water, the remaining ½ cup (3.5 oz.) granulated sugar, brown sugar and butter in a large saucepan. Bring to boil over medium-high heat, stirring until sugars are dissolved. Pour the hot liquid over the apple mixture. Bake for 45–50 minutes, until filling is bubbly and a toothpick inserted into the center comes out clean. Allow to cool slightly before serving.

Apple Cranberry Crisp

The addition of oats to the streusel topping gives it a pleasant, crunchy texture. The combination of apples and cranberries makes it perfect for an autumn or holiday breakfast.

SERVES 6

- 3 large baking apples, peeled, cored and thinly sliced
- ½ cup (3.5 oz.) granulated sugar
- 1 tsp. finely grated lemon zest
- 1 cup (4.4 oz.) all-purpose flour
- 1 tsp. freshly grated ginger

- 12 tbsps. unsalted butter
- 1 cup (3.5 oz.) fresh cranberries
- ¾ cup (2.5 oz.) old-fashioned oats
- ¼ cup (2 oz.) light brown sugar
- ½ tsp. salt

Preheat the oven to 350 degrees F. Grease a 9" x 9" baking dish (or grease 6 individual ramekins and place them on baking sheet).

Combine the apples, granulated sugar, lemon zest, ¼ cup (1.1 oz.) flour and fresh ginger in a medium bowl and toss to coat. Melt 4 tbsps. butter in a large skillet over medium heat and add the apple mixture. Cook for 5 minutes, stirring often. Add the cranberries and cook for 3-4 minutes longer, until cranberries just begin to pop. Spoon the mixture into the baking dish.

Combine the remaining ¾ cup (3.3 oz.) flour, oats, brown sugar and salt in a medium bowl. Cut the remaining 8 tbsps. butter into bits and cut in the mixture with a pastry blender until crumbly. Sprinkle the mixture evenly over the fruit.

Bake for 25–30 minutes until topping is golden brown and fruit is bubbling. Allow to cool for 5 minutes before serving.

Peach Pecan Crumble

Here the peaches are lightly caramelized to accent their fresh seasonal flavor.

SERVES 6

- 4 large peaches, peeled, pitted and sliced thinly
- ⅓ cup (2.6 oz.) plus 2 tbsps. light brown sugar
- 1 ½ cups (6.6 oz.) all-purpose flour
- ⅓ cup (2.35 oz.) granulated sugar
- 8 tbsps. unsalted butter, melted
- 1 large egg yolk
- ½ tsp. vanilla extract
- ½ cup (2oz.) chopped pecans

Preheat the broiler on high and position a rack about 4" from the heat. Line a rimmed baking sheet with foil and lightly grease. Grease an 8" x 8" baking dish (or grease 6 individual ramekins and place them on a baking sheet) and set aside.

Combine the peaches and 2 tbsps. brown sugar in a medium bowl. Place the peaches in a single layer onto the baking sheet. Broil the peaches for about 5 minutes. Turn the peaches and broil for 4-5 minutes longer, until just caramelized. Spoon the peaches into the baking dish. Lower the oven temperature to 375 degrees F.

Combine the flour, granulated sugar and remaining ⅓ cup brown sugar in a medium bowl. Whisk the butter, egg yolk and vanilla together in a small bowl. Pour the mixture into the dry ingredients, stirring with a fork to combine. Cut in the butter until crumbly. Stir in the pecans. Sprinkle the crumb topping evenly over the peaches.

Bake until the topping is golden and the fruit is bubbling, about 25-30 minutes. Let cool for 5 minutes before serving.

Apricot Buckle

This traditional Southern-style buckle gets an update with the addition of cornmeal. The batter will rise to the top during baking, forming a golden crust.

SERVES 6-8

- 5 tbsps. unsalted butter, melted
- ¾ cup (3.3 oz.) all-purpose flour
- ¼ cup (1.4 oz.) cornmeal, yellow or white
- 1 ½ tsps. baking powder
- 1 ½ cups (10.5 oz.) granulated sugar
- ½ tsp. salt
- ½ tsp. freshly grated nutmeg
- 1 tsp. finely grated lemon zest
- ¾ cup (6 fl. oz.) whole milk
- 1 tsp. vanilla extract
- 10 apricots, peeled, pitted and thinly sliced

Preheat the oven to 375 degrees F.

Pour the melted butter into an 8" x 8" baking dish or pan.

Combine flour, cornmeal, baking powder, ½ cup (3.5 oz.) granulated sugar, salt, nutmeg and lemon zest in a medium bowl. Stir in the milk and vanilla until just combined. Pour the mixture into the pan without stirring.

Combine the remaining 1 cup (7 oz.) sugar and apricots in a medium saucepan over medium heat. Bring to a boil and stir until all of the sugar is melted. Spoon the apricots over the batter (again, do not stir). Bake for 35-40 minutes, until the topping is golden. Let cool for 5 minutes before serving.

Blackberry Cobbler

We lived on Whidbey Island in the Puget Sound for several years, where summer time meant sunny weather and wild blackberries growing along the hillsides down to the water. This quickly assembled cobbler was the delicious result of a bounty of fresh berries.

SERVES 6

- 3 cups (13 oz.) blackberries
- 1 ¼ cups (8.8 oz.) plus 2 tbsps. granulated sugar
- 1 tbsp. lemon juice
- 3 tbsps. cornstarch
- 1 tsp. ground cinnamon
- 1 cup (4.4 oz.) all-purpose flour
- 1 ¼ tsps. baking powder
- ½ tsp. salt
- ½ tsp. baking soda
- 4 tbsps. unsalted butter, cut into bits
- ⅔ cup (5.3 fl. oz.) buttermilk
- 1 tsp. vanilla extract

Preheat the oven to 375 degrees F. Grease a 9" x 9" baking pan.

Combine the blackberries, ¾ cup (5.3 oz.) sugar, lemon juice, cornstarch and cinnamon in a medium bowl. Pour the mixture into the baking pan and bake until the fruit begins to bubble, about 15 minutes.

In the meantime, combine the flour, remaining ¼ cup (1.8 oz.) sugar, baking powder, salt and baking soda in a medium bowl. Cut in the butter with a pastry blender until crumbly. Stir in the buttermilk and vanilla until just combined.

Remove the pan from the oven and drop the batter in heaping tablespoons evenly on top of the blackberries. Bake until the topping is golden brown, about 15-20 minutes longer.

Raspberry Lemon Buckle

In this lemon-scented buckle, some of the raspberries will still show through the crust. Fresh raspberries make a lovely appearance, but frozen ones will taste delicious as well.

SERVES 6 - 8

- 2 cups (8.6 oz.) raspberries
- 1 tbsp. lemon juice
- 2 tbsps. granulated sugar
- 8 tbsps. unsalted butter, softened
- 1 cup (7.76 oz.) light brown sugar
- 3 large eggs
- 1 cup (4.4 oz.) all-purpose flour
- 1 tsp. baking powder
- ½ tsp. salt
- 1 tsp. lemon zest

Preheat the oven to 350 degrees F. Grease an 8" x 8" baking dish or pan.

Combine the raspberries, lemon juice and granulated sugar in a medium bowl and toss to combine. Set aside.

Combine the butter and brown sugar in the bowl of a stand mixer. Cream until fluffy, about 3-4 minutes. Add the eggs one at a time and beat to combine. In a large bowl, whisk together the flour, baking powder, salt and lemon zest. Add the flour mixture to the butter mixture and mix until just combined.

Spread the batter in the baking dish. Scatter the raspberries on top. Bake until a toothpick inserted in center of the cake comes out clean and the top is golden brown, about 45-50 minutes. Let cool for 5 minutes before serving.

Strawberry Rhubarb Crumble

This classic spring combination balances sweet and tart in every bite.

SERVES 6-8

- 2 rhubarb stalks, cut into ½" pieces (about 2 cups)
- ⅔ cup (4.7 oz.) granulated sugar
- 3 cups (16 oz.) strawberries, hulled and quartered
- 2 tbsps. cornstarch
- 2 tsps. lemon juice
- 1 ½ cups (6.6 oz.) all-purpose flour
- 1 ½ cups (11.6 oz.) light brown sugar
- 1 ½ tsps. ground cinnamon
- ½ tsp. salt
- 8 tbsps. unsalted butter, softened

Preheat the oven to 375 degrees F. Grease an 8" x 8" baking dish (or grease 6 individual ramekins and place them on a baking sheet).

Combine the rhubarb with ⅓ cup (2.35 oz.) granulated sugar in a medium bowl and allow the pieces to macerate for 10 minutes. In a separate medium bowl, toss the strawberries with the remaining ⅓ cup (2.35 oz.) sugar and allow them to macerate for 10 minutes. Drain any liquid off of the rhubarb and discard. Stir the rhubarb into the strawberries. Whisk the cornstarch and lemon juice together and stir it into the fruit. Spoon the mixture into the baking dish. Cover with foil and bake for 15 minutes.

In the meantime, combine the flour, brown sugar, cinnamon and salt in a large bowl. Cut in the butter with a pastry blender until the mixture is crumbly. Sprinkle the topping evenly over the filling.

Bake for 20-25 minutes longer, until the topping is golden and the fruit is bubbling. Allow the cobbler to cool for 5 minutes before serving.

Apricot Sour Cream Crumble

Adding sour cream to the standard fruit filling gives this apricot crumble a unique, creamy texture.

SERVES 6

- ¾ cup (5.3 oz.) granulated sugar
- ¼ cup (2 oz.) sour cream
- 1 large egg yolk
- 1 tsp. vanilla extract
- 6 apricots, pitted and thinly sliced
- 1 tbsp. lemon juice
- 1 cup (4.4 oz.) all-purpose flour
- 3 tbsps. cornmeal, white or yellow
- 1 tsp. finely grated lemon zest
- ¼ tsp. freshly grated nutmeg
- 1 tsp. ground cinnamon
- 8 tbsps. unsalted butter, cold

Preheat the oven to 375 degrees F. Butter an 8" x 8" baking dish (or use individual ramekins).

Whisk together ¼ cup (1.8 oz.) sugar, sour cream, egg yolk and vanilla in a medium bowl. Stir in the apricots and lemon juice. Spoon the apricot mixture into the baking dish. Mix the flour, cornmeal, remaining ½ cup (3.5 oz.) sugar, lemon zest, nutmeg and cinnamon in a medium bowl. Cut in the butter until the mixture is crumbly. Spoon the topping over the apricots. Bake for 25 minutes or until the top is golden brown. Cool for 10–15 minutes before serving.

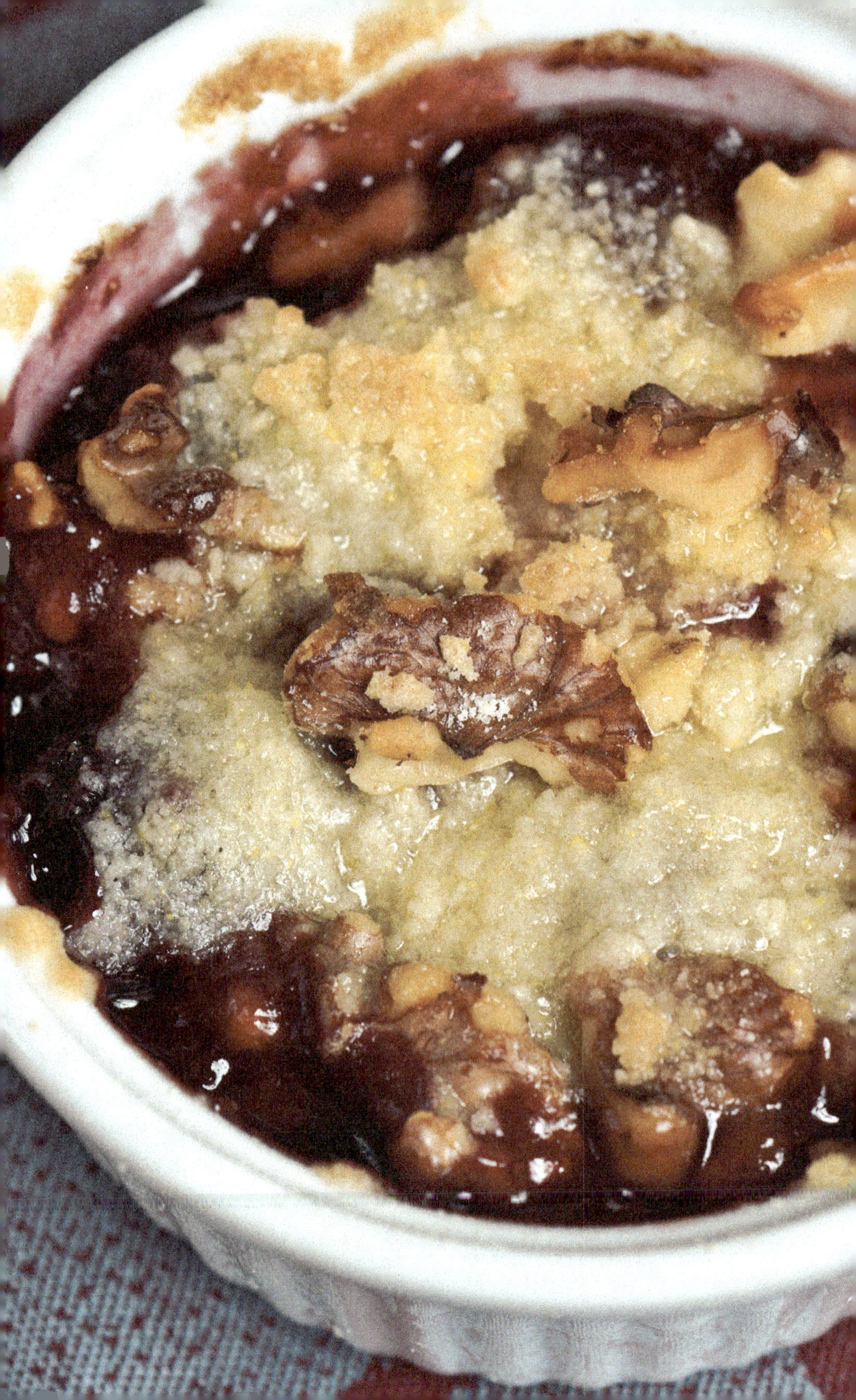

Cherry Walnut Crumble

This crisp topping with a hint of orange and ginger is the perfect foil to sweet dark cherries.

SERVES 6

- 3 cups (24 oz.) dark cherries, pitted
- 2 tbsps. honey
- 1 tsp. vanilla bean paste
- ¼ cup (1.8 oz.) granulated sugar
- ¾ cup (3.3 oz.) all-purpose flour

- ¼ cup (2 oz.) light brown sugar
- 1 tsp. finely grated orange zest
- 1 tsp. finely grated ginger
- ¼ cup (1 oz.) coarsely chopped walnuts
- 6 tbsps. unsalted butter, melted

Preheat the oven to 375 degrees F. Grease an 8" x 8" baking dish (or grease 6 individual ramekins and place them on a baking sheet).

Combine the cherries, honey and vanilla bean paste in a medium bowl. Spoon the mixture into the baking dish.

Combine the sugar, flour, brown sugar, orange zest, ginger and walnuts. Stir in the melted butter. Press the topping into clumps. Sprinkle the topping over the cherries. Bake for 25-30 minutes, until golden brown and bubbling. Allow to cool for 5 minutes before serving.

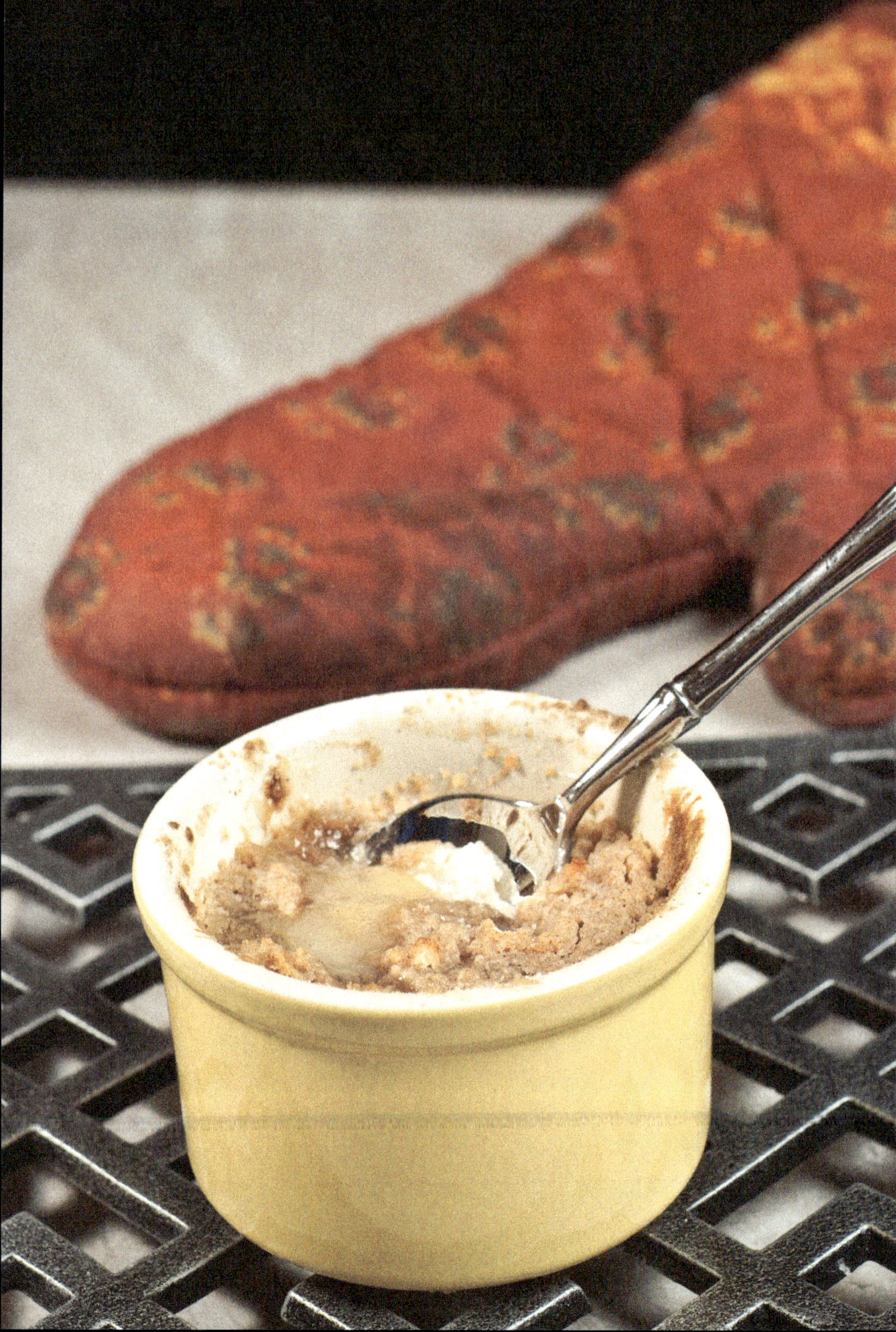

Apple Raisin Sour Cream Crumble

The filling of this crumble is reminiscent of Dutch apple pie.

SERVES 6

- ¾ cup (5.3 oz.) granulated sugar
- ¼ cup (2 oz.) sour cream
- 1 tsp. vanilla
- 3 baking apples, peeled, cored and thinly sliced
- ¼ cup (1.5 oz.) dark raisins
- 1 tbsp. lemon juice
- 1 cup (4.4 oz.) all-purpose flour
- ½ cup (4 oz.) light brown sugar
- 1 tsp. ground cinnamon
- 8 tbsps. unsalted butter, cut into bits

Preheat the oven to 375 degrees F. Butter an 8" x 8" baking dish (or use individual ramekins).

Whisk together ¼ cup sugar, sour cream and vanilla in a medium bowl. Stir in the apples, raisins and lemon juice. Spoon the apple mixture into the baking dish. Bake for 15 minutes.

In the meantime, mix the flour, remaining ½ cup sugar, brown sugar and cinnamon in a medium bowl. Cut in the butter with a pastry blender until the mixture is crumbly. Spoon the topping over the apple filling. Bake for 15–20 minutes longer, until the top is golden brown and the fruit is bubbling. Cool for 5 minutes before serving.

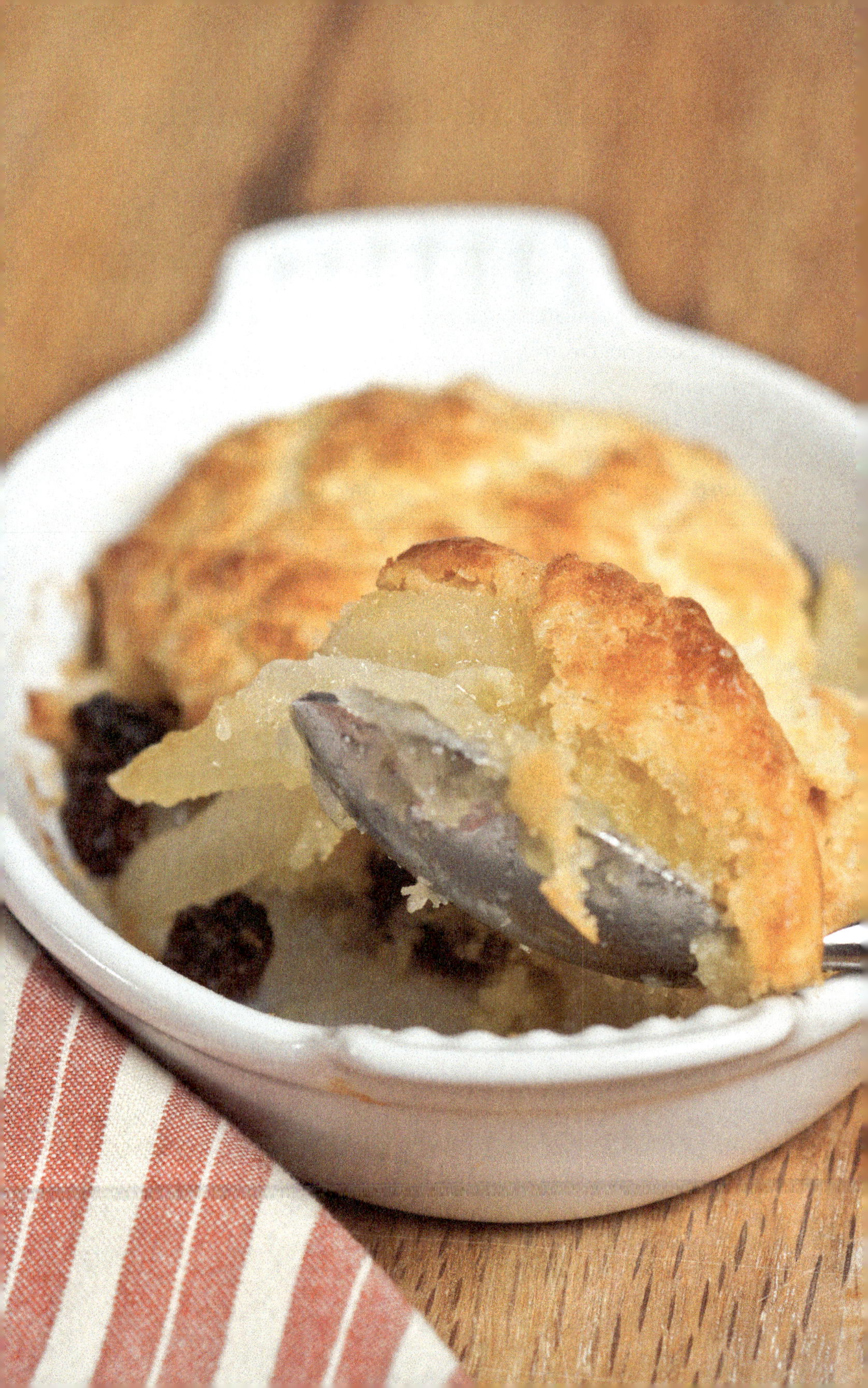

Pear Raisin Cobbler

Slices of pear balance nicely with the flavor of raisins in this biscuit-topped breakfast treat.

SERVES 6

- 4 large pears, peeled, cored and thinly sliced
- ½ cup (2.9 oz.) golden raisins
- 1 ½ cups (6.6. oz.) plus 2 tbsps. all-purpose flour
- ½ cup (3.5 oz.) granulated sugar
- 1 tsp. ground all-spice
- ½ tsp. ground ginger
- 1 ½ tsps. baking powder
- ½ tsp. salt
- 8 tbsps. unsalted butter, cut into bits
- ½ cup (4 fl. oz.) buttermilk
- 1 large egg

Preheat the oven to 350 degrees F. Grease an 8" x 8" baking dish (or grease 6 individual ramekins and place them on a baking sheet).

Combine the pears, raisins, 2 tbsps. flour, ¼ cup (1.8 oz.) granulated sugar, all-spice and ginger in a medium bowl. Spoon the mixture into the baking dish. Dot the top with 2 tbsps. butter. Cover with foil and bake for 10 minutes.

In the meantime, combine the remaining 1 ½ cups flour (6.6. oz.), ¼ cup (1.8 oz.) granulated sugar, baking powder and salt in a medium bowl. Cut in the remaining 6 tbsps. butter with a pastry blender until crumbly. Whisk together the buttermilk and egg in a measuring cup. Stir the buttermilk mixture into the dry ingredients with a fork until just combined. Remove the fruit from the oven and drop the batter over top in heaping tablespoons.

Bake for 25-30 minutes longer, until the topping is golden brown and the fruit is bubbling. Allow to cool for 5 minutes before serving.

Mixed Berry Crisp

The mixture of berries balances the crunchy oat topping in this easy-to-make crisp.

SERVES 6-8

- 1 cup (5.2 oz.) blueberries
- 1 cup (4.3 oz.) blackberries
- 1 cup (4.3 oz.) raspberries
- 2 tbsps. lemon juice
- ¼ cup (1.8 oz.) granulated sugar

- 1 cup (4.4. oz.) all-purpose flour
- ½ cup (1.7 oz.) old-fashioned oats
- ½ cup (4 oz.) brown sugar
- 10 tbsps. unsalted butter, melted

Preheat oven to 400 degrees F. Grease an 8" x 8" baking dish.

Combine the blueberries, blackberries, raspberries, lemon juice and granulated sugar in a medium bowl and toss to combine. Pour the berries into the baking dish.

Combine the flour, oats and brown sugar in a medium bowl. Pour in the butter and combine the ingredients with a fork until clumps form. Sprinkle the topping evenly over the berries.

Bake 20–25 minutes until the berries are bubbling and topping is golden brown. Cool for 5 minutes before serving.

Pear Cranberry Tart with Almond

A layer of creamy almond custard is layered in a buttery crust and topped with slices of pear and tart cranberries.

SERVES 8-10

- 1 recipe Sweet Tart Dough (see p. 281)
- ¾ cup (2.5 oz.) finely ground almonds or almond flour
- ⅓ cup (2.35 oz.) granulated sugar
- ½ tsp. almond extract
- 2 large eggs
- 4 tbsps. unsalted butter, melted

- ¼ cup (1.1. oz.) all-purpose flour
- 1 tsp. finely grated lemon zest
- 2 Bartlett or other large pears, peeled, cored and thinly sliced
- ¼ cup (.8 oz.) fresh cranberries (or substitute defrosted frozen cranberries)
- ½ cup (5.6 oz.) apricot fruit spread or preserves (see recipe p. 305)

Lightly grease a 9" tart pan with a removable bottom (or a spring form pan) and set it on a baking sheet.

On a lightly floured work surface, roll the dough into a 12" circle about ⅛" thick. Press the dough firmly around the sides and bottom of the tart pan. Trim off any excess dough by running a rolling pin across the top of the pan. Press the dough into the sides to extend it slightly above the rim to offset any shrinkage during baking. Place in the refrigerator for 30 minutes.

Preheat the oven to 375 degrees F.

Line the bottom of the pastry shell with a 9" to 10" round of parchment paper and fill with pie weights. Bake for 20 minutes. Remove the weights and parchment and bake for 10–12 minutes longer, until lightly golden. Set aside.

Combine the ground almonds and sugar in the bowl of a stand mixer. Add the almond extract and 1 egg and mix until frothy and light-colored. Add the melted butter and beat until smooth. Add the remaining egg and beat until smooth. Add the flour and mix until just combined.

Spread the mixture evenly in the tart shell. Arrange the pear slices slightly overlapping in a circular pattern and press them into the filling. Arrange the cranberries evenly over the exposed areas of almond filling.

Bake the tart until the filling is firm to the touch in the center, about 40–45 minutes. Transfer to a rack to cool.

In a small saucepan over low heat, warm the apricot spread until it liquefies. Pour through a fine-mesh sieve set over a small bowl or measuring cup and discard any pieces. Brush the top of the tart evenly with the apricot glaze. Allow the glaze to set completely before serving.

Make Ahead Tip: The tart dough may be made 2 days ahead. The pastry shell may be assembled and baked off the night before serving.

Blackberry Shortbread Tart

Strips of buttery shortbread are woven over a fresh berry filling in this simply assembled tart.

SERVES 8-10

- 3 cups (13 oz.) blackberries
- 1 cup (7 oz.) granulated sugar
- 2 tsps. lemon juice
- 16 tbsps. unsalted butter
- 2 egg yolks
- 1 tsp. finely grated lemon zest
- 2 ½ cups (11 oz.) all-purpose flour
- 2 tsps. baking powder
- ¼ tsp. salt

Combine the blackberries, ½ cup (3.5 oz.) sugar and 2 tbsps. water in a medium saucepan. Crush the berries lightly to release their juices. Bring to a boil over medium heat. Reduce heat to a simmer and cook for 8–10 minutes, until mixture has thickened (temperature should reach 220 degrees F). Remove from the heat and stir in the lemon juice. Cool completely. Cover and refrigerate until ready to use.

Lightly grease a 9" tart pan with a removable bottom (or a spring form pan) and set it on a baking sheet.

Combine the butter and remaining ½ cup (3.5 oz.) sugar in the bowl of a stand mixer until fluffy, about 3–4 minutes. Add the egg yolks and mix until smooth. Mix in the lemon zest, flour, baking powder and salt until dough just comes together. Gather the dough into a ball and place on a lightly floured work surface. Divide the dough into two pieces, one slightly larger. Wrap the smaller piece in plastic wrap and refrigerate for 30 minutes or until firm. Place the larger piece of dough and press it evenly into the bottom and sides of the pan. Cover with plastic wrap and place in the refrigerator for 30 minutes.

Preheat the oven to 350 degrees F.

Spread the blackberry mixture over the bottom of the crust. Roll the remaining dough into a 12" square. Cut the pastry into ¾" strips. Lay half the strips across the filling, evenly spaced. Turn the pan a quarter turn and lay the remaining strips across the first strips. If desired, weave the top strips over and under the bottom strips. Press and seal the edges into the crust, trimming off any excess.

Bake for 30–35 minutes, until crust is golden brown. Cool for 5 minutes, then transfer to a cooling rack. Cool for 5 minutes longer. Dust with confectioners' sugar to serve.

Make Ahead Tip: Make the blackberry filling and the crust up to 2 days before serving and refrigerate. Assemble the tart the night before and refrigerate. Bring the tart to room temperature before baking.

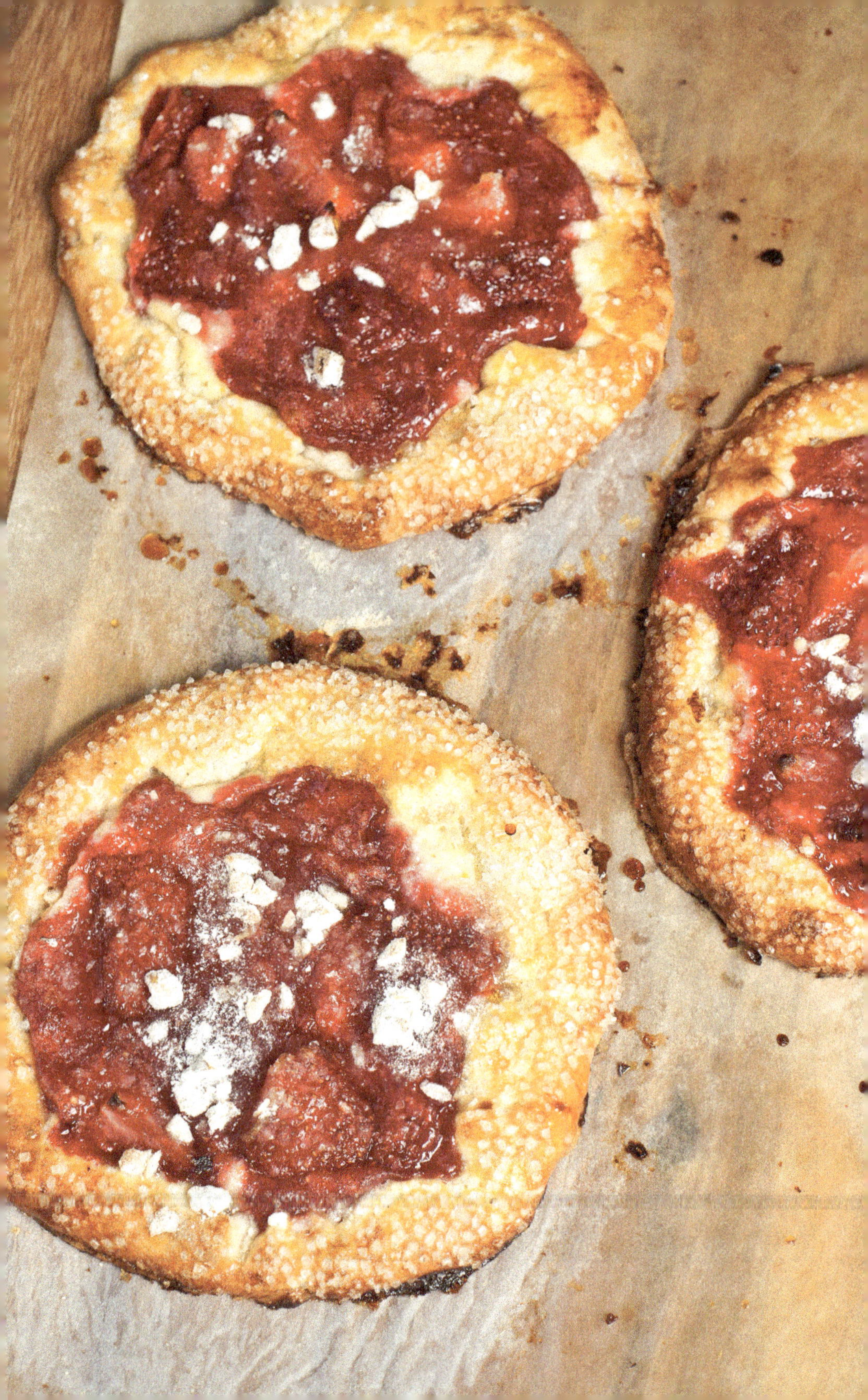

Rustic Strawberry Ricotta Tart

Rustic tarts are made without tart pans and may be made with a variety of fillings. Here ricotta and sweet strawberries combine for a delicious morning treat.

MAKES 1 LARGE 12" TART OR 2 SMALL 6" TARTS

- 1 ½ cup (6.6. oz.) all-purpose flour
- ¼ cup (1.8 oz.) plus 6 tbsps. granulated sugar
- ½ tsp. salt
- 8 tbsps. unsalted butter
- 2 cups (8.7 oz.) strawberries, hulled and quartered
- 1 tbsp. lemon juice
- 1 ½ tbsps. cornstarch
- 1 ¼ cups (12.2 oz.) ricotta cheese
- 1 tsp. finely grated orange zest
- 1 tbsp. orange juice
- 2 tbsps. ground walnuts
- 1 large egg
- 1 tbsp. sanding sugar

In a large bowl, combine the flour, 2 tbsps. sugar and salt. Cut in the butter using a pastry blender until the butter is evenly distributed but still in large pieces. Add ¼ cup ice water and mix until the dough just pulls together. Gather the dough into a ball and wrap in plastic. Refrigerate for at least 1 hour.

Combine the ½ cup (2.7 oz.) strawberries, the remaining ¼ cup (1.8 oz.) sugar, lemon juice and 1 tbsp. water in a medium saucepan. Bring the mixture to a boil over medium heat. Whisk the cornstarch and 3 tbsps. water together in a small bowl. Pour the mixture into the strawberries and bring to a boil. Cook, stirring constantly, until the liquid is clear, about 3–4 minutes. Remove from the heat and allow the mixture to cool. Stir in the remaining strawberries.

Preheat the oven to 400 degrees F. Line a baking sheet with parchment.

Combine the ricotta, 2 tbsps. sugar, orange zest and orange juice in a medium bowl. Combine the remaining 2 tbsps. sugar and walnuts in a small bowl. Whisk the egg with a pinch of salt in a separate bowl.

On a lightly floured surface, roll the dough into a 16" round (alternatively, divide it into 2 pieces and roll each out to about an 8" round). Transfer the dough by folding it in half and unfolding it on the lined baking sheet. Spoon the strawberry mixture onto the pastry, leaving a 2" border. Fold the edge of the dough inward toward the filling, pleating the edges to seal. Sprinkle the walnut mixture over the strawberries.

Brush the edge of the dough with the egg wash and sprinkle on the sanding sugar. Bake until the crust is lightly browned, about 25-35 minutes. Allow to cool for 5 minutes, then transfer to a rack for 10 minutes longer before serving.

Make Ahead Tip: Make the crust and filling the day before serving and refrigerate.

Raspberry Cream Tart

Fresh seasonal raspberries make this simple fruit tart shine at the breakfast table. This recipe will also make 4 individual 4" tarts.

SERVES 6-8

- 1 recipe Sweet Tart Dough (see recipe p. 281)
- 1 cup (8 fl. oz.) whole milk
- 1 tsp. vanilla bean paste
- ⅓ cup (2.35 oz.) granulated sugar
- 1 ½ tbsps. all-purpose flour
- 3 large egg yolks
- 4 tsps. unsalted butter
- ½ cup (5.6 oz.) raspberry jam (see recipe p. 307)
- 3 cups (13 oz.) fresh raspberries

Preheat the oven to 350 degrees F.

Line the bottom of the pastry shell with a 9" to 10" round of parchment paper and fill with pie weights. Bake 20 minutes. Remove the weights and parchment. Bake until lightly golden, about 8–10 minutes longer. Cool the shell completely.

To make the pastry cream, combine the milk and vanilla bean paste in a small saucepan over medium heat. Bring just to a boil, then remove from the heat and set aside.

Whisk the sugar and flour together in a medium bowl. Add the egg yolks and beat until pale yellow and frothy. Whisking constantly, add half of the hot milk to the egg mixture to temper it. Pour the mixture into the saucepan with the remaining milk. Heat the mixture over medium heat, whisking constantly until thickened, about 3–5 minutes longer. Remove from the heat and strain through a fine mesh strainer into a clean bowl. Stir in the butter. Cover with plastic wrap, pressing down against the surface to prevent a skin from forming. Refrigerate until completely cool, at least 2 hours.

In a small saucepan, heat the jam until liquefied. Remove from the heat and pour through a strainer to remove the seeds. Allow the strained jam to cool slightly.

Spread the pastry cream evenly over the pastry crust. Arrange the raspberries in a circular pattern over the cream and brush them lightly with the jam glaze. Let the glaze cool and set up for 10 minutes before serving.

Make Ahead Tip: Make the pastry cream the day before and refrigerate it until ready to assemble the tart. Make the pastry dough the day before and transfer it to the pan. Bake the tart shell off the day before.

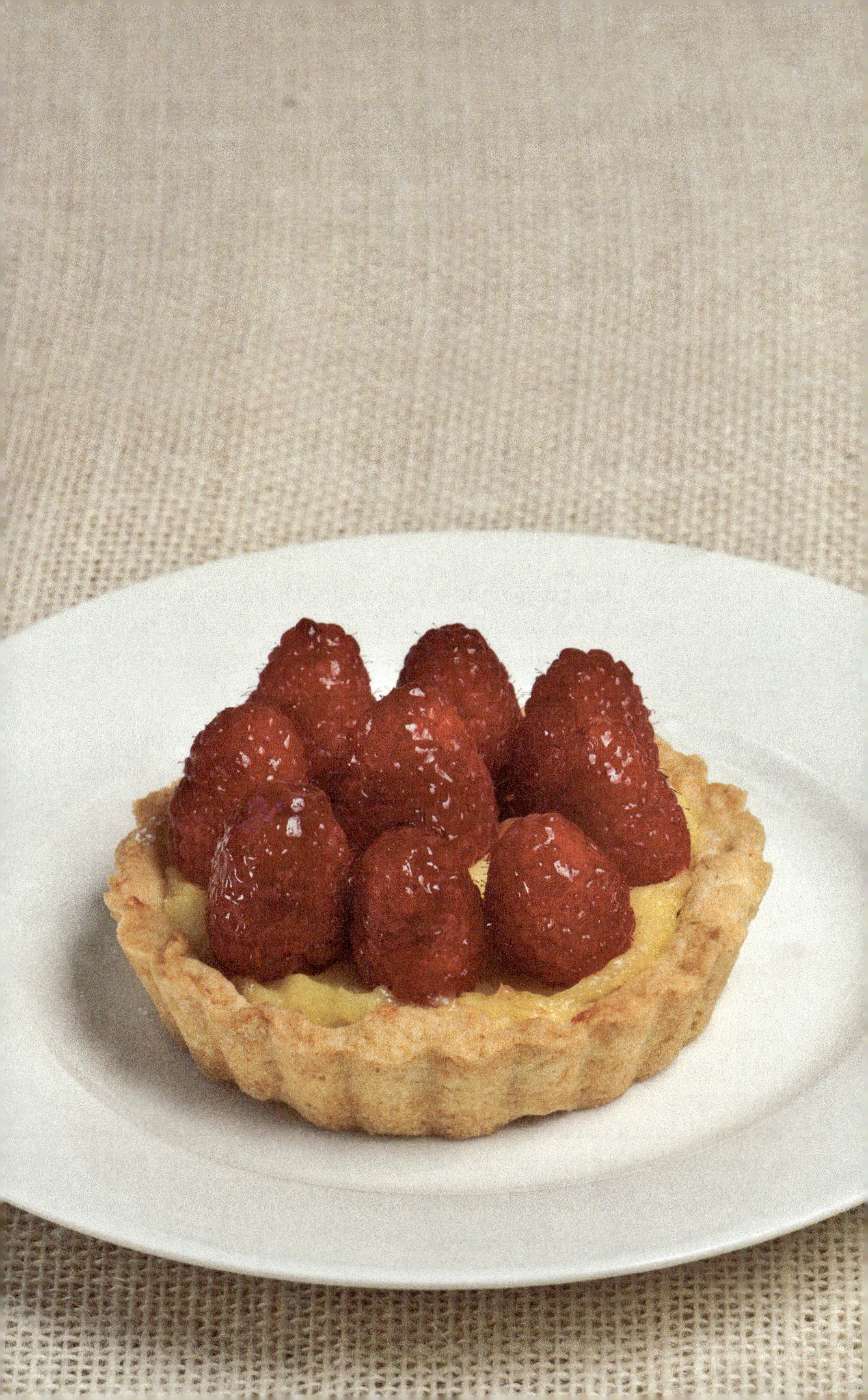

Blueberry Lemon Tart

This simple-to-assemble tart features a creamy lemon filling and fresh blueberries. The recipe will also make 4 individual 4" tarts.

SERVES 6-8

- 12 tbsps. unsalted butter
- ¾ cups (5.3 oz.) granulated sugar
- 1 large egg
- 2 large egg yolks
- ⅓ cup (2.6 fl. oz.) lemon juice
- 1 tsp. finely grated lemon zest

- 1 ¼ cups (5.5. oz.) all-purpose flour
- 1 tsp. baking powder
- ¼ tsp. salt
- 3 cups (15.7 oz.) fresh blueberries

In a large bowl, beat 4 tbsps. butter and ¼ cup (1.8 oz.) sugar until smooth, about 2–3 minutes. Add the egg and 1 egg yolk and beat until combined, about 1 minute. Stir in the lemon juice. (The mixture will appear curdled but will smooth out as the butter melts.)

In a medium saucepan, cook the mixture over low heat, stirring constantly, until the mixture thickens and coats the back of a spoon, about 10–12 minutes. Pour the mixture into a bowl and allow to cool completely. Cover with plastic wrap, pressing the wrap against the surface to prevent a skin from forming, and refrigerate until ready to use.

Lightly grease a 9" tart pan with a removable bottom (or use a 9" pie dish).

Combine the remaining 8 tbsps. butter and ½ cup (3.5 oz.) sugar in the bowl of a stand mixer until fluffy, about 3–4 minutes. Add the remaining egg yolk and mix until smooth. Mix in the lemon zest, flour, baking powder and salt until dough just comes together. Gather the dough into a ball and place on a lightly floured work surface. Roll the dough into a 12"circle about ⅛" thick and press it evenly into the bottom and sides of the pan, trimming any excess. Cover with plastic wrap and chill in the refrigerator for 30 minutes.

Preheat the oven to 350 degrees F.

Line the bottom of the pastry shell with a 9" to 10" round of parchment paper and fill with pie weights. Bake 20 minutes. Remove the weights and parchment. Bake until lightly golden, about 8–10 minutes longer.

Cool the shell completely. Stir the blueberries into the lemon filling. Spoon the lemon blueberry filling into the shell to serve.

Make Ahead Tip: Make the dough and bake off the tart shell the day before serving. Make the filling the day before and refrigerate until ready to assemble.

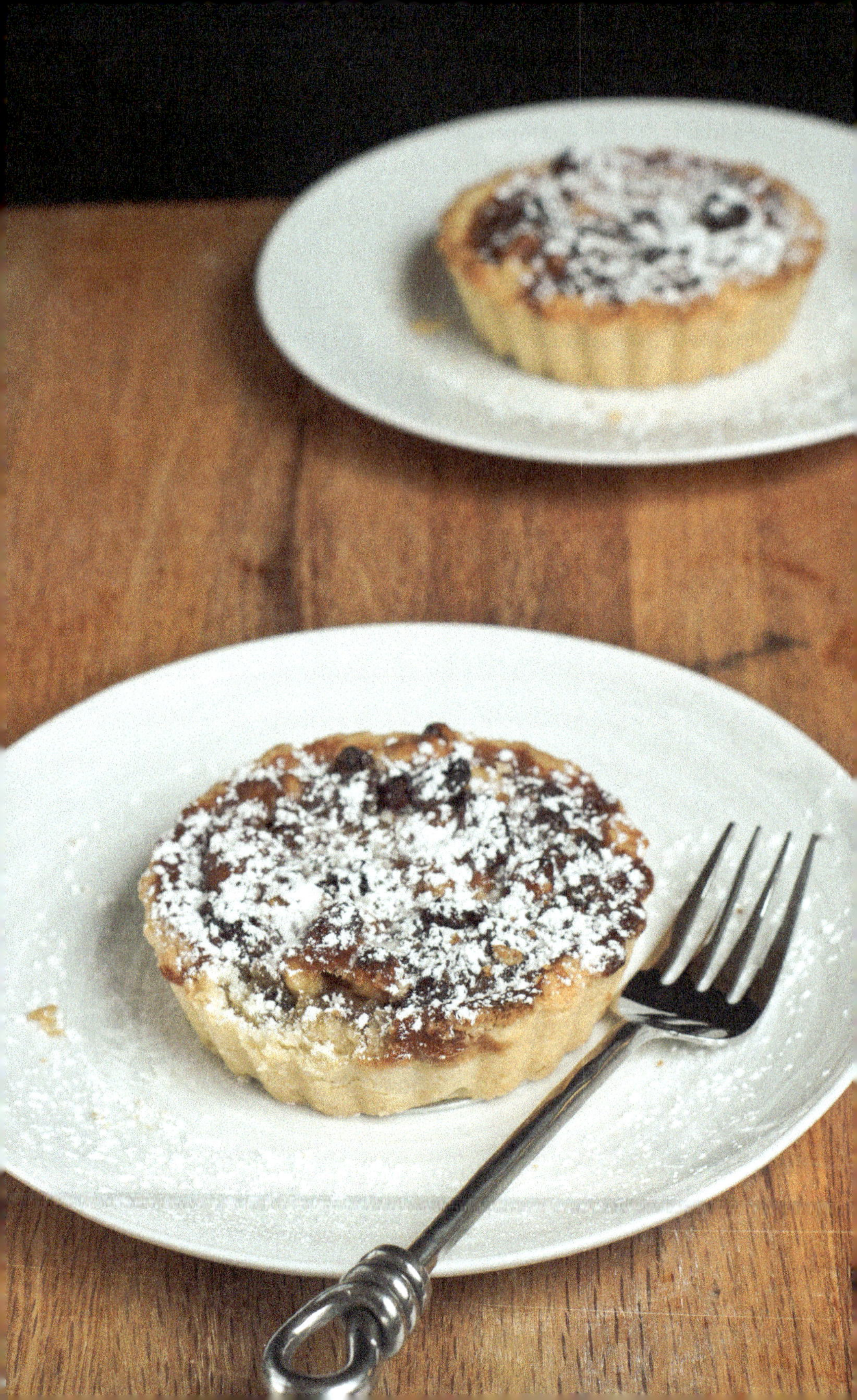

Cranberry Raisin Tart

This tart has a buttery, maple-scented filling studded with dried fruit and walnuts. The recipe may also be made into four individual tarts.

SERVES 6 - 8

- 1 recipe Sweet Tart Dough (see recipe p. 281)
- ½ cup (5.6 oz.) maple syrup
- 1 cup (7.76 oz.) light brown sugar
- 6 tbsps. unsalted butter
- 3 large eggs
- 1 cup (5.8 oz.) dried cranberries
- 1 cup (5.8 oz.) raisins, dark or golden
- 1 tsp. orange zest
- ½ cup chopped walnuts

Lightly grease a 9" tart pan with a removable bottom (or use a 9" pie dish).

On a lightly floured work surface, roll the dough into a 12" circle about ⅛" thick. Press the dough firmly around the sides and bottom of the pan. Trim off any excess dough by running a rolling pin across the top of the pan. Cover with plastic wrap and chill for 30 minutes.

In the meantime, combine the maple syrup and brown sugar in a small saucepan. Bring to a boil and stir to dissolve the sugar. Remove from the heat and stir in the butter. In a medium bowl, whisk the eggs. Stir in the syrup mixture until just combined. Stir in the cranberries, raisins, orange zest and walnuts.

Preheat the oven to 400 degrees F. Pour the filling into the shell. Bake for 30–35 minutes, until the center is just set. Cool on a rack before serving.

Make Ahead Tip: Make the dough and bake off the tart shell the day before. Make the filling the day before and refrigerate until ready to assemble and bake.

Plum Custard Tart

Any variety of sweet plums will work in this delicious tart. In this version, an early variety of golden-hued plums were in season.

SERVES 6 – 8

- 1 recipe Sweet Tart Dough (see recipe p. 281)
- 8 plums, pitted and sliced
- 3 large eggs
- ¾ cup (5.3 oz.) granulated sugar
- 3 tbsps. heavy cream
- 1 tbsp. unsalted butter, melted
- 3 tbsps. all-purpose flour

Lightly grease a 9" tart pan with a removable bottom (or use a 9" pie dish).

On a lightly floured work surface, roll the dough into a 12" circle about ⅛" thick. Press the dough firmly around the sides and bottom of the pan. Trim off any excess dough by running a rolling pin across the top of the pan. Cover with plastic wrap and chill for 30 minutes.

Preheat the oven to 350 degrees F.

Spread the plums in the bottom of the tart shell. Whisk together the eggs and sugar until light and lemony. Whisk in the heavy cream and butter. Stir in the flour until just combined. Pour the custard over the plums. Bake for 45–50 minutes until center is just firm. Cool on a rack before serving.

Make Ahead Tip: Make the tart dough and press it into the pan the day before baking.

Apple Sour Cream Tart

SERVES 6-8

- 1 recipe Sweet Tart Dough (see recipe p. 281)
- 3 large eggs
- 1 ¼ cups (8.8 oz.) granulated sugar
- ¾ cup (6 oz.) sour cream
- ¾ cup (3.3. oz.) plus 3 tbsps. all-purpose flour
- 3 large baking apples, peeled, cored and thinly sliced
- 4 tbsps. unsalted butter, cut into bits

Lightly grease a 9" tart pan with a removable bottom (or use a 9" pie dish).

On a lightly floured work surface, roll the dough into a 12" circle about ⅛" thick. Press the dough firmly around the sides and bottom of the pan. Trim off any excess dough by running a rolling pin across the top of the pan. Cover with plastic wrap and chill for 30 minutes.

Preheat the oven to 350 degrees F.

Whisk together the eggs and ½ cup (3.5 oz.) sugar in a medium bowl until light and lemony. Whisk in the sour cream. Stir in the flour until just combined. Stir in the apples to coat. Spread the apples in the bottom of the tart shell.

In a small bowl, combine the remaining ¾ cup (5.3 oz.) sugar and ¾ cup (3.3. oz.) flour. Cut in the butter with a pastry blender until crumbly. Sprinkle the crumb topping evenly over the custard.

Bake for 50–55 minutes, until golden brown and center is set. Cool on a rack before serving.

Make Ahead Tip: Make the tart dough the day before baking and serving.

Pear Sour Cream Turnovers

Turnovers are perfect for buffet and family-style service, and are easy to prepare. Here they are formed into squares for easy preparation, but the dough may be also cut into rounds to form a half-moon shape. Sour cream adds a moist, creamy texture to this pear filling.

MAKES 6 TURNOVERS

- 2 large eggs
- ¼ cup (1.8 oz.) granulated sugar
- 1 tbsp. all-purpose flour
- ¼ cup (2 oz.) sour cream
- ½ tsp. vanilla extract
- ¼ tsp. nutmeg

- ¼ tsp. salt
- ½ tsp. finely grated lemon zest
- 2 large pears, peeled, cored and cut into ½" dice
- 1 recipe Simple Puff Pastry Dough (see recipe p. 295)
- 1 tbsp. sanding sugar

Preheat the oven to 375 degrees F. Line a baking sheet with parchment and lightly grease.

In a large bowl, whisk together 1 egg with the sugar until the mixture is light and lemony. Add the flour, sour cream, vanilla, nutmeg, salt and lemon zest and whisk to combine. Fold in the pears to evenly coat them. Set aside.

Whisk the remaining egg with a pinch of salt in a small bowl or measuring cup. Roll out the pastry dough into a 12" x 18" rectangle. Cut the dough into 6 (6") squares. Brush the edges of each square with the egg wash. Divide the pear mixture evenly among the pastry squares. Fold the dough over diagonally to enclose the filling on each square and transfer them to the baking sheet. Use a fork to press the edges of the dough together, completely sealing them. Refrigerate the pastries on the baking sheet for 15 minutes.

Brush the pastries with the remaining egg wash. Sprinkle the sanding sugar evenly over the pastries. Bake for 20-25 minutes until the pastries are golden and the filling is bubbling slightly through the holes. Allow the pastries to cool on the baking sheet for 5 minutes. Transfer the pastries to a cooling rack for 5–10 minutes before serving.

Make Ahead Tip: Make the puff pastry ahead of time and freeze it. Defrost the pastry overnight in the refrigerator a day before assembling the turnovers. Cut fruit may be refrigerated overnight for up to 8 hours in a solution of Fruit Fresh, or other ascorbic acid fruit preserver.

Mixed Berry Turnovers

This version of turnovers features simple-to-prepare pastry dough, a little less buttery than the puff pastry typically used in turnovers.

MAKES 6 TURNOVERS

- 1 ½ cups (6.6. oz.) all-purpose flour
- ¼ tsp. salt
- 7 tbsps. granulated sugar
- 5 tbsps. unsalted butter, cut into bits
- ½ cup (2.6 oz.) blueberries
- 2 tsps. lemon juice
- 2 tbsps. cornstarch
- ½ cup (2.2 oz.) raspberries
- ½ cup (2.2 oz.) blackberries
- 1 large egg
- 1 tsp. sanding sugar

Combine the flour, salt and 2 tbsps. sugar in a large bowl. Cut in the butter with a pastry blender until the mixture is crumbly. Add water 1 tbsp. at a time until the mixture can be formed into a ball. Wrap the dough in plastic and refrigerate it for 30 minutes.

In the meantime, combine the remaining 5 tbsps. sugar, blueberries and lemon juice in a medium saucepan. Heat over medium until the sugar is melted and the mixture is beginning to boil. Whisk together the cornstarch and 2 tbsps. water in a measuring cup. Add the cornstarch mixture to the blueberries and bring to a boil. Cook for 2–3 minutes until the liquid is clear and the mixture is slightly thickened. Remove from the heat and stir in the raspberries and blackberries. Allow to cool.

Preheat the oven to 425 degrees F. Line a baking sheet with parchment and lightly grease. Whisk together the egg and a pinch of salt in a small bowl.

Divide the dough into 6 balls. Lightly flour a work surface. Roll out the dough into 3 ½" circles. Brush the edges of the pastry with the egg wash. Divide the filling evenly among the centers of each round of dough. Fold the pastry over and seal the edges. Transfer the folded turnovers to the baking sheet. Use a fork to completely seal the edges. Prick the tops of the turnovers with the fork to allow the filling to vent. Brush the tops with the remaining egg wash. Sprinkle the sanding sugar evenly over the turnovers.

Bake for 18–20 minutes, until tops are golden and filling is beginning to bubble through the vents. Allow the turnovers to cool on the baking sheet for 5 minutes. Transfer to a cooling rack and allow to cool 10 minutes longer before serving.

Make Ahead Tip: Make the pastry dough and filling the day before serving.

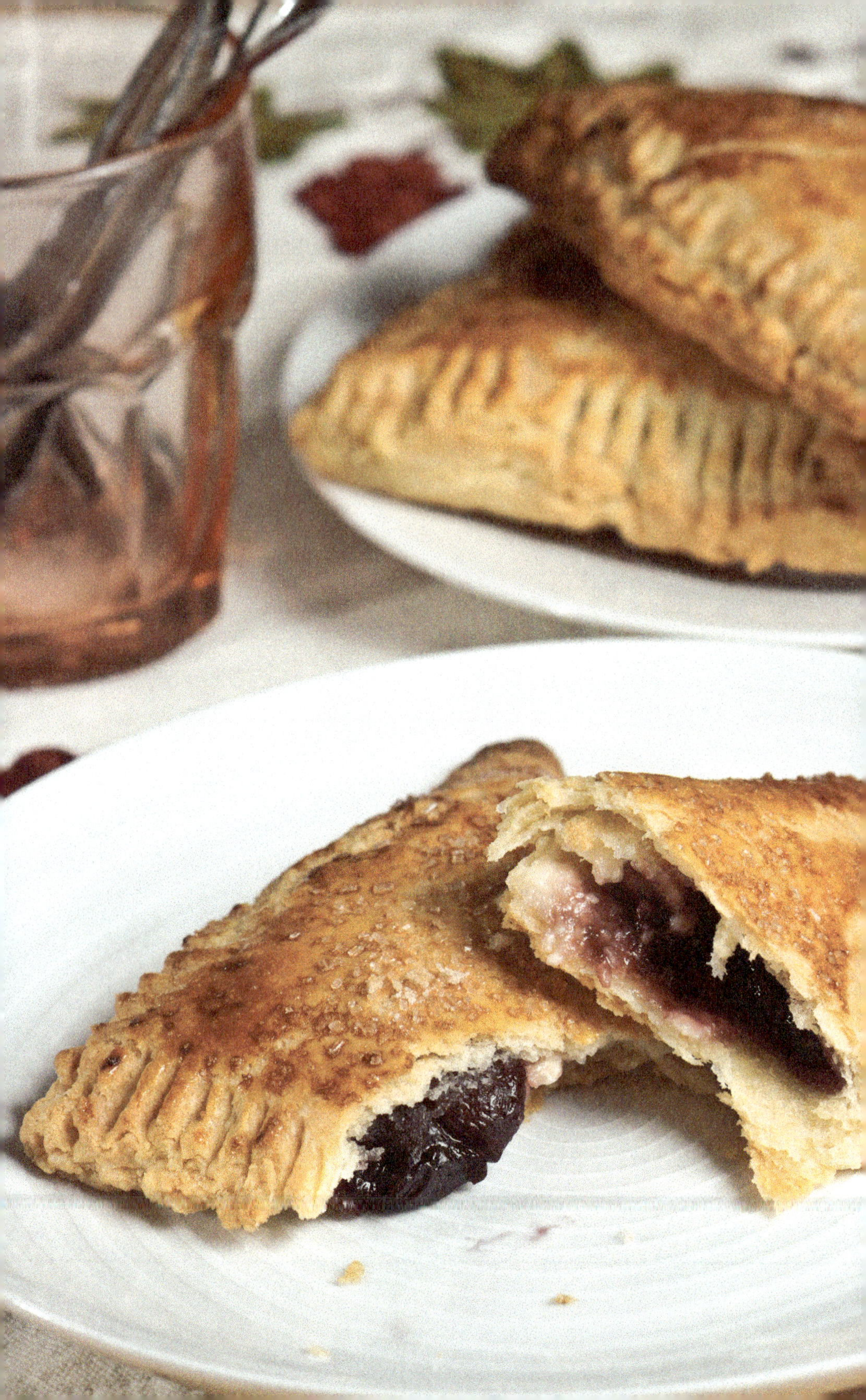

Cherry Cream Turnovers

In this turnover, sour cream pastry encases a sweet filling of cherries and cream cheese.

MAKES 6 TURNOVERS

- 1 cup (4.4. oz.) all-purpose flour
- ½ tsp. baking powder
- ¼ tsp. salt
- 8 tbsps. unsalted butter
- ¼ cup (2 oz.) sour cream
- 3 cups (24 oz.) cherries, pitted and halved
- ¼ cup (1.8 oz.) plus 2 tbsps. granulated sugar
- 2 tsps. lemon juice
- 1 tsp. cornstarch
- 3 oz. cream cheese
- 1 large egg
- 1 tsp. sanding sugar

Combine the flour, baking powder and salt in a large bowl. Cut in the butter with a pastry blender until crumbly. Stir in the sour cream. Gather the dough by hand into a ball. Turn the dough onto a lightly floured work surface.

Pat the dough into a rectangle and roll it to 8" x 10". Fold the 2 short ends of the dough into the center, leaving a small (about ¼") space between them. Fold one half over the other half. Lightly flour and roll it out again to about 8" x 10". Brush off the excess flour and repeat the folding. Wrap the dough in plastic wrap and refrigerate for 30 minutes.

In the meantime, combine the cherries, ¼ cup (1.8 oz.) granulated sugar and lemon juice in a medium saucepan. Bring to a boil over medium heat. Simmer for 5 minutes, until the cherries have released their juices. Whisk together the cornstarch with 1 tbsp. water until combined. Stir the cornstarch mixture into the cherries and cook for 2–3 minute longer, until thickened and the liquid is clear. Pour the cherries into a heat-proof bowl or measuring cup and cool completely.

Combine the cream cheese and remaining 2 tbsps. granulated sugar until smooth.

Preheat the oven to 400 degrees F. Line a baking sheet with parchment paper.

Roll the dough into a 10" x 15" rectangle. Cut the rectangle into 6 (5") squares.

Divide the cream cheese filling among the squares. Divide the cherry filling among the squares. Fold the dough over diagonally to enclose the filling on each square and transfer them to the baking sheet. Use a fork to press the edges of the dough together, completely sealing them. Refrigerate the pastries on the baking sheet for 15 minutes.

Whisk the egg with a pinch of salt in a small bowl or measuring cup. Brush the pastries with the egg wash. Sprinkle the sanding sugar evenly over the pastries. Bake for 20–25 minutes until the pastries are golden and the filling is bubbling slightly through the holes. Allow the pastries to cool on the baking sheet for 5 minutes. Transfer the pastries to a cooling rack for 5–10 minutes before serving.

Bake the turnovers for 18–20 minutes, until golden brown and cooked through. Cool for 15 minutes before serving.

Make Ahead Tip: Make the dough and fruit filling the day before and refrigerate.

Apricot Raisin Turnovers

Dried apricots and raisins are blended with cream cheese and baked in a flaky butter crust.

MAKES 6 TURNOVERS

- 1 recipe Simple Puff Pastry (see recipe p. 295)
- 4 oz. cream cheese
- 2 tbsps. granulated sugar
- 1 tsp. lemon zest
- ½ cup (3.4 oz.) dried apricots, coarsely chopped
- ¼ cup (1.5 oz.) raisins, dark or golden
- 1 large egg
- 1 cup (4.23 oz.) confectioners' sugar
- 1 tbsp. lemon juice

Preheat the oven to 400 degrees F. Line a baking sheet with parchment paper.

Roll the dough into a 10" x 15" rectangle. Cut the rectangle into 6 (5") squares.

Combine 2 oz. cream cheese, sugar and lemon zest until smooth. Divide the cream cheese filling among the squares. Toss the dried apricots and raisins together in a small bowl and divide among the squares. Fold the dough over diagonally to enclose the filling on each square and transfer them to the baking sheet. Use a fork to press the edges of the dough together, completely sealing them. Refrigerate the pastries on the baking sheet for 15 minutes.

Whisk the egg with a pinch of salt in a small bowl or measuring cup. Brush the pastries with the egg wash. Bake for 20-25 minutes until the pastries are golden. Allow the pastries to cool on the baking sheet for 5 minutes.

Combine the remaining 2 oz. cream cheese, confectioners' sugar and lemon juice until smooth. Drizzle the glaze over the turnovers. Transfer the pastries to a cooling rack for 5-10 minutes before serving.

Make Ahead Tip: Make the dough and glaze the day before and refrigerate. Assemble the pastries the night before, refrigerate and bake off in the morning.

CHAPTER FOUR

Donuts, Biscotti, Bars and Granola

- Yeast Donuts
- Buttermilk Donuts
- Pumpkin Donuts with Maple Glaze
- Chocolate Donuts with Chocolate Glaze
- Apple Spice Donuts
- Coconut Donuts with Lemon Glaze
- Powdered Sugar Donuts
- Coffee Chocolate Chunk Biscotti with Caramel Glaze
- Apricot Ginger Walnut Biscotti
- Almond Biscotti
- Cinnamon Biscotti
- Peanut Butter Oatmeal Biscotti
- Orange Hazelnut Biscotti
- Cranberry, Pistachio and White Chocolate Biscotti
- Anise Almond Biscotti
- Sun-Dried Tomato and Goat Cheese Biscotti
- Fruit and Nut Bars
- Fig Almond Bars

- Strawberry Bars
- Peanut Coconut Bars
- Granola Bars
- Apricot Pecan Bars
- Granola Two Ways
- Pumpkin Spice Granola
- Cherry Pistachio Granola

Yeast Donuts

Fried donuts are so very delicious, but they can be time-consuming and a little messy. To enjoy fresh donuts at home, baking may be an easier alternative. These baked yeast donuts are slightly denser than their fried counterparts. Dipping them in chocolate ganache (see recipe p. 312) and sprinkling them with peanuts is one of my favorite variations.

MAKES 12 DONUTS

- 1 cup (8 fl. oz.) whole milk
- 2 tbsps. unsalted butter
- 3 cups (13.2 oz.) plus 3–5 tbsps. all-purpose flour
- 1 ½ tsps. instant yeast
- ⅓ cup (2.35 oz.) granulated sugar
- ½ tsp. salt
- 1 tsp. ground cinnamon
- 2 large eggs
- 1 cup (4.23 oz.) confectioners' sugar
- 1 tsp. vanilla extract

Warm the milk in a small saucepan over medium heat. Stir in the butter until melted, and set aside.

Combine 3 cups (13.2 oz.) flour, yeast, granulated sugar, salt and cinnamon in the bowl of a stand mixer. Mix in the milk mixture until smooth. Add the eggs one at a time and beat until combined. Add the remaining flour 1 tbsp. at a time until the dough pulls away from the sides of the bowl. Switch to the dough hook and knead until smooth, about 3–4 minutes. Gather the dough into a ball. Transfer the dough to a large greased bowl and cover. Allow the dough to rise until doubled in size, about 1–1 ½ hours or in the refrigerator for at least 8 hours (or overnight).

Line 2 baking sheets with parchment and grease the parchment. Transfer the dough to a floured work surface and roll it to ½" thickness (about a 10" circle). Flour a 3" donut cutter (or a 3" round and ½" round pastry cutter) and cut out as many donuts as possible.

Transfer the donuts to the baking sheets with a spatula. Gather up the remaining dough and roll it out again to ½" thickness. Continue to cut rounds with holes until 12 donuts are formed. Cover with a large unscented plastic bag and allow the donuts to rise for 30–40 minutes, until puffy and almost doubled.

In the meantime, preheat the oven to 375 degrees F.

Bake until the bottom of the donuts are just golden, about 8–10 minutes. Whisk the confectioners' sugar, vanilla and 1 tbsp. water in a shallow bowl. Dip the donuts in the glaze, allowing any excess to drain off. Place the donuts on a rack and allow the glaze to set 10 minutes before serving.

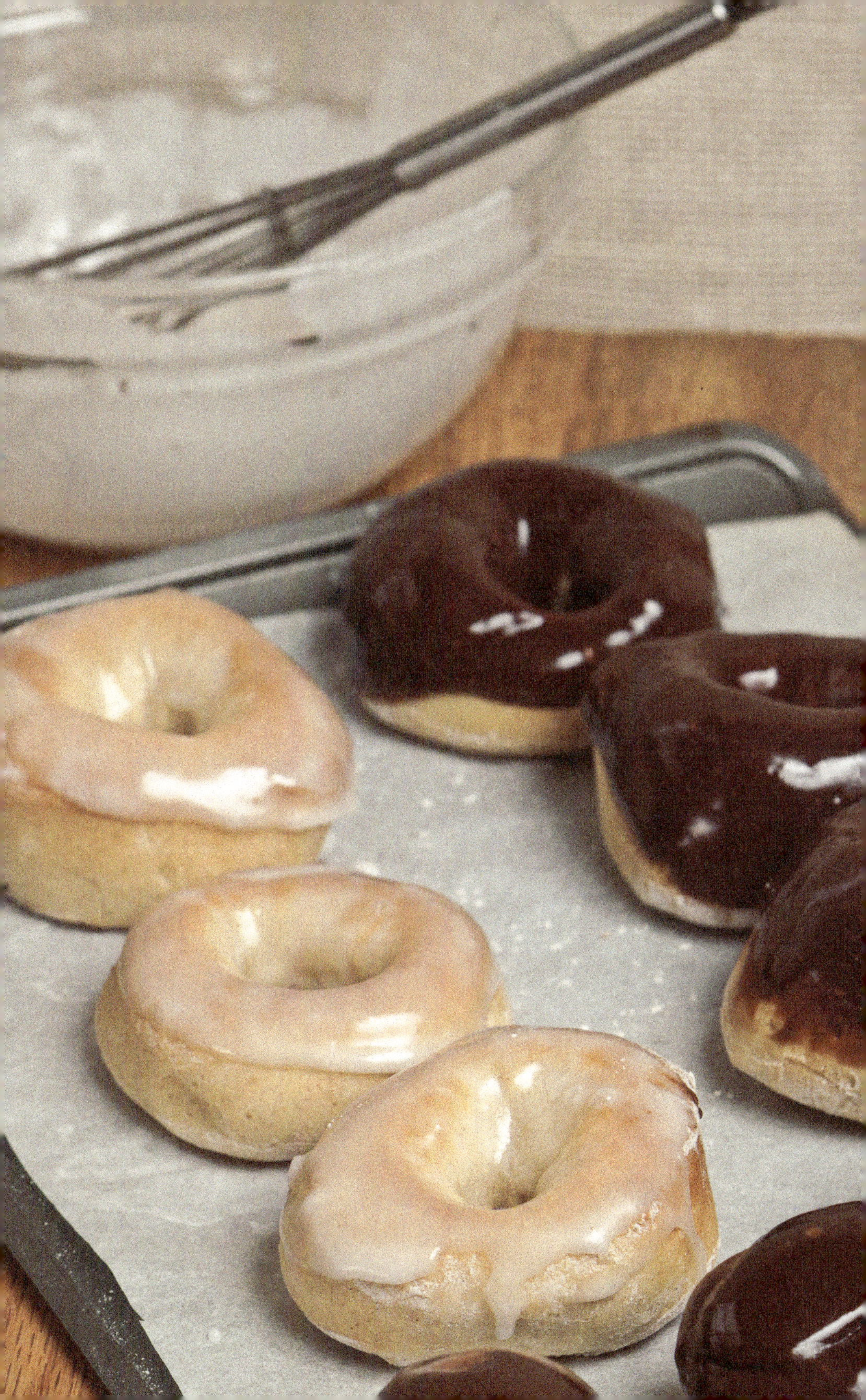

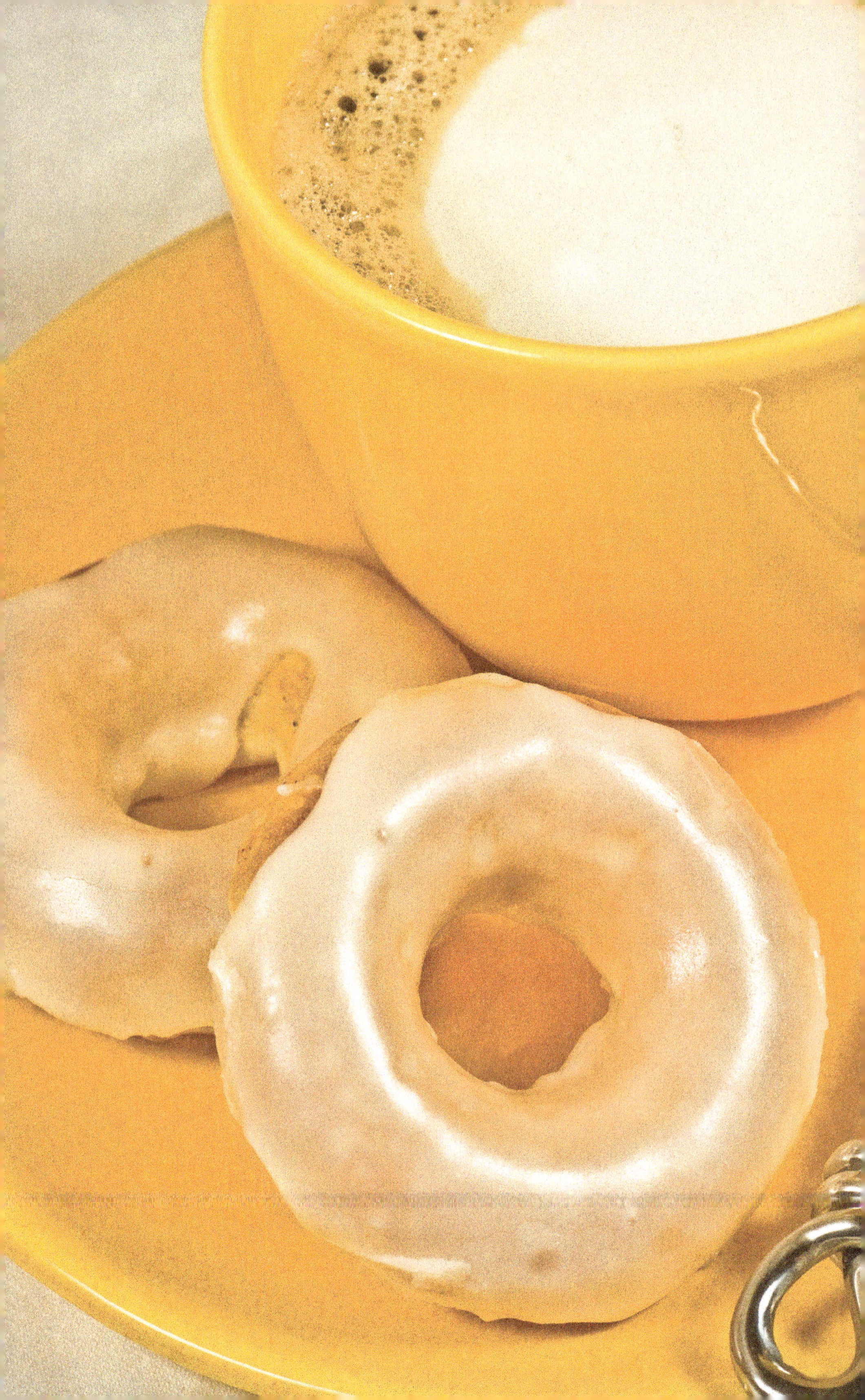

Buttermilk Donuts

To get a true donut shape for many baked donut recipes, a donut pan is required. As with fried donuts, toppings for these are limited only to your imagination—lemon glaze, cinnamon sugar and maple glaze with crumbled bacon are just a few ideas for variations. There are a variety of recipe options in the Pantry chapter.

MAKES 12 DONUTS

- 2 cups (8.75 oz.) all-purpose flour
- ½ cup (3.5 oz.) granulated sugar
- 1 tbsp. baking powder
- ½ tsp. ground nutmeg
- 1 tsp. salt
- ½ cup (4 fl. oz.) buttermilk
- 1 large egg
- 5 tbsps. unsalted butter, melted
- 1 cup (4.23 oz.) confectioners' sugar

Combine the flour, sugar, baking powder, nutmeg and salt in a large bowl. In a separate bowl, whisk together the buttermilk, egg and 3 tbsps. melted butter. Pour the wet ingredients into the dry and mix till just combined. Cover and refrigerate the dough for 30 minutes.

Preheat the oven to 400 degrees F. Lightly grease 2 standard donut pans.

Fill each donut cup ⅔ full. (You can use a pastry bag with a round tip or plastic bag with the end snipped off to make it easier to fill the pans).

Bake 15–17 minutes until the top of the donuts are lightly browned and spring back when touched. Let cool for 3–4 minutes before removing from pan. Place on a wire cooling rack and cool 5 minutes longer.

In the meantime, whisk together the remaining 2 tbsp. butter with the confectioners' sugar and 1 tbsp. water. Drizzle the glaze evenly over the donuts and allow the glaze to set for a few minutes before serving.

Pumpkin Donuts with Maple Glaze

These spice-scented baked donuts are finished with a sweet maple glaze.

MAKES 12 DONUTS

- 1 ¾ cups (7.7 oz.) all-purpose flour
- 2 tsps. baking powder
- ½ tsp. salt
- ¾ tsp. ground cinnamon
- ¼ tsp. ground nutmeg
- 6 tbsps. canola oil
- 3 large eggs
- 1 ½ cups (10.6 oz.) granulated sugar
- 1 ½ cups (13 oz.) pumpkin purée
- 2 tbsps. whole milk
- 1 cup (4.23 oz.) confectioners' sugar
- 1 tsp. vanilla extract
- 2 tbsps. maple syrup

Preheat the oven to 350 degrees F. Lightly grease 2 standard donut pans.

Combine the flour, baking powder, salt, cinnamon and nutmeg in a large bowl. In a separate medium bowl, whisk the oil, eggs, sugar, pumpkin and milk until smooth. Stir the pumpkin mixture into the flour mixture until just combined. Divide the batter evenly among the donut pans (each will be about ¾ full).

Bake the donuts for 12–15 minutes, until the top of the donuts are lightly browned and spring back when touched (or until a toothpick inserted into the center of one comes out clean). Cool the donuts in the pans for 3–4 minutes before transferring to a rack.

Whisk together the confectioners' sugar, vanilla, 1 tbsp. water and maple syrup in a medium shallow bowl. Dip the donuts in the glaze, allowing any excess to drain off. Place the donuts on a rack and allow the glaze to set 10 minutes before serving.

Chocolate Donuts with Chocolate Glaze

These moist and tender donuts with rich chocolate glaze may be my favorite baked donut.

MAKES 12 DONUTS

- 2 cups (8.75 oz.) all-purpose flour
- ½ cup (1.5 oz.) Dutch process cocoa powder
- ½ cup (4 oz.) light brown sugar
- ½ cup (3.5 oz.) granulated sugar
- 1 tsp. baking powder
- ½ tsp. baking soda
- ¼ tsp. salt
- 1 tsp. espresso powder (optional)

- 2 large eggs
- 1 cup (8 fl. oz.) buttermilk
- 6 tbsps. unsalted butter, melted
- 1 tsp. vanilla bean paste
- 6 oz. bittersweet chocolate, finely chopped
- 1 cup (4.23 oz.) confectioners' sugar
- 1 tsp. vanilla extract
- 4 tbsps. heavy cream

Preheat the oven to 350 degrees F. Lightly grease 2 standard donut pans.

Combine the flour, cocoa, brown sugar, granulated sugar, baking powder, baking soda, salt and espresso powder (if using) in a large bowl. In a separate medium bowl, whisk together the eggs, buttermilk, 4 tbsps. butter and vanilla bean paste. Pour the wet ingredients into the flour mixture and stir to combine. Fold in 2 oz. chocolate. Divide the batter evenly among the donut pans (each will be about ¾ full).

Bake the donuts until puffed, about 10–12 minutes, until the top of the donuts are lightly browned and spring back when touched. Cool the donuts in the pan for 3–4 minutes before transferring to a rack.

Combine the remaining 2 tbsps. butter and 4 oz. chocolate in a medium saucepan over medium heat. Stir until the chocolate is melted. Remove from the heat and stir in the confectioners' sugar, vanilla and heavy cream. Dip the donuts into the chocolate glaze to coat one side, allowing any excess to drain off. Place the donuts on a rack and allow the glaze to set 10 minutes before serving.

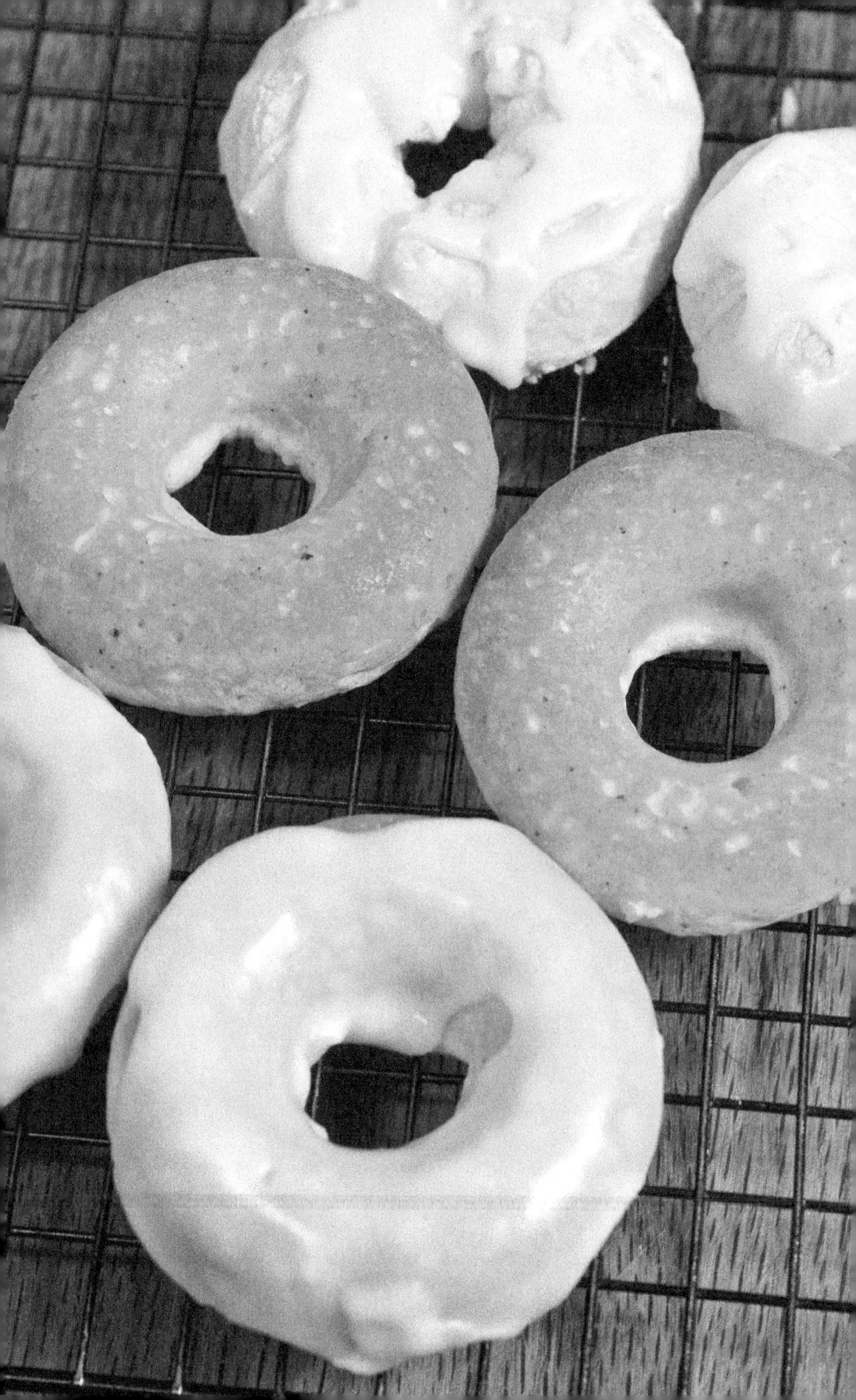

Apple Spice Donuts

These spiced donuts are the perfect comfort food addition to a cool weather breakfast.

MAKES 12 DONUTS

- 2 cups (8.75 oz.) all-purpose flour
- ¾ cup (5.8 oz.) light brown sugar
- 1 ½ tsps. baking powder
- ½ tsp. baking soda
- 1 tsp. ground cinnamon
- ½ tsp. ground ginger
- ¼ tsp. ground cloves

- ½ tsp. salt
- 2 large eggs
- ½ cup (4.3 oz.) applesauce (see recipe p. 309)
- 4 tbsps. whole milk
- 4 tbsps. unsalted butter, melted
- ½ cup (2.11 oz.) confectioners' sugar

Preheat the oven to 350 degrees F. Lightly grease 2 standard donut pans.

Combine the flour, ½ cup (4 oz.) brown sugar, baking powder, baking soda, cinnamon, ginger, cloves and salt in a large bowl. In a separate medium bowl, whisk together the eggs, applesauce, 2 tbsps. milk and 2 tbsps. butter. Pour the wet ingredients into the flour mixture and stir to combine. Divide the batter evenly among the donut pans, filling each about ¾ full.

Bake the donuts for 12–15 minutes until the top of the donuts are lightly browned and spring back when touched (or until a toothpick inserted into the center of one comes out clean). Cool the donuts in the pans for 3–4 minutes before transferring to a rack.

Combine the remaining ¼ cup (2 oz.) brown sugar, 2 tbsps. milk and 2 tbsps. butter in a small saucepan. Bring to a boil over medium heat and stir to dissolve the sugar. Remove from the heat and stir in the confectioners' sugar. Dip the donuts in the glaze, allowing any excess to drain off. Place the donuts on a rack and allow the glaze to set 10 minutes before serving.

Coconut Donuts with Lemon Glaze

I love the combination of coconut and lemon in these baked treats. Sprinkle some toasted coconut flakes onto the glaze for even more coconut flavor. They are also delicious with the vanilla glaze on p. 311 according to preference.

MAKES 12 DONUTS

- 1 ¾ cups (7.7 oz.) all-purpose flour
- 2 cups (8.46 oz.) confectioners' sugar
- 2 tsps. baking powder
- ½ tsp. baking soda
- ¼ tsp. salt
- ½ cup (1.6 oz.) sweetened shredded coconut
- 2 large eggs
- ½ cup (4 fl. oz.) buttermilk
- 6 tbsps. unsalted butter, melted
- 1 tsp. lemon zest
- 2 tbsps. large toasted coconut flakes

Preheat the oven to 350 degrees F. Lightly grease 2 standard donut pans.

Combine the flour, 1 cup (4.23 oz.) confectioners' sugar, baking powder, baking soda and shredded coconut in a large bowl. In a separate medium bowl, whisk together the eggs, buttermilk and butter. Pour the wet ingredients into the flour mixture and stir to combine. Divide the batter evenly among the donut pans (each will be about ¾ full).

Bake the donuts for 12–15 minutes, or until the top of the donuts are lightly browned and spring back when touched (or until a toothpick inserted into the center of one comes out clean). Cool the donuts in the pans for 3–4 minutes before transferring to a rack.

Whisk together the remaining 1 cup (4.23 oz.) confectioners' sugar, lemon zest and 2 ½ tbsps. water in a medium shallow bowl. Dip the donuts in the glaze, allowing any excess to drain off. Place the donuts on a rack and sprinkle on the coconut flakes. Allow the glaze to set 10 minutes before serving.

Powdered Sugar Donuts

These nutmeg-scented donuts have an old-fashioned flavor that's perfect for the morning meal. Dipping the warm donuts in granulated sugar will help the confectioners' sugar stick when the donuts cool.

🍩 MAKES 12 DONUTS

- 2 ¾ cups (12.2 oz.) all-purpose flour
- 1 ½ tsps. baking powder
- ½ tsp. baking soda
- ½ tsp. freshly grated nutmeg
- ½ tsp. salt
- 8 tbsps. unsalted butter
- ¾ cup (5.3 oz.) granulated sugar
- ⅓ cup (2.6 oz.) light brown sugar
- 2 large eggs
- 1 cup (8 fl. oz.) whole milk
- 1 tsp. vanilla extract
- 1 cup (4.23 oz.) confectioners' sugar

Preheat the oven to 425 degrees F. Lightly grease 2 standard donut pans.

Combine the flour, baking powder, baking soda, nutmeg and salt in a medium bowl and set aside.

Combine the butter, ½ cup (3.5 oz.) granulated sugar and brown sugar in the bowl of a stand mixer. Beat until fluffy. Beat in the eggs one at a time. Add half the flour mixture and beat to combine. Stir in the milk and vanilla until smooth. Beat in the remaining flour mixture until just combined.

Bake the donuts for 10–12 minutes until the top of the donuts are lightly browned and spring back when touched (or until a toothpick inserted into the center of one comes out clean). Cool the donuts in the pans for 3–4 minutes before turning them onto a rack. Dip the donuts in the remaining ¼ cup granulated sugar and place them on a rack to cool completely. Dip the cooled donuts in the confectioners' sugar to coat.

Coffee Chocolate Chunk Biscotti with Caramel Glaze

Biscotti are easy to make ahead and are the perfect breakfast accompaniment to coffee. Here the flavor of coffee is also highlighted in these cocoa-scented biscotti. The creamy glaze adds a sweet touch. I prefer to make biscotti smaller (3-4"), but there are also directions on how to form the logs to make larger biscotti according to preference.

MAKES 36-40 SMALL BISCOTTI

- 2 cups (8.75 oz.) all-purpose flour
- ¾ cup (5.3 oz.) granulated sugar
- 2 tsps. baking powder
- ½ tsp. salt
- 1 tbsp. cocoa powder
- 2 tsps. espresso powder (or substitute instant coffee)
- 8 tbsps. unsalted butter
- 8 oz. bittersweet chocolate, chopped into chunks
- 2 large eggs
- ½ cup (4 oz.) light brown sugar
- ¼ cup (2 fl. oz.) heavy cream
- 1 ½ cups (6.35 oz.) confectioners' sugar

Preheat the oven to 350 degrees F. Line 2 baking sheets with parchment paper or lightly grease.

Combine the flour, sugar, baking powder, salt, cocoa powder and espresso powder in a large bowl. Cut 4 tbsps. butter into bits and mix the butter into the flour mixture with a pastry blender until crumbly. Stir in the chocolate chunks. Whisk the eggs and 1 tsp. vanilla in a measuring cup or small bowl and pour them into the flour mixture. Stir until just combined.

Turn the dough onto a lightly floured work surface. Divide the dough into 4 balls. Form each ball into a loaf approximately 10" long and 1 ½" wide. (For larger biscotti, divide the dough in half and form the loaves 10" x 3".) Place logs at least 3" apart on baking sheets and press down slightly to flatten them. Bake for 25-30 minutes until logs are golden brown. Remove the logs from the oven and lower the oven to 325 degrees F. Allow the logs to cool for 10 minutes.

Slice each of the logs into ½" thick pieces and lay the slices flat on the parchment-lined baking sheets. Place in the oven for 8–10 minutes, until they are just turning golden. Turn the cookies over and bake until golden brown, about 8–10 minutes longer. Cool the biscotti on baking racks.

In the meantime, make the caramel glaze. In a medium saucepan, melt the remaining 4 tbsps. butter over medium heat. Stir in the brown sugar until melted. Stir in the cream and bring just to a boil. Remove from the heat and stir in the remaining 1 tsp. vanilla. Cool to room temperature. Whisk in the confectioners' sugar to form a glaze. Dip one side of each cooled biscotti into the glaze to coat. Allow the glaze to set before serving, at least 15 minutes.

Make Ahead Tip: Store baked biscotti in an airtight container for up to 3 days.

Apricot, Ginger and Walnut Biscotti

Tender, moist apricots and spicy-sweet ginger combine in these crunchy biscotti.

🍩 **MAKES ABOUT 36-40 SMALL BISCOTTI.**

- 2 ¼ cups (10 oz.) all-purpose flour
- 1 ¼ cups (9.7 oz.) light brown sugar
- 1 ¼ tsps. baking powder
- ½ tsp. baking soda
- ½ tsp. salt
- 1 tsp. ground cinnamon
- 2 tsps. ground ginger
- ¼ tsp. ground nutmeg
- ¼ tsp. ground cloves
- ½ cup (2.5 oz.) dried apricots, coarsely chopped
- 1 cup (4 oz.) walnuts, coarsely chopped
- ¼ cup (1.5 oz.) chopped crystallized ginger
- 2 large eggs
- ¼ cup (3 oz.) unsulphured dark molasses

Preheat the oven to 350 degrees F. Line a large cookie sheet with parchment.

In a large bowl (or use a stand mixer), combine the flour, brown sugar, baking powder, baking soda, salt, cinnamon, ginger, nutmeg and cloves. Stir in the apricots, walnuts and crystallized ginger. In a measuring cup or small bowl, whisk the eggs until frothy. Whisk in the molasses. Add the egg mixture to the dry ingredients and mix until just combined.

Turn the dough onto a lightly floured work surface. Divide the dough into 4 balls. Form each ball into a loaf approximately 10" long and 1 ½" wide. (For larger biscotti, divide the dough in half and form the loaves 10" x 3"). Place logs at least 3" apart on baking sheets and press down slightly to flatten them. Bake for 25-30 minutes until logs are golden brown. Remove the logs from the oven and lower the oven to 325 degrees F. Allow the logs to cool for 10 minutes.

Slice each of the logs into ½" thick pieces and lay the slices flat on the parchment-lined baking sheets. Place in the oven for 8–10 minutes, until they are just turning golden. Turn the biscotti over and bake until golden brown, about 8–10 minutes longer. Cool the biscotti on baking racks before serving.

Make Ahead Tip: Store baked biscotti in an airtight container for up to 3 days.

Almond Biscotti

Ground almonds give these biscotti a softer, slightly crumbly texture.

MAKES 36–40 SMALL BISCOTTI

- 2 ¾ (12.2. oz.) cups all-purpose flour
- 1 ¼ cups (5.5. oz.) granulated sugar
- ½ cup (1.7 oz.) finely ground almonds (or almond meal)
- 2 tsps. baking powder
- ½ tsp. salt
- 4 tbsps. unsalted butter, cut into bits
- 2 large eggs
- 2 large egg yolks
- 1 tsp. vanilla extract
- 1 tsp. almond extract
- 1 cup (3.8 oz.) sliced almonds

Preheat the oven to 350 degrees F. Line 2 baking sheets with parchment paper or set aside.

In a large mixing bowl, combine the flour, sugar, ground almonds, baking powder and salt. Cut in the butter with a pastry blender until crumbly. In a separate bowl, whisk together the eggs, egg yolks, vanilla and almond extracts. Mix the egg mixture into the dry ingredients until just combined. Stir in the sliced almonds.

Turn the mixture onto a lightly floured work surface. Knead for 2–3 minutes, adding flour a little at a time as necessary, until the dough is still sticky but easier to handle. Divide the dough into 4 balls. Form each ball into a loaf approximately 10" long by 1 ½" wide. (For larger biscotti, divide the dough in half and form the loaves 10" x 3"). Place logs at least 3" apart on baking sheets. Bake for 25–30 minutes until logs are golden brown. Remove the logs from the oven and lower the oven to 325 degrees F. Allow the logs to cool for 10 minutes.

Slice each of the logs into about ½" thick pieces and lay the slices flat on the parchment-lined baking sheets. Bake for 8–10 minutes, until they are just turning golden. Turn the biscotti and cook for

8–10 minutes longer, until just golden. Cool the biscotti on baking racks before serving.

Make Ahead Tip: Store baked biscotti in an airtight container for up to 3 days.

Cinnamon Biscotti

In addition to being twice-baked, these easy-to-make biscotti are brushed with butter and dipped in cinnamon sugar for added flavor.

MAKES 36–40 SMALL BISCOTTI

- 2 ¾ cups (12.2 oz.) all-purpose flour
- 1 ½ cups (10.6 oz.) granulated sugar
- 2 tsps. ground cinnamon
- 1 tsp. baking powder
- ¼ tsp. salt
- 7 tbsps. unsalted butter, cut into bits
- 2 large eggs
- 1 tsp. vanilla extract

Preheat the oven to 350 degrees F. Line 2 large baking sheets with parchment.

Combine the flour, 1 cup (7 oz.) sugar, 1 tsp. cinnamon, baking powder and salt in a large bowl and set aside. Cut 4 tbsps. butter into the flour mixture with a pastry blender until crumbly. Whisk together the eggs and vanilla. Add the wet ingredients to the flour mixture and stir until just combined.

Turn the dough onto a lightly floured work surface. Divide the dough into 4 balls. Form each ball into a loaf approximately 10" long and 1 ½" wide. (For larger biscotti, divide the dough in half and form the loaves 10" x 3"). Place logs at least 3" apart on baking sheets and press down slightly to flatten them. In a shallow bowl or plate, combine the remaining ½ cup granulated sugar with the remaining 1 tsp. cinnamon. Sprinkle a little of the mixture evenly over the logs, reserving the remainder for the dipping. Bake for 25–30 minutes until logs are golden brown. Remove the logs from the oven and lower the oven to 325 degrees F. Allow the loaves to cool for 10 minutes.

Use a serrated knife to cut the loaves into about ½" thick slices. Place biscotti cut side down on parchment-lined baking sheets. Bake for 8-10 minutes, until they are just turning golden. Turn the biscotti and cook for 8-10 minutes longer, until just golden. Allow the logs to cool for 10 minutes.

Melt the remaining 3 tbsps. butter and brush it over the tops of the biscotti. Dip the buttered side of the biscotti into the sugar mixture to coat. Allow the biscotti to dry on the rack, sugar side up, for 5 minutes before serving.

Make Ahead Tip: Store baked biscotti in an airtight container for up to 3 days.

Peanut Butter Oatmeal Biscotti

Peanut butter and oatmeal come together in these peanut-studded cookies. Dip one side of these biscotti in melted dark chocolate for a decadent treat.

MAKES 36–40 SMALL BISCOTTI

- 2 ¼ cups (10 oz.) all-purpose flour
- ½ cup (1.7 oz.) old-fashioned oats
- 2 tsps. baking powder
- ½ tsp. salt
- 3 large eggs
- 2 tsps. vanilla extract

- ¾ cup (5.3 oz.) granulated sugar
- ½ cup (4 oz.) light brown sugar
- 10 tbsps. unsalted butter, melted
- ½ cup (4.55 oz.) smooth peanut butter
- 1 cup (5.15 oz.) roasted peanuts, finely chopped

Preheat the oven to 350 degrees F. Line 2 baking sheets with parchment paper, or lightly grease.

Combine the flour, oats, salt and baking powder in a large bowl.

In a separate bowl, whisk together the eggs and vanilla extract. Whisk in the granulated sugar until mixture is light and pale yellow. Whisk in the brown sugar until combined. Whisk in the melted butter, vanilla and peanut butter. Stir the egg mixture into the dry ingredients until just combined. Fold in the peanuts.

Turn the dough onto a lightly floured work surface. Divide the dough into f4 balls. Form each ball into a loaf approximately 10" long and 1 ½" wide. (For larger biscotti, divide the dough in half and form the loaves 10" x 3"). Place logs at least 3" apart on baking sheets and press down slightly to flatten them. Bake for 25–30 minutes until logs are golden brown. Remove the logs from the oven and lower the oven to 325 degrees F. Allow the logs to cool for 10 minutes.

Slice each of the logs into ½" thick pieces and lay the slices flat on the parchment-lined baking sheets. Place in the oven for 8–10 minutes, until they are just turning golden. Turn the biscotti over and bake until golden brown, about 8–10 minutes longer. Cool the biscotti on baking racks before serving.

Make Ahead Tip: Store baked biscotti in an airtight container for up to 3 days.

Orange Hazelnut Biscotti

Using olive oil instead of butter gives these orange biscotti a unique flavor. Licorice-scented anise seeds add a unique twist, but feel free to omit them according to taste.

MAKES 36–40 SMALL BISCOTTI

- 2 ¾ cups (12. 2 oz.) all-purpose flour
- 1 ½ cups (10.6 oz.) granulated sugar
- 2 tsps. baking powder
- ½ tsp. salt
- 1 tbsp. finely grated orange zest

- 1 cup (4.76 oz.) hazelnuts, skinned and coarsely chopped (see Chef's Tip p. 75)
- 3 large eggs
- 5 tbsps. olive oil
- 2 tbsps. fresh orange juice
- 1 tsp. anise seeds (optional)

Preheat the oven to 350 degrees F. Line 2 baking sheets with parchment paper, or lightly grease.

Combine the flour, sugar, baking powder, salt, orange zest and hazelnuts in a large bowl.

In a separate bowl, whisk together the eggs, olive oil and orange juice. Pour the wet ingredients into the center of the dry ingredients and mix to combine.

Turn the dough onto a lightly floured work surface. Divide the dough into 4 balls. Form each ball into a loaf approximately 10" long and 1 ½" wide. (For larger biscotti, divide the dough in half and form the loaves 10" x 3"). Place logs at least 3" apart on baking sheets and press down slightly to flatten them. Bake for 25–30 minutes until logs are golden brown. Remove the logs from the oven and lower the oven to 325 degrees F. Allow the logs to cool for 10 minutes.

Slice each of the logs into ½" thick pieces and lay the slices flat on the parchment-lined baking sheets. Place in the oven for 8–10 minutes, until they are just turning golden. Turn the cookies over and bake until golden brown, about 8–10 minutes longer. Cool the biscotti on baking racks.

Make Ahead Tip: Store baked biscotti in an airtight container for up to 3 days.

Cranberry, Pistachio and White Chocolate Biscotti

White chocolate chips add a subtle sweetness to these pistachio-studded breakfast cookies.

🍩 MAKES 36–40 SMALL BISCOTTI

- 6 tbsps. unsalted butter, softened
- ¾ cup (5.3 oz.) granulated sugar
- 2 large eggs
- 1 tsp. vanilla extract
- 2 cups (8.75 oz.) all-purpose flour
- 2 tsps. baking powder
- ¼ tsp. salt
- 1 cup (4 oz.) unsalted pistachio nuts
- ¾ cup dried cranberries
- ½ cup (3 oz.) white chocolate chips

Preheat the oven to 350 degrees F. Line 2 baking sheets with parchment paper.

Combine the butter and sugar in the bowl of a stand mixer until light and fluffy, about 3-4 minutes. Mix in the eggs and vanilla until smooth. Combine the flour, baking powder and salt until just combined. Add the flour mixture to the wet ingredients. Fold in the pistachios, cranberries and white chocolate.

Turn the dough onto a lightly floured work surface. Divide the dough into 4 balls. Form each ball into a loaf approximately 10" long and 1 ½" wide. (For larger biscotti, divide the dough in half and form the loaves 10" x 3"). Place logs at least 3" apart on baking sheets and press down slightly to flatten them. Bake for 25–30 minutes until logs are golden brown. Remove the logs from the oven and lower the oven to 325 degrees F. Allow the logs to cool for 10 minutes.

Slice each of the logs into ½"-thick pieces and lay the slices flat on the parchment-lined baking sheets. Place in the oven for 8–10 minutes, until they are just turning golden. Turn the cookies over and bake until golden brown, about 8–10 minutes longer. Cool the biscotti completely on baking racks.

Anise Almond Biscotti

Unlike most of my biscotti recipes, which include shortening to soften them slightly, these traditional biscotti (similar to the Italian cookie cantucci) have a crunchier texture and are perfect for dipping.

🍩 MAKES 36–40 SMALL BISCOTTI

- 2 ½ cups (11 oz.) all-purpose flour
- 1 cup (7 oz.) granulated sugar
- 1 ½ tsps. baking powder
- ¼ tsp. salt
- 2 tsps. anise seeds, crushed
- 2 tsps. lemon zest

- 2 large eggs
- 2 large egg yolks
- 1 tsp. vanilla extract
- 1 tbsp. anisette, Sambuca or other anise liqueur (optional)
- 1 cup (3.8 oz.) almonds, chopped
- 1 large egg white

Preheat the oven to 350 degrees F. Line 2 baking sheets with parchment paper or set aside.

Combine the flour, sugar, baking powder, salt, anise seeds and lemon zest in a large bowl. In a separate bowl, whisk together the eggs, egg yolks, vanilla extract and anisette (if using). Mix the egg mixture into the dry ingredients until just combined. Fold in the almonds.

Turn the mixture onto a lightly floured work surface. Knead for 2–3 minutes, adding flour a little at a time as necessary until the dough is still sticky but easier to handle. Divide the dough into 4 balls. Form each ball into a loaf approximately 10" long by 1 ½" wide. (For larger biscotti, divide the dough in half and form the loaves 10" x 3"). Place logs at least 3" apart on baking sheets, as the dough will spread as it cooks. Whisk the egg white lightly and brush it over the tops of the loaves.

Bake for 25–30 minutes until logs are golden brown. Remove the logs from the oven and lower the oven to 325 degrees F. Allow the logs to cool for 10 minutes.

Slice each of the logs into about ½"-thick pieces and lay the slices flat on the parchment-lined baking sheets. Bake for 8–10 minutes, until they are just turning golden. Turn the biscotti and cook for 8–10 minutes longer, until just golden. Cool the biscotti on baking racks before serving.

Make Ahead Tip: Store baked biscotti in an airtight container for up to 7 days.

Sun-Dried Tomato and Goat Cheese Biscotti

These savory biscotti are delicious paired with omelets and are perfect for dipping into soft-cooked eggs.

MAKES 24–30 BISCOTTI SMALL BISCOTTI

- 2 ¼ cups (10 oz.) all-purpose flour
- 1 tbsp. herbs de Provence
- 1 ½ tsps. baking powder
- ¾ tsp. salt
- 4 tbsps. unsalted butter, softened
- 4 tbsps. extra virgin olive oil
- 2 oz. goat cheese, crumbled
- 1 tbsp. granulated sugar
- 2 large eggs
- ⅓ cup sliced oil-packed sun-dried tomatoes, drained and coarsely chopped

Preheat the oven to 350 degrees F. Line a baking sheet with parchment paper and set aside.

In a medium bowl, whisk together the flour, herbs de Provence, baking powder and salt. Set aside.

In a medium bowl (or with an electric mixer), beat the butter, olive oil and goat cheese together until smooth. Whisk in the sugar and eggs. Add the butter mixture to the dry ingredients and mix until just combined. Fold in the sun-dried tomatoes.

Turn the dough onto a lightly floured work surface. Divide the dough into 4 balls. Form each ball into a loaf approximately 10" long and 1 ½" wide. (For larger biscotti, divide the dough in half and form the loaves 10" x 3"). Place logs at least 3" apart on baking sheets and press down slightly to flatten them. Bake for 25–30 minutes until logs are golden brown. Remove the logs from the oven and lower the oven to 325 degrees F.

Allow the logs to cool for 5 minutes. Slice each of the logs into ¾"-thick pieces and lay the slices flat on the parchment-lined baking sheets. Place in the oven for 8–10 minutes, until they are just turning golden. Turn the biscotti over and bake until golden brown, about 8–10 minutes longer. Cool the biscotti on baking racks before serving.

Make Ahead Tip: Store baked biscotti in an airtight container for up to 3 days.

Fruit and Nut Bars

These fruit- and nut-studded bars are delicious as part of a breakfast buffet or as a satisfying meal on the go.

MAKES 8 BARS OR 16 SQUARES

- ½ cup (1.7 oz.) old-fashioned oats
- ¼ cup (1.1 oz.) all-purpose flour
- ½ cup (1.67 oz.) finely ground almonds (or almond meal)
- ½ tsp. baking powder
- ¼ tsp. salt
- 1 tsp. ground ginger
- ¼ cup (1.1 oz.) dried apricots, finely chopped
- ¼ cup (1.5 oz.) dried cranberries
- ¼ cup (1 oz.) hazelnuts, peeled and chopped (see Chef's Tip on p. 75)
- ¼ cup (3 oz.) honey
- 2 large egg whites

Preheat the oven to 250 degrees F. Grease an 8" x 8" baking pan, line with parchment and grease again.

Combine the oats, flour, almond meal, baking powder, salt and ginger in a large bowl. Stir in the apricots, cranberries and hazelnuts. Stir in the honey. Whisk the egg whites to soft peaks. Fold in the egg whites. Press the mixture into the prepared pan.

Bake for 1 hour, until firm and golden brown. Cool for 10 minutes. Cut into 2" x 4" bars or 2" squares and cool completely.

Make Ahead Tip: Store bars in an airtight container for up to a week.

Fig Almond Bars

These layered bars are a wholesome, home-baked version of fig bars. Substitute dried cherries for the figs for a tasty variation.

🍩 MAKES 8 BARS (OR 16 SQUARES)

- 1 ½ cups (6.6 oz.) all-purpose flour
- ¼ cup (.83 oz.) finely ground almonds (or almond meal)
- ⅓ cup (2.6 oz.) light brown sugar
- ½ tsp. baking soda
- ½ tsp. salt
- 4 tbsps. unsalted butter, softened
- ¼ cup (3 oz.) honey
- ¼ cup (2 fl. oz.) whole milk
- 1 cup (5.25 oz.) finely chopped dried figs
- ½ cup (2.9 oz.) chopped almonds

Preheat oven to 350 degrees F. Grease an 8" x 8" baking dish or pan, line with parchment and grease again.

Combine the flour, almonds, brown sugar, baking soda and salt in large bowl. Cut in the butter with a pastry blender until crumbly. Stir in the honey and milk. Press half the mixture in the baking pan. Combine the figs and chopped almonds in a small bowl and press the mixture evenly over top. Press the remaining flour mixture over the fig almond filling. Bake for 20 minutes, until firm and lightly browned. Allow the bars to cool in the pan for 20 minutes, then cut into 2" x 4" bars or 2" squares to serve.

Make Ahead Tip: Store bars in an airtight container for up to a week.

Strawberry Bars

These easy-to-make fruit bars are topped with a crumbly streusel. A good quality strawberry jam may be substituted for the strawberry filling.

MAKES 8 BARS OR 16 SQUARES

- 2 cups (10.7 oz.) fresh strawberries, hulled and quartered
- ⅔ cup (4.7 oz.) granulated sugar
- 1 tbsp. lemon juice
- 1 ¼ cups (5.5 oz.) all-purpose flour
- ⅔ cup (4.7 oz.) granulated sugar
- ½ tsp. salt
- 10 tbsps. unsalted butter, cut into bits
- ¼ cup (2 oz.) light brown sugar
- ½ cup (1.7 oz.) old-fashioned oats

To make the strawberry filling, combine the strawberries, ⅓ cup (2.35 oz.) granulated sugar and lemon juice in a medium bowl. Mash the strawberries slightly and allow them to macerate and release their juices for 20 minutes. Bring the strawberry mixture to a boil in a medium saucepan over medium heat. Allow the mixture to bubble until thickened, about 8–10 minutes. Remove from the heat and pour into a heat-proof measuring cup to cool.

Preheat the oven to 375 degrees F. Grease an 8" x 8" baking dish or pan, line with parchment and grease again.

Combine the flour, remaining ⅓ cup (2.35 oz.) granulated sugar and salt in a large bowl. Cut in 8 tbsps. butter with a pastry blender until crumbly. Reserve ½ cup (2.5 oz.) of the mixture for the topping.

Press the remaining flour mixture evenly into bottom of prepared pan. Bake for 15–18 minutes, until edges begin to brown lightly. Leave the oven on.

In the meantime, combine the reserved flour mixture, brown sugar and oats in a medium bowl. Cut in the remaining 2 tbsps. butter with a pastry blender until crumbly.

Spread the strawberries evenly over the crust. Sprinkle on the streusel topping. Bake until topping is deep golden brown and filling is bubbling, 22–25 minutes. Allow the bars to cool in the pan for 20 minutes, then cut into 2" x 4" bars or 2" squares to serve.

Make Ahead Tip: Store bars in an airtight container in the refrigerator for 1–2 days.

Peanut Coconut Bars

Baking these bars at a low temperature results in a crunchy texture.

🍩 MAKES 8 BARS OR 16 SQUARES

- ½ cup (4 fl. oz.) heavy cream (or ½ cup evaporated milk)
- ¾ cup (5.3 oz.) granulated sugar
- ¼ cup (2.3 oz.) smooth peanut butter
- 1 ½ cups (5 oz.) old-fashioned oats
- 1 cup (3.28 oz.) shredded sweetened coconut
- 1 cup (5.15 oz.) unsalted peanuts
- ½ cup (3 oz.) pepitas (optional)

Combine the cream and sugar in a small saucepan and bring just to a boil. Remove from the heat and allow the mixture to cool slightly. Whisk in the peanut butter and set aside.

Preheat the oven to 250 degrees F. Lightly grease an 8" x 8" baking dish, line with parchment and grease parchment.

Combine the oats, coconut, peanuts and pepitas (if using) in a medium bowl. Stir in the warm cream mixture and mix to combine. Spread the mixture in the baking dish and press down evenly.

Bake for 1 hour. Remove from the oven and allow to cool for 5 minutes. Cut into 2" x 4" bars or 2" squares and transfer to a rack to finish cooling completely.

Make Ahead Tip: Store bars in an airtight container for up to a week.

Granola Bars

Baking granola into bars makes an on-the-go breakfast that satisfies. You can make the bars up to one week ahead, but don't be surprised if they don't last that long.

MAKES 8 BARS OR 16 SQUARES

- 2 cups (6.7 oz.) old-fashioned oats
- ½ cup (3 oz.) pepitas
- 1 cup (3.8 oz.) sliced almonds
- ½ cup (1.6 oz.) unsweetened coconut flakes
- ½ cup (6 oz.) honey
- 3 tbsps. light brown sugar
- 2 tbsps. unsalted butter
- 2 tsps. vanilla extract
- ½ tsp. salt
- 1 cup (5.8 oz.) dried blueberries or other dried fruit

Preheat the oven to 350 degrees F. Grease an 8" x 8" baking dish and set aside. Line a baking sheet with parchment.

Spread the oats, pepitas and almonds on the baking sheet and toast for 7 minutes. Stir in the coconut and toast for 7–8 minutes longer, until coconut is just golden.

In the meantime, combine the honey, brown sugar, butter, vanilla and salt in a medium saucepan. Whisk over medium heat until the brown sugar has completely dissolved. Stir in the blueberries. Pour into a large bowl.

Reduce the oven temperature to 300 degrees F.

Stir the oatmeal mixture into the honey mixture to combine. Spread it into the prepared baking dish and press down, evenly distributing the mixture in the dish. Bake for 25 minutes. Allow to cool for 10 minutes. Cut into 2" x 4" bars or 2" squares and allow to cool completely.

Make Ahead Tip: Store bars in an airtight container for up to a week.

Apricot Pecan Bars

These easy-to-make-ahead bars are an excellent addition to a breakfast or brunch buffet. A good quality apricot preserve may be substituted for the fruit spread.

MAKES 8 BARS OR 16 SQUARES

- 1 ½ cups (6.6 oz.) all-purpose flour
- 1 ½ cups (5 oz.) old-fashioned oats
- 1 cup (7.76 oz.) light brown sugar
- 1 tsp. baking powder
- ½ tsp. salt
- 14 tbsps. unsalted butter, softened
- 1 cup (11.3 oz.) apricot fruit spread (see recipe p. 305)
- ½ cup (2 oz.) chopped pecans

Preheat the oven to 350 degrees F. Grease an 8" x 8" baking dish or pan, line with parchment and grease again.

Combine the flour, oats, sugar, baking powder and salt in a large bowl. Cut in the butter with a pastry blender until crumbly. Press half the mixture into the prepared pan. Spoon the apricot spread evenly over the crust. Sprinkle on the pecans. Spoon on the remaining flour-butter mixture and press lightly with the back of a spoon.

Bake for 25–30 minutes, until golden brown. Cool completely. Cut into 2" x 4" bars or 2" squares.

Make Ahead Tip: Store bars in an airtight container for up to a week.

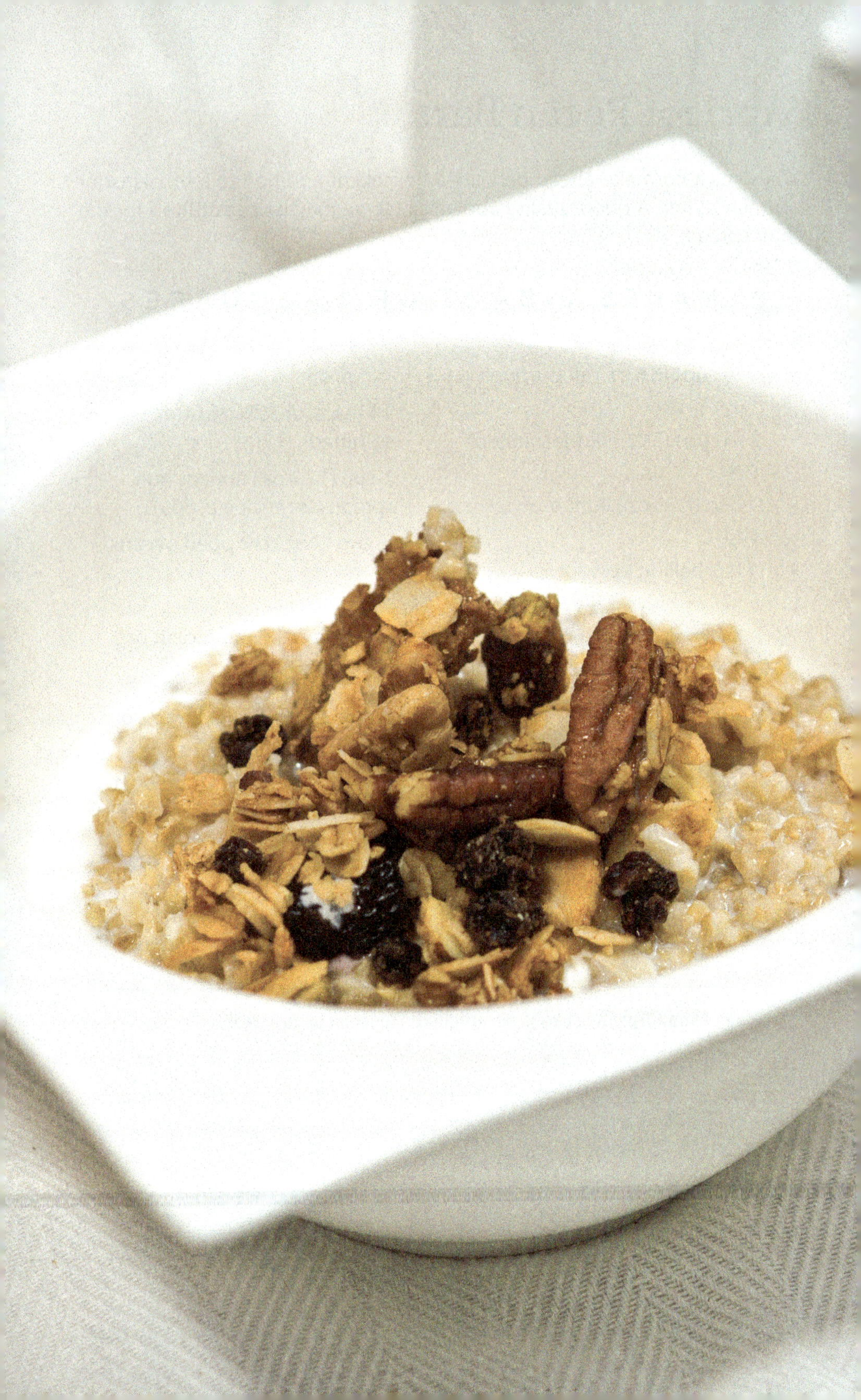

Granola Two Ways

Granola recipes often used to include butter and a lot of sugar—perhaps not the healthiest way of eating toasted oats and nuts. However, there are times when I find that a chunky texture is desirable, which does require adding sugar. I've developed a two-step approach that results in half of the granola being lower sugar and more crumbly, and the second half being more in the chunky style. Both are delicious. If you prefer all of the granola in the crumbly, lower-sugar style, then simply skip the last step.

MAKES ABOUT 7 CUPS

- 2 ½ cups (8.5 oz.) old-fashioned oats
- ½ cup (2.8 oz.) steel cut oats
- 1 cup (3.28 oz.) large unsweetened coconut flakes
- ½ cup (2.9 oz.) sliced almonds
- 1 cup (5.8 oz.) pecan halves
- ½ cup (2.9 oz.) coarsely chopped walnuts
- ¼ cup (1.5 oz.) pistachios
- 3 tbsps. chia, flax or pumpkin seed
- 1 egg white, whipped to soft peaks
- 2 tbsps. coconut oil or other neutral oil

- ½ tsp. salt
- ¼–½ cup (2–4 oz.) light brown sugar
- ¼ cup (3 oz.) honey
- ¼–½ (2.8–5.6 oz.) cup maple syrup
- ½ tsp. ground cinnamon
- ¼ tsp. ground allspice
- 1 tsp. vanilla extract
- ½ cup (3 oz.) dried cherries
- ½ cup (2.9 oz.) dried currants or cranberries

Preheat the oven to 300 degrees F. Line 2 large baking sheets with parchment or aluminum foil and lightly grease.

Combine the old-fashioned oats, steel cut oats, coconut flakes, almonds, pecans, walnuts, pistachios and chia in a large bowl. Fold in the egg white. In a medium saucepan, stir together the coconut oil, salt, ¼ cup (2 oz.) brown sugar, honey, ¼ cup (2.8 oz.) maple syrup, cinnamon, allspice and vanilla. Bring to a simmer over medium heat, then pour over the dry ingredients and stir to coat. Spread the mixture out evenly on the baking sheets.

Bake in the preheated oven for 20 minutes, then stir the mixture so it browns evenly. Continue cooking for 15 minutes longer, until mixture is evenly golden brown and crisp. Remove the pans from the oven and place them on cooling racks. Allow the mixture to cool. If you are not proceeding to the chunky step, toss the mixture with the cherries and currants and store in an airtight container. If you are proceeding below, divide the cherries and currants in half and toss them with half the mixture. Store this half crumbly mixture in a separate airtight container. Reserve the remaining cherries and currants for the second batch.

To make the chunky granola, leave the oven on. Combine the remaining ¼ cup (2 oz.) brown sugar and ¼ cup (2.8 oz.) maple syrup over medium heat. Pour the second half of the toasted granola into a large bowl. Toss the mixture with the maple syrup and brown sugar mixture and spread it out on the parchment. Bake for 12–15 minutes longer without stirring, until mixture looks glossy and evenly dark brown but not burnt. The granola will not be crunchy when it's done baking, but will set and harden as it cools. Cool slightly then break into bits according to your preference. Cool completely and then stir in the cherries and currants.

Make Ahead Tip: Store granola in an airtight container for up to a week.

Pumpkin Spice Granola

Spices and pumpkin puree combine in this granola for a tasty breakfast treat. If you prefer a chunkier texture, press the granola by hand or use tongs to form clusters before baking.

🍩 MAKES ABOUT 7 CUPS

- 3 cups (10 oz.) old -fashioned oats
- ¾ cup (4.2 oz.) steel cut oats
- 1 cup (3.3 oz.) large unsweetened coconut flakes
- ½ cup (2oz.) sliced almonds
- 1 cup (3.8 oz.) pecan halves
- ½ cup (2 oz.) coarsely chopped walnuts
- ¼ cup (1 oz.) pepitas
- 2 egg whites, whipped to soft peaks
- ⅓ cup coconut oil or other neutral oil
- 1 tsp. salt
- ½ cup (4 oz.) light brown sugar
- 3 tbsps. honey
- ½ cup (5.6 oz.) maple syrup
- 1 tsp. vanilla
- 2 tsps. ground cinnamon
- 1 tsp. ground allspice
- 1 tsp. ground nutmeg
- 1 tsp. ground ginger
- ½ tsp. ground cloves
- ¾ cup pumpkin puree
- 1 cup (5.8 oz.) dried cranberries

Preheat the oven to 300 degrees F. Line 2 large baking sheets with parchment or aluminum foil and lightly grease.

Combine the old-fashioned oats, steel cut oats, coconut flakes, almonds, pecans, walnuts and pepitas in a large bowl. Fold in the egg white. In a medium saucepan, stir together the coconut oil, salt, brown sugar, honey, maple syrup, vanilla, cinnamon, allspice, nutmeg, ginger and cloves. Bring just to a simmer over medium heat. Remove from heat and whisk in the pumpkin puree until combined. Pour the wet ingredients over the dry ingredients and stir to coat. Spread the mixture out evenly on the baking sheets.

Bake in the preheated oven for 20 minutes, then stir the mixture so it browns evenly. Continue cooking for 20 minutes longer, until mixture is evenly golden brown and crisp. Remove the pans from the oven and place them on cooling racks. Allow the mixture to cool. Toss the mixture with the cranberries.

Make Ahead Tip: Store granola in an airtight container for up to a week.

Cherry Pistachio Granola

Crystallized ginger adds a spicy accent to this delicious take on granola.

MAKES ABOUT 7 CUPS

- 3 cups (10 oz.) old-fashioned oats
- 1 cup (5.8 oz.) pistachios, coarsely chopped
- ¾ cup (2.5 oz.) large unsweetened coconut flakes
- ½ cup (2.9 oz.) pepitas
- 1 egg white, whipped to soft peaks
- ⅓ cup (2.6 fl. oz.) coconut oil
- ¼ cup (1.8 oz.) light brown sugar
- ⅓ cup maple syrup
- ½ tsp. salt
- ½ tsp. ground cinnamon
- ½ tsp. ground cardamom
- 1 tsp. vanilla extract
- 1 cup (6 oz.) dried cherries, coarsely chopped
- ¼ cup (1.5 oz.) chopped crystallized ginger

Preheat the oven to 300°F. Line 2 large baking sheets with parchment or foil and lightly grease.

Combine the old-fashioned oats, pistachios, coconut flakes and pepitas in a large bowl. Fold in the egg white. In a medium saucepan, stir together the coconut oil, brown sugar, maple syrup, salt, cinnamon, cardamom and vanilla. Bring to a simmer over medium heat, then pour over the dry ingredients and stir to coat. Spread the mixture out evenly on the baking sheets.

Bake in the preheated oven for 20 minutes, then stir the mixture so it browns evenly. Continue cooking for 15 minutes longer, until mixture is evenly golden brown and crisp. Remove the pans from the oven and place them on cooling racks. Allow the mixture to cool. Add the cherries and ginger and toss to combine.

Make Ahead Tip: Store granola in an airtight container for up to a week.

CHAPTER FIVE

Classic Baked Goods, Breads and Doughs

- Traditional English Muffins
- Simple English Muffins
- Crumpets
- Traditional Bagels
- Simple Bagels
- Buttermilk Biscuits
- Cinnamon Bread
- Panettone Loaf
- Sweet Roll Dough
- Sweet Tart Dough
- Cream Cheese Pastry Dough
- Sour Cream Pastry Dough
- Traditional Brioche
- Simple Brioche
- Danish Pastry Dough
- Traditional Puff Pastry
- Simple Puff Pastry
- Traditional Croissant Dough
- Simple Croissant Dough

Traditional English Muffins

Something happened to store-bought English muffins—something very wrong. They last for weeks. So even if you never thought of making them before, please do. This muffin recipe features a very soft batter that requires rings to form the traditional round shape. The rings give the muffins a little extra rise and the texture is somewhat lighter than the recipe for Simple English Muffins. Both are delicious. Splitting them with a fork highlights the bounty of holes created by using both yeast and baking soda in the batter.

MAKE 6 MUFFINS

- ¾ cup (6 fl. oz.) whole milk, warmed
- 1 tbsp. unsalted butter
- 1 tbsp. granulated sugar
- 1 large egg
- 2 cups (8.75 oz.) all-purpose flour (or substitute 2 cups/9.6 oz. bread flour)
- 1 tsp. instant yeast
- ½ tsp. salt
- ½ tsp. baking soda
- ¼ cup (1.4 oz.) cornmeal (optional)

Combine the milk, butter and granulated sugar in the bowl of a stand mixer. Whisk in the egg. Combine the flour, yeast and salt in a separate bowl. Add the flour mixture and beat to combine. Continue to beat the mixture on low for 4 minutes. Place the dough in a greased bowl and cover with plastic wrap. Allow the dough to rise until doubled, about 1–1 ½ hours (or refrigerate overnight).

Stir the baking soda into 1 tbsp. warm water. Add the baking soda mixture to the batter.

Grease 6 (3–4") rings and grease a large baking sheet. Heat a griddle or large skillet over medium heat and brush the surface with oil. Place the rings on the griddle to heat up. Lower the heat to low and spoon batter into the rings about ½" deep. Sprinkle the tops lightly with cornmeal (if using). Cover the rings with a baking sheet. Cook the batter in the rings for 5–6 minutes, until golden brown. Loosen the muffins from the rings with a thin knife and set the rings aside. Turn the muffins and cook for 5–6 minutes longer, until golden brown and cooked through. If your muffins brown too quickly, place them on a rack in a preheated oven at 350 degrees F to cook through.

Simple English Muffins

This is a simple version of muffins that doesn't require rings. Even though they are easy to prepare, the dough has a rich, complex flavor.

MAKES 6 MUFFINS

- 2 cups (8.75 oz.) all-purpose flour
- 1 tbsp. granulated sugar
- ½ tsp. salt
- 1 tsp. instant yeast
- ½ tsp. baking soda
- 1 tbsp. unsalted butter, softened
- ¾ cup (6 fl. oz.) buttermilk
- ¼ cup (1.4 oz.) cornmeal

Mix together the flour, sugar, salt, yeast and baking soda in the bowl of an electric mixer. On low speed, mix in the butter and buttermilk until the ingredients form a ball. Switch to the dough hook (or use lightly floured hands) and knead for 10 minutes. Form the dough into a ball, adding a little flour if necessary. Lightly grease a large bowl and place the dough ball into the bowl. Turn the dough to coat it with oil and cover with plastic wrap. Leave in a warm place to rise for 1 ½ hours, until dough is doubled in size.

Divide the dough into 6 equal pieces with lightly floured hands. Shape the pieces into balls. Line a sheet pan with baking parchment and lightly grease the parchment. Spread half the cornmeal onto the parchment. Transfer the balls of dough to the sheet pan at least 2 inches apart. Press the balls down to form 3 ½" rounds. Sprinkle them loosely with the remaining cornmeal and cover the pan loosely with plastic wrap. Allow the muffins to rise in a warm place for 1 hour, or until pieces are almost double in size.

Heat a griddle or large skillet over medium-low heat. Preheat the oven to 350 degrees F.

Brush the griddle with a little oil. Uncover the muffin rounds and gently transfer them to the griddle at least 1" apart. Cover any remaining rounds with plastic wrap while cooking. Cook the muffins for 5–8 minutes, or until the bottoms are golden brown. Turn the muffins over and cook on the other side for 5–8 minutes longer, until just golden. Immediately transfer the muffins to a baking sheet. Bake for 5–8 minutes, until the muffins spring back and are cooked through. Continue until all muffins are complete. Transfer the baked muffins to a cooling rack and cool for at least 30 minutes before slicing or serving.

Crumpets

Crumpets have holes on the top sides (which are not browned), and are less bready than English muffins. The thin batter is cooked on the stovetop in rings to prevent the dough from spreading, and to maximize the bubbles that form throughout the batter. If you only have a few rings, you can remove the rings after the first crumpets set up, and start a second batch. Keep the heat on the lowest setting to avoid overbrowning the bottoms. You can also make a single crumpet in a small 8" skillet and cut it into wedges for sharing.

MAKES 6-8 CRUMPETS

- 1 cup (4.4 oz.) all-purpose flour
- 1 ½ tsps. instant yeast
- ¼ tsp. salt
- ⅓ cup (2.6 fl. oz.) whole milk
- ½ tsp. granulated sugar
- ¼ tsp. baking soda

Combine the flour, yeast and salt in a large bowl. Heat the milk in a small saucepan until it steams but is not boiling. Stir the sugar into the warm milk. Stir ⅓ cup (2.6 fl. oz.) water into the milk. Make a well in the center and pour in the warm milk mixture. Stir the mixture until it forms a smooth batter, about 3-4 minutes. Cover and allow the mixture to rise in a warm place until almost doubled (it may begin to fall but that's OK), about 1 hour.

Mix the baking soda with 2 tbsps. warm water. Stir the mixture into the batter. Cover and allow the dough to rest for 20 minutes.

In the meantime, grease 6 (3-4") rings. Heat a griddle or large skillet over medium heat and brush the surface with oil. Place the rings on the griddle to heat up. Lower the heat to low. Spoon batter into the rings no more than ½" deep. Cook the batter in the rings for 10-12 minutes, until the bottom is golden brown and the top surface is no longer wet or glossy and is just cooked through. Loosen the crumpets from the rings with a thin knife and set the rings aside. If you are planning to serve them immediately, turn the crumpets and brown the tops lightly for 2-3 minutes. For best results, let the crumpets cool and set completely, then toast them to serve.

Traditional Bagels

This overnight version is my first choice for the most authentic NY-style bagels to make at home. They are foolproof as long as you follow the directions and only allow them to rise for 20 minutes before refrigerating them (imagine my sadness the next morning when my over-risen bagels had become hockey pucks!). Baking soda is used here as a safer home alternative to the solution of food-grade lye bagels are typically dipped into.

MAKES 8 LARGE BAGELS (5-6"), 12 MEDIUM BAGELS (3-4") OR 24 MINI BAGELS (1-2").

- 3 ½ cups (16.9 oz.) bread flour or high-gluten flour
- 1 tsp. instant yeast
- 1 tsp. salt
- 1 tsp. diastatic malt (optional)
- 3 tbsps. baking soda

Line a baking sheet with parchment and grease the parchment.

Combine the bread flour, 1 cup (8 fl. oz.) warm water, instant yeast, salt and diastatic malt (if using) into the bowl of a stand mixer and mix on low speed for 3 4 minutes, until combined. Stop the mixer and gather the dough together, adding water 1 tsp. at a time if dough seems too dry. Switch to the dough hook and knead for 9–10 minutes until the dough is stiff but smooth. Place the dough on a lightly floured work surface and continue to knead by hand for 3 minutes longer. The dough should be stiff and smooth on the surface. If the dough seems too soft or overly tacky, mix or knead in a little more flour.

Clean any flour off the work surface and divide the dough into the desired number of bagels. Shape each piece into a smooth ball. Cover the pieces with plastic wrap and allow them to rest for 20 minutes.

Take a piece of dough and roll it out by hand to form a log approximately ¾" thick and 7–8" long, making the ends slightly thicker than the center. Make a ring with the dough around your hand and pinch the ends together. Roll the dough slightly to secure the 2 ends together. Place the bagel on the prepared sheet and repeat until all are formed.

Cover the sheet pan with plastic wrap, forming a tent (or place it inside a large unscented plastic bag). Allow the bagels to rise at room temperature for 20 minutes. Drop 1 bagel into a bowl of cold water. If it floats within 10 seconds, the bagels are ready for the overnight rise. Pat the bagel dry and return it to the pan. If it doesn't float within 10 seconds, pat it dry, return it to the pan and test it again every 5 minutes until it floats.

Place the bagels on the baking sheet into the refrigerator at least 8 hours, or up to 2 days.

Preheat the oven to 450 degrees F. Allow the bagels to sit at room temperature for 30 minutes. Combine 6 cups water and baking soda together in a large stockpot or Dutch oven and bring to a boil. Lower the heat to barely a simmer. Drop bagels 2–3 at a time into the simmering water for 1 minute. The bagels should float at the top of the water. Turn them over and let simmer for 30 seconds longer. Remove the bagels, allowing water to drain off, and place them on a rack to drain. If using toppings (such as sesame or poppy seeds), immediately sprinkle the tops of the bagels with the topping while the bagels are still moist.

Place bagels on the baking sheet and bake for 5 minutes. Rotate the pan and lower the heat to 400 degrees F. Continue baking for 10–15 minutes, until golden brown. Cool for at least 10 minutes before serving. Freeze any bagels not eaten the same day for up to 1 month.

Chef's Tip: For cinnamon raisin bagels, soak ¾ cup raisins in warm water for 10 minutes. Drain the raisins and roll them in paper towels to dry them. Add 2 tsps. ground cinnamon, 2 tbsps. granulated sugar and the raisins to the other dough ingredients and proceed as above.

Simple Bagels

If you want to make the bagels all in one day, this version is a tasty choice. I find the dough is a little more temperamental because of the added yeast, so handle it carefully throughout the rising, shaping and boiling.

🥖 MAKES 8 LARGE BAGELS (5-6"), 12 MEDIUM BAGELS (3-4") OR 24 MINI BAGELS (1-2").

- 3 ½ cups (16.9 oz.) bread flour or high-gluten flour
- 2 tsps. instant yeast
- 1 tsp. salt
- 1 tsp. diastatic malt (optional)
- 2 tbsps. baking soda

Place bread flour, 1 cup (8 fl. oz.) warm water, instant yeast, salt and diastatic malt (if using) into the bowl of a stand mixer and mix on low speed for 3-4 minutes, until combined. Stop the mixer and gather the dough together, adding water 1 tsp. at a time if dough seems too dry. Switch to the dough hook and knead for 9-10 minutes, until the dough is stiff but smooth. Place the dough on a lightly floured work surface and continue to knead by hand for 3 minutes longer. Form dough into a ball. Place the dough in a greased bowl and turn it to coat. Cover with plastic wrap and allow it to rise for 1 hour.

Punch the dough down and let it rest for 10 minutes. Line a baking sheet with parchment and lightly grease the parchment.

Divide the dough into 12 equal pieces. Shape each piece into a ball. Take a piece of dough and roll it out using your hands to form a log approximately ¾" thick and 7-8" long, making the ends just a bit thicker than the center. Make a ring with the dough around your hand and pinch the ends together. Roll the dough slightly to secure the 2 ends together. Place the bagel on the prepared sheet. (Alternately, poke a hole in the center of the ball and work the dough into a ring from the inside.) Repeat until all are formed.

Cover the sheet pan with plastic wrap, forming a tent (or place it inside a large unscented plastic bag). Allow the bagels to rest at room temperature for 10 minutes.

In the meantime, preheat the oven to 450 degrees F. Allow the bagels to sit at room temperature for 30 minutes. Combine 6 cups water and baking soda together in a large stockpot or Dutch oven and bring to a boil. Lower the heat to barely a simmer. Drop bagels 3 at a time into the simmering water for 1 minute (the bagels should float on the top of the water). Turn them over and let simmer for 30 seconds. Remove the bagels, allowing water to drain off. Place them on a rack to drain. If using toppings such as sesame or poppy seeds, immediately sprinkle the tops of the bagels with the topping while the bagels are still moist.

Grease the parchment on the baking sheet again. Transfer the bagels to the baking sheet and bake for 5 minutes. Rotate the pan and lower the heat to 400 degrees F. Continue baking for 10–15 minutes, until golden brown. Cool for at least 10 minutes before serving. Freeze any bagels not eaten the same day for up to 1 month.

Chef's Tip: For cinnamon raisin bagels, soak ¾ cup raisins in warm water for 10 minutes. Drain the raisins and roll them in paper towels to dry them. Add 2 tsps. ground cinnamon, 2 tbsps. granulated sugar and the raisins with the other dough ingredients and proceed as above.

Buttermilk Biscuits

Buttermilk biscuits are a joy—buttery, flaky and slightly sour from the buttermilk. They are perfect foil for scrambled eggs and bacon, or simply slathered with butter and jam. Plan to consume them the same day you make them.

MAKES 8 BISCUITS

- 2 cups (8.75 oz.) all-purpose flour
- 1 tsp. salt
- 4 tsps. baking powder
- ½ tsp. baking soda
- 3 tbsps. vegetable shortening, chilled
- 7 tbsps. unsalted butter
- 1 cup (8 fl. oz.) buttermilk

Preheat the oven to 425 degrees F. Line a baking sheet with parchment and set aside.

Whisk the flour, salt, baking powder and baking soda in a medium bowl. Using a pastry blender, cut in the shortening until the mixture is crumbly. Cut in 5 tbsps. butter with the pastry blender. Press the dough into a disk, cover with plastic wrap and place the bowl into the freezer for 15 minutes.

Stir the buttermilk into the dough. Transfer the dough to a lightly floured work surface and press into a 6" x 9" rectangle, about ¾" thick. Fold the 2 short ends of the dough into the center, leaving a small (about ¼") space between them. Fold one half over the other. Reshape the edges of the dough into an even rectangle. Repeat this step of rolling and folding, dusting the dough with a little flour as necessary and scraping any dough off the rolling pin and work surface. Roll the dough into a circle about 1" thick. Using a 3" round cutter, cut 4 biscuits and place them on the baking sheet. Gather the remaining dough and roll it out to 1" thick. Cut 4 more biscuits from the remaining dough, gathering and reshaping it as necessary. Place the biscuits on the baking sheet.

Melt the remaining 2 tbsps. butter and brush it over the tops of the biscuits. Bake until golden, about 15–18 minutes.

Cinnamon Bread

This bread is delicious fresh from the oven, lightly toasted or as French toast. Add ½ cup reconstituted raisins to the cinnamon filling for cinnamon raisin bread.

🥖 MAKES ONE LOAF

- ½ cup (4 fl. oz.) whole milk
- 6 tbsps. unsalted butter
- ½ cup (3.5 oz.) granulated sugar
- ½ tsp. salt
- 2 ½ tsps. instant yeast
- 3 cups (13.2 oz.) all-purpose flour
- 2 large eggs
- 1 tbsp. ground cinnamon

Bring the milk just to a boil in a medium saucepan over medium-high heat and remove from the heat. Add 3 tbsps. butter, ¼ cup (1.8 oz.) sugar and salt and stir until the butter is melted. Add ¼ cup (2 fl. oz.) water to the mixture. Combine the yeast with 2 cups (8.75 oz.) flour in a large bowl. When the milk mixture has cooled to lukewarm (about 110–115 degrees F), whisk in the eggs. Pour the milk into the flour-yeast mixture and stir to combine (or use a stand mixer). Turn the dough onto a lightly floured work surface (or switch to the dough hook on the stand mixer) and add the remaining flour a little at a time until a soft dough forms. Knead the dough for 5 minutes, until the surface is smooth. Place the dough into a greased bowl, turning it to cover the top with grease. Cover and let rise in a warm place until double in size, about 1 ½ hours. Punch down the dough and return it to the bowl. Let the dough rise at room temperature until not quite doubled in volume, about 1 ½ hours.

Grease a 9" x 5" x 3" loaf pan. Roll out the dough into a 12" x 17" rectangle on a lightly floured work surface. Combine the remaining ¼ cup sugar with the cinnamon and reserve 1 tbsp. of the mixture. Melt 1 tbsp. butter and brush it all over the dough. Sprinkle the mixture evenly over the dough. Roll up the dough like a jellyroll, starting at the narrow end. Seal the dough along the edge and tuck the ends under.

Place the dough, sealed edge down, into the pan. Cover and let the dough rise until almost doubled, about 1–1 ½ hours.

Preheat the oven to 350 degrees F.

Brush the top of the loaf with the remaining butter and sprinkle with the reserved cinnamon sugar. Bake for 40–45 minutes, covering the loaf with foil if the top starts to get too brown. Allow the bread to cool on a rack, then store in a Zip-lock bag until ready to use.

Panettone Loaf

This loaf is reminiscent of the traditional egg-based Italian Christmas cake, scented with citrus and studded with golden raisins. I originally developed it to use as French toast or in bread pudding. Making it in a loaf pan makes it perfect for toasting.

MAKES ONE LOAF

- 3 ½ tsps. instant dry yeast
- 3 ½ cups (17.6 oz.) plus 3–5 tbsps. all-purpose flour
- ½ cup (3.5 oz.) granulated sugar
- 1 tsp. salt
- ¼ cup (2 fl. oz.) warm whole milk (110–115 degrees F)
- 2 large eggs
- 3 large egg yolks

- 1 tsp. vanilla extract
- 8 tbsps. unsalted butter, softened
- 1 tsp. grated lemon zest
- 1 tsp. grated orange zest
- ½ cup (2.9 oz.) golden raisins
- ½ cup (2.9 oz.) candied lemon and orange peel (see Chef's Tip on p. 73)

Pour ¼ cup (2 fl. oz.) warm water into a small bowl and sprinkle 2 tsps. yeast over it. Whisk in ½ cup (2.2 oz.) flour. Cover loosely with plastic wrap and allow to rise until doubled, about 1 hour.

Whisk together the remaining yeast, sugar, salt, milk, eggs, egg yolks and vanilla in a large bowl (or use a stand mixer). Stir in the yeast mixture until combined. In a medium bowl, cut the butter into 3 cups (13.2 oz.) flour until crumbly. Add the flour mixture to the milk yeast mixture and stir until dough is combined. Turn the dough onto a lightly floured surface and knead, adding flour 1 tbsp. at a time as necessary, until dough is smooth but still slightly sticky, about 10 minutes (or use the dough hook on a stand mixer). Place dough in large, lightly buttered bowl. Cover with plastic wrap and allow the dough to rise until doubled, about 2–2 ½ hours.

Lightly grease a 9" x 5" x 3" loaf pan, line with parchment and grease again.

Turn out dough onto a lightly floured work surface and knead in the lemon zest, orange zest, raisins and citrus peel evenly. Pat the dough into a rectangle approximately 10" x 20", fold the long sides to the middle and fold the ends under to form a loaf. Place the log into the prepared loaf pan. Cover and allow dough to rise until doubled, about 1 ½–2 hours.

Preheat oven to 400 degrees F and set the rack in center of the oven. Bake for 10 minutes. Reduce temperature to 375 degrees F and bake for 10 minutes longer. Reduce temperature to 350 degrees F and bake for 25–30 minutes, until loaf is baked through (a toothpick inserted should come out clean). Cool the loaf briefly and unmold it onto a rack to cool completely.

Sweet Roll Dough

This simple, easy-to-handle dough is perfect for baking off first thing in the morning.

🥖 **MAKES 12-16 ROLLS**

- 2 ½ cups (11 oz.), plus 1–4 tbsps. all-purpose flour
- ¼ cup (1.8 oz.) granulated sugar
- ½ tsp. salt
- 1 tbsp. instant yeast
- 1 tsp. diastatic malt (optional)
- ½ cup (4 fl. oz.) buttermilk
- 1 large egg
- 5 tbsps. unsalted butter, softened

Combine 2 ½ cups (11 oz.) flour, granulated sugar, salt, yeast and diastatic malt (if using) in the bowl of a stand mixer until the yeast is evenly dispersed, about 2 minutes. Whisk together the buttermilk and egg until combined. Add the buttermilk-egg mixture to the flour and mix on low to combine. With the mixer running, add the butter, 1 tbsp. at a time, until each is combined. Mix until the dough pulls away from the side of bowl, adding additional flour 1 tbsp. at a time if necessary.

Switch to the dough hook and knead for 5-7 minutes, until the dough is smooth and slightly elastic. With lightly floured hands, knead the dough for 1 minute (dough should be soft and slightly tacky but holding its shape). Form the dough into a ball. Place the dough a lightly greased bowl, turn and cover with plastic wrap. Let the dough rise for 2 hours. The dough may be covered and refrigerated for 8 hours (or overnight) before shaping and second rise.

Sweet Tart Dough

This buttery dough makes the perfect crust for fruit tarts.

MAKES 1 LARGE 9-10" TART CRUST OR 4 INDIVIDUAL 3" CRUSTS

- 1 egg yolk
- 1 tsp. vanilla extract
- 1 ½ cups (6.6 oz.) all-purpose flour

- ⅓ cup (2.35 oz.) granulated sugar
- ¼ tsp. salt
- 8 tbsps. unsalted butter, cut into bits

In a small bowl or measuring cup, whisk together the egg yolk, 2 tbsps. cold water and vanilla. Set aside.

Combine the flour, sugar and salt in a large bowl. Cut in the butter with a pastry blender until crumbly (you can also use a food processor—just be careful to not over-process). Stir in the egg mixture until the dough pulls together.

Transfer the dough to a lightly floured work surface and pat into a ball. Place the dough on a piece of plastic wrap and flatten into a disk. Cover the top with plastic wrap and refrigerate for at least 30 minutes before using, or up to 3 days. The tart dough may be frozen for up to 1 month.

Cream Cheese Pastry Dough

Two-bite crescents made from this dough are great for buffets where you are serving a lot of different things. Baked crescents stay fresh and crisp for up to 5 days, so they are perfect for making ahead of time.

MAKES 36 SMALL PASTRIES OR CRESCENTS

- 4 oz. cream cheese, softened
- 4 tbsps. unsalted butter, softened
- 2 tbsps. granulated sugar
- ¼ tsp. salt
- 1 tsp. vanilla extract
- 1 cup (4.4 oz.) all-purpose flour

Combine the cream cheese and butter in the bowl of a stand mixer. Add the sugar, salt and vanilla and mix until fluffy and combined. Add the flour and mix until just combined. Divide the dough in half and wrap it in plastic wrap. Refrigerate for at least 2 hours, or overnight. The dough will keep in the refrigerator for up to 3 days.

Sour Cream Pastry Dough

A variation on the cream cheese dough for making individual crescents and pastries.

🥖 MAKES 36 SMALL PASTRIES OR CRESCENTS

- 1 ½ cups (6.6 oz.) all-purpose flour
- 2 tbsps. granulated sugar
- ½ tsp. salt
- 14 tbsps. unsalted butter, cut into bits
- ½ cup (4 oz.) sour cream

Combine the flour, sugar and salt in a medium bowl. Cut the butter into the flour mixture using a pastry blender (alternatively, use a food processor and pulse until it forms a coarse meal). Add the sour cream and mix until just combined. Divide the dough in half and wrap it in plastic wrap. Refrigerate for at least 2 hours, or overnight. The dough will keep in the refrigerator for up to 3 days.

Traditional Brioche

Buttery, flaky brioche is an enriched dough that requires a few days of advance preparation, but is easy to make. The dough may be frozen for up to one month. If you'd like to enjoy brioche warm from the oven, leave the final rising for the morning you plan to serve it. There are instructions to shape the dough into traditional individual brioche, or see the Chef's Tip below if you would like to make the dough into loaves.

MAKES 1 RECIPE BRIOCHE DOUGH OR 20-24 BRIOCHES A TETE

- 1 cup (8 fl. oz.) whole milk, warmed
- 1 ½ tbsps. instant yeast
- 4 cups (17.6 oz.) plus 3–5 tbsps. all-purpose flour
- 3 tbsps. granulated sugar
- 1 tsp. salt
- 4 large eggs
- 1 large egg yolk
- 12 tbsps. unsalted butter, cut into bits

Combine the milk, yeast and 1 cup (4.4 oz.) flour in a medium bowl. Cover with plastic wrap and allow it to ferment and rise for 30 minutes.

Place the remaining 3 cups (13.2 oz.) flour, sugar and salt in the bowl of a stand mixer and mix to combine. Whisk together 3 eggs and the egg yolk in a measuring cup. Add the yeast mixture and whisked eggs and mix to combine (the dough will be very sticky). With the mixer running on low, add the butter 1 tbsp. at a time until all is incorporated.

Switch to the dough hook. Mix the dough on medium, adding flour 1 tbsp. at a time, until the dough releases from the sides of the bowl, about 7–8 minutes. The dough should be smooth, glossy but still very soft, and slightly sticky.

With lightly floured hands, gather the dough into a ball and place it into a lightly greased bowl. Turn the dough and cover the bowl with plastic wrap. Allow the dough to rise until doubled, about 1 hour. Pat the dough down with lightly floured hands, stretch one side and fold the stretched dough over the rest, like folding a letter. Stretch the other side and fold it over in the same manner. Repeat this entire process and tuck the dough ends underneath to form a round. Cover and allow the dough to rise for 1 more hour.

Press the dough to deflate it, then refrigerate for at least 6 hours, or overnight. Press the dough down once after about an hour to keep it from rising too quickly. The dough is now ready to be shaped into traditional brioche or used in other recipes. It may be refrigerated for up to 24 hours or frozen for 1 month. Remove the dough from the refrigerator 20 minutes before shaping.

For traditional brioche a tete (basically a roll with a smaller top-knot), turn half the dough onto a lightly floured surface and press it into a 12" x 12" square. Divide the square in half. Divide each half into 6 equal pieces, for a total of 12 pieces of dough. Cover the dough with plastic to prevent it from drying out while you roll out the brioche into balls.

Place a piece of the dough onto the work surface and roll it into a ball. Form the top-knot by pressing down onto the ball with the side of your hand about ⅓ of the way from one of the edges of the dough ball. Gently roll back and forth until the shape resembles a bowling pin (little ball on top, thin neck, large ball on the bottom). Pick up the dough by the thin end and press it into the thicker end (this will form the traditional "tete" or top-knot). Place it into a brioche pan with the top-knot centered. Press down lightly around the top-knot to center it. Repeat with the remaining dough. Transfer the molds to a large rimmed baking sheet.

In a small bowl, whisk the remaining egg with 1 tsp. water and a pinch of salt. Lightly brush the top of the brioches with the egg wash, being careful to not drip any excess down into the pans (this will make them difficult to get out of the pans after baking). Cover and allow them to rise until puffy and doubled in size, about 1 hour. Reserve the remaining egg wash in the refrigerator.

Preheat the oven to 375 degrees F.

Uncover the brioche and lightly brush them again with the remaining egg wash. Use lightly oiled kitchen shears to snip around the bases of the top-knots. Bake until golden-brown on top and golden on the sides, about 18–20 minutes. Cool on a wire rack for 10 minutes before unmolding and serving.

Chef's Tip: To make this dough into loaves, divide it into 20 pieces and roll each piece into a ball. Grease 2 large loaf pans. Place 2 rows of 5 pieces in each loaf pan and continue with proofing and baking.

Traditional Brioche

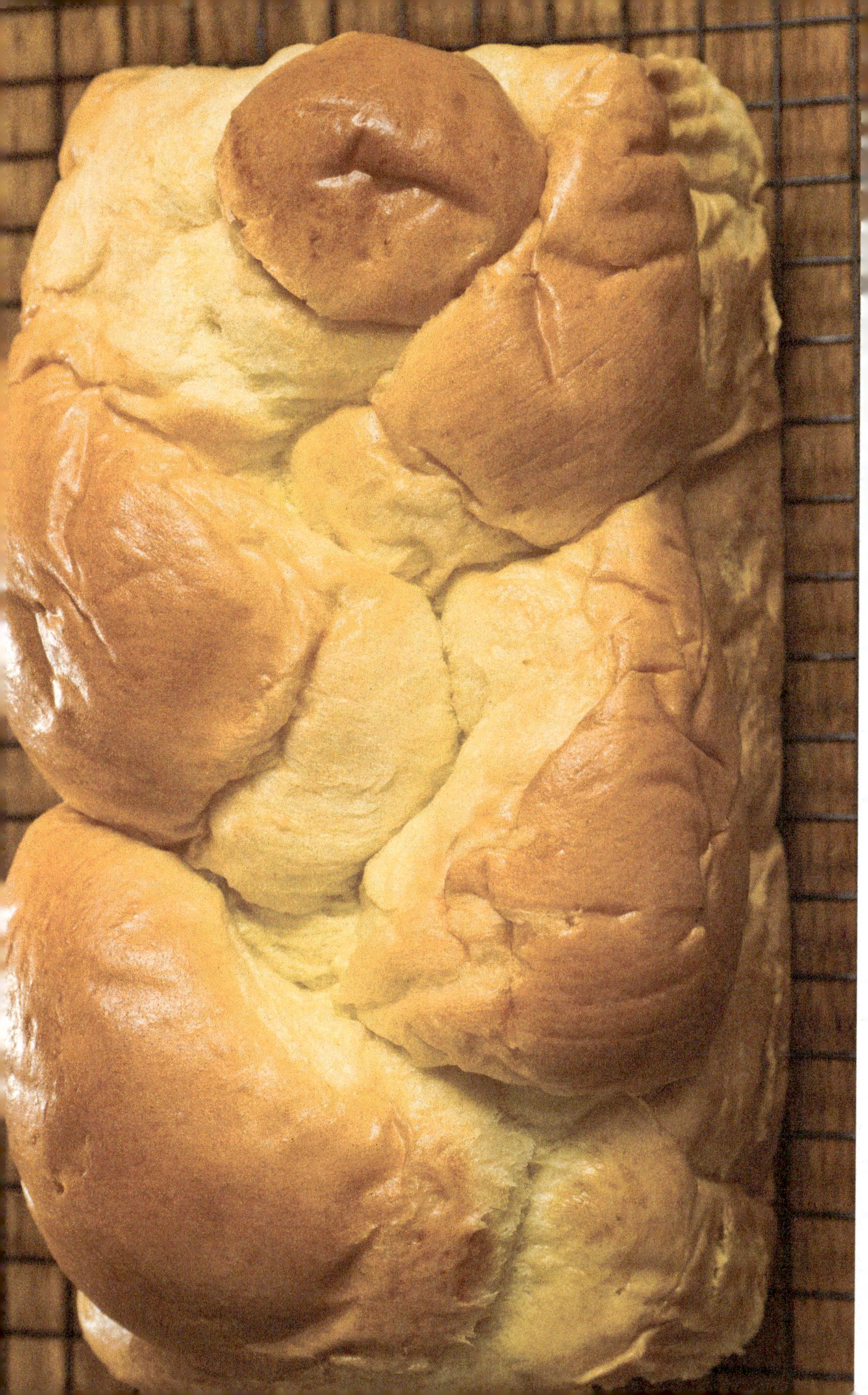

Simple Brioche

This version of brioche has been simplified for use as a component in dishes like French toast or bread pudding. Here it is baked in a standard loaf pan, but it can also be baked in traditional brioche tins.

MAKES 1 LOAF

- ¼ cup (2 fl. oz.) whole milk
- 3 tbsps. granulated sugar
- ¼ tsp. salt
- 3 large eggs
- 3 cups (13.2 oz.) plus 3–5 tbsps. all-purpose flour

- 2 ½ tsps. instant yeast
- 5 tbsps. unsalted butter, cut into bits
- 1 egg yolk

Heat the milk just to a boil in a small saucepan over medium-high heat. Remove from the heat, stir in the sugar and salt and stir to dissolve. Allow the mixture to cool to lukewarm. Pour the milk mixture into the bowl of a stand mixer. Add the eggs and mix until smooth. In a separate bowl, combine 3 cups flour with the yeast so that the yeast is evenly distributed. Pour the flour and yeast into the milk mixture and beat on low until just combined, scraping dough together as necessary. Add the pieces of butter a few at a time until all is incorporated.

Switch to the dough hook and knead for 10 minutes, adding flour 1 tbsp. at a time, until the dough is smooth but still very sticky. Lightly grease a large bowl. With floured hands, gather the dough into a ball. Turn the dough out onto a lightly floured work surface and knead by hand for 3 minutes, adding only enough flour to be able to handle it if necessary. Form the dough into a round mound and place it into the bowl. Cover the bowl loosely with plastic wrap and let it rise until about doubled, about 1 ½–2 hours. Pat the dough down and transfer it to the floured work surface. With lightly floured hands, stretch one side and fold the stretched dough over the rest, like folding a letter. Stretch the other side and fold it over in the same manner. Repeat this entire process and tuck the dough ends underneath to form a round. Return the dough to the bowl and cover it with plastic wrap. Place the bowl into the refrigerator for at least 6 hours, or ideally overnight.

Remove the dough from the refrigerator for 20 minutes before shaping. Place it on a lightly floured work surface. Lightly grease a 9" x 5" x 3" loaf pan. Pat the dough into a rectangle approximately 10" x 20", fold the long sides to the middle and fold the ends under to form a loaf. Place in the loaf pan and cover loosely with plastic wrap. Allow the dough to rise until it reaches the top of the pan, about 1 ½–2 hours. Preheat the oven to 375 degrees F. Whisk the egg yolk with 1 tsp. water and brush the top of the loaf, being careful to not let the egg wash drip down the sides. Bake for 25–30 minutes until golden brown and loaf is baked through (a wooden skewer inserted should come out clean). Cool the brioche loaf briefly and unmold onto a rack to cool completely.

Danish Pastry Dough

Layering butter between layers of dough—known as laminating—yields a flaky pastry perfect for crescents and Danish pastries. This Danish dough includes yeast to help the layers separate as they rise. Plan to give yourself a few days to get to the finish line, as the steps involved cannot be rushed without sacrificing the flaky quality you want. This recipe yields professional results with simple, easy-to-follow steps. Using butter with higher butterfat content for layering will result in an even flakier pastry (see the note on Butter on p. 20). See the Chef's Tip below for how to assemble a quick version of cinnamon rolls with this dough like those on the cover.

MAKES 12–24 PASTRIES, DEPENDING ON SIZE AND SHAPE

- 4 cups (17.6 oz.) all-purpose flour
- 1 tbsp. instant yeast
- ¼ cup (1.8 oz.) granulated sugar
- 2 large eggs
- 1 tsp. salt
- 1 cup (8 fl. oz.) whole milk
- 22 tbsps. unsalted butter (11 oz.)

Combine the flour with the yeast in a large bowl and mix to distribute yeast evenly. Combine ¼ cup (2 fl. oz.) warm water, sugar, eggs, salt and the milk in the bowl of a stand mixer. Add the flour-yeast mixture and 2 tbsps. butter. Mix on low until combined, about 3 minutes. Switch to the dough hook and mix on medium for 2–3 minutes longer, until dough pulls together into a ball. Place the dough into a lightly greased large bowl and turn it over to coat the top. Cover the bowl with plastic wrap and allow the dough to rise and ferment at room temperature for 1 hour. Loosely shape the dough into a rectangle about 6" x 10", place it on a parchment-lined baking sheet and cover with plastic wrap. Refrigerate for 4 hours, or overnight.

In the meantime, lay 2 pieces of parchment paper (at least 10" x 12") on top of each other. Fold the sheets in on each side to form a 6" x 8" rectangle in the center. (The folds will make it easier to form the butter block into the proper size.) Open the folds and remove the top sheet. Place the remaining 20 tbsps. butter in the center of the bottom sheet and place the second sheet on top. Using a rolling pin, pound out the butter within the center rectangle about 4" wide x 6" long, using a bench scraper to trim and shape as necessary. Fold the edges of the parchment to form the 6" x 8" enclosure around the butter. Continue pounding out the butter to fill the enclosure in an even layer. Refrigerate for 4 hours, or overnight.

Lightly flour a work surface. Press the dough into a rough rectangle, then roll it out to a 8" x 16" rectangle. Remove the butter block from the refrigerator. Lightly pound the butter block with a rolling pin to make it pliable. (Check to see if the butter is pliable by trying to bend the parchment-covered block over the edge of the counter. It should bend but not break.) Place the butter in the center of the dough, leaving 4 inches on either side of it. Fold each side over the butter to completely encase it with dough. Pinch the seam together to seal it.

Rotate the dough so the seam is going across instead of top to bottom. Roll the dough out into an 8" x 16" (top to bottom) rectangle. Trim the short ends with a sharp knife or pastry wheel. Turn the dough so that the longer side is facing you. Fold ⅓ of the dough towards the center. Fold the other third into the center, as if folding a letter. (If any butter breaks through the surface as you are rolling, lightly flour the spot and place the dough into the refrigerator for 30 minutes.) Repeat this step, then cover the dough with plastic wrap and place the dough into the freezer for 30 minutes. Repeat the process a third and final time. Cover with plastic wrap and freeze the dough block for 30 minutes. Move the dough to the refrigerator for at least 8 hours, or overnight. The dough may now be rolled out for baking or frozen for future use.

Chef's Tip: To make 6 cinnamon rolls, grease a 9" x 13" baking dish. Combine 2 tbsps. unsalted butter and ½ cup light brown sugar in a medium bowl. Stir in 1 tbsp. cinnamon and 1 tbsp. all-purpose flour.

Remove half the dough from the refrigerator and roll out to a rectangle about 6" x 15" with the long side towards you. Spread the cinnamon sugar evenly over the dough, leaving a 1" border uncovered along the top. Starting at the side close to you, tightly roll the dough up. Press on the seam to seal. Trim off the ends. Wrap the log in plastic wrap and refrigerate for 30 minutes. Slice the dough into 6 pieces. Place the pieces cut side down into the baking pan. Tuck the end of each pastry underneath to prevent it from unravelling.

Preheat the oven to 350 degrees F. Whisk a large egg with a pinch of salt. Brush the buns all over with the egg wash. Bake until golden brown, about 18–20 minutes, turning the pans halfway through baking. Transfer to a rack and cool for 10 minutes before glazing.

Danish Pastry Dough

Traditional Puff Pastry

Traditional puff pastry is laminated dough (similar to the process for Danish pastry dough, except it does not contain yeast).

🥖 **MAKES MAKES TWO 10" X 14" X ¼" SHEETS**

- 3 ½ cups (15.4 oz.) all-purpose flour
- 22 tbsps. unsalted butter
- 1 tsp. salt

Combine the flour, 4 tbsps. butter cut into bits and the salt in a medium bowl. Use a pastry blender to cut the butter into the flour until it's completely incorporated. Pour 1 ¼ cups (10 fl. oz.) water into the bowl of a stand mixer. Add the flour mixture and mix until just combined. Switch to the dough hook and knead for 4–5 minutes, until the dough forms a smooth ball. Loosely shape the dough into a rectangle, place it on a parchment-lined baking sheet and cover with plastic wrap. Refrigerate for 8 hours, or overnight.

In the meantime, lay 2 pieces of parchment paper (at least 10" x 12") on top of each other. Fold the sheets in on each side to form a 6" x 8" rectangle in the center. (The folds will make it easier to form the butter block into the proper size.) Open the folds and remove the top sheet. Place the remaining 20 tbsps. butter in the center of the bottom sheet and place the second sheet on top. Using a rolling pin, pound out the butter within the center rectangle about 4" wide x 6" long, using a bench scraper to trim and shape as necessary. Fold the edges of the parchment to form a 6" x 8" enclosure around the butter. Continue pounding out the butter to fill the enclosure in an even layer. Refrigerate at least 1 hour, or overnight.

Lightly flour a work surface. Press the dough into a rough rectangle, then roll it out to a 8" x 16" rectangle. Remove the butter block from the refrigerator. Lightly pound the butter block with a rolling pin to make it pliable. (Check to see if the butter is pliable by trying to bend the parchment-covered block over the edge of the counter. It should bend but not break.) Place the butter in the center of the dough, leaving 4 inches on either side of it. Fold each side over the butter to completely encase it with dough. Pinch the seam together to seal it.

Lightly flour the surface of the dough and roll it into a rectangle measuring about 12" x 20". Brush off any excess flour. Fold the 2 short ends of the dough into the center, leaving a small (about ¼") space between them. Fold one half over the other half. Lightly flour and roll it out again to about 12" x 20". Brush off the excess flour and repeat the folding. Place the dough on a baking sheet, cover it with a plastic bag and refrigerate for 20–30 minutes.

Repeat this step of rolling and folding 3 more times, refrigerating the dough at least 1 hour in between. After the final fold, cover the dough with plastic wrap and refrigerate at least 4 hours, or overnight. The dough may be refrigerated for up to 3 days and frozen for up to 1 month.

Simple Puff Pastry

This quick version of puff pastry will not rise as much as a traditional puff pastry, but features the same crisp, buttery texture. A bench scraper is a helpful tool for making this recipe.

MAKES ONE 10" X 14" X ¼" SHEET

- 16 tbsps. cold unsalted butter, cut into ½" dice
- 1 ⅔ cups (7.3 oz.) all-purpose flour
- ½ tsp. salt

Place the butter cubes on a lightly floured work surface. Sprinkle on the flour and salt and toss to coat. Cut the butter into the flour with a bench scraper or chef's knife until just crumbly. Add ⅓ cup (2.3 fl. oz.) ice-cold water a little at a time until the dough just hangs together. Shape the shaggy dough into a rough rectangle about 6" x 18" and ½" thick. (Making the dough the approximate width of the bench scraper will make it easier to use it to fold the dough. You can also use a wide spatula).

Using the bench scraper, fold the 2 short ends of the dough into the center, leaving a small (about ¼") space between them (this will be very messy). Fold one half over the other. Reshape the edges of the dough into an even rectangle. Repeat this step of rolling and folding, dusting the dough with a little flour as necessary and scraping any dough off the rolling pin and work surface. Repeat the rolling and folding 2 more times, then cover with plastic wrap and refrigerate for at least 2 hours before using. Dough may be refrigerated for up to 2 days or frozen for up to 1 month.

Traditional Croissant Dough

Our Maine B & B was located on the beautiful Passamaquoddy Bay, part of the ecosystem of the Bay of Fundy. The area was prone to some wicked fog, and one summer it never left. Literally. That summer I dedicated myself to mastering the art of croissant dough. Later, at our Pennsylvania inn, the croissants usually took the form of the Croissant Cinnamon Rolls on p. 121, and occasionally the Raisin Buns on p. 127. I recently revisited the dough recipe in an effort to make it foolproof but not overly complicated. This recipe also includes the instructions for shaping this dough into traditional croissants.

MAKES 24 TRADITIONAL-SHAPED CROISSANTS OR 1 RECIPE CROISSANT DOUGH

- 23 tbsps. unsalted butter (14 oz.)
- 1 cup (2 fl. oz.) whole milk
- 3 cups (13.2 oz.) plus 3–5 tbsps. all-purpose flour
- 1 tbsp. instant yeast
- ¼ cup (1.8 oz.) granulated sugar
- 1 tsp. salt
- 1 tsp. diastatic malt (optional)

Melt 3 tbsps. butter in a small saucepan over low heat. Remove from the heat and stir in the milk.

Combine 3 cups (13.2 oz.) flour, yeast, sugar, salt and diastatic malt (if using) in the bowl of a stand mixer until yeast in evenly dispersed. Add the milk-butter mixture and mix to combine, adding flour 1 tbsp. at a time until the dough comes together.

Knead the dough for about 1 minute with lightly floured hands, stretching one side and folding the stretched dough over the rest, like folding a letter. Stretch the other side and fold it over in the same manner. Repeat this entire process one more time and tuck the dough ends underneath to form a round.

Place the dough into a lightly greased bowl and cover it with plastic wrap. Allow the dough to ferment and rise for 2 hours. Loosely shape the dough into a rectangle about 6" x 12", place it on a parchment-lined baking sheet and cover with plastic wrap. Refrigerate for at least 4 hours, or overnight.

In the meantime, lay 2 pieces of parchment paper (at least 10" x 12") on top of each other. Fold the sheets in on each side to form a 6" x 8" rectangle in the center. (The folds will make it easier to form the butter block into the proper size.) Open the folds and remove the top sheet. Place the remaining 20 tbsps. butter in the center of the bottom sheet and place the second sheet on top. Using a rolling pin, pound out the butter within the center rectangle about 4" wide x 6" long, using a bench scraper to trim and shape as necessary. Fold the edges of the parchment to form a 6" x 8" enclosure around the butter. Continue pounding out the butter to fill the enclosure in an even layer. Refrigerate at least 1 hour, or overnight.

Lightly flour a work surface. Press the dough into a rough rectangle, then roll it out to an 8" x 16" rectangle. Remove the butter block from the refrigerator. Lightly pound the butter block with a rolling pin to make it pliable. (Check to see if the butter is pliable by trying to bend the parchment-covered block over the edge of the counter. It should bend but not break.) Place the butter in the center of the dough, leaving 4 inches on either side of it. Fold each side over the butter to completely encase it with dough. Pinch the seam together to seal it. Rotate the dough so the seam is going across instead of top to bottom.

Roll the dough out into an 8" x 16" (top to bottom) rectangle, about ½" thick. Trim the short ends with a sharp knife or pastry wheel. Turn the dough so that the longer side is facing you. Fold ⅓ of the dough towards the center. Fold the other third over to cover the center, as if folding a letter. (If any butter breaks through the surface as you are rolling, lightly flour the spot and place the dough in the refrigerator for 30 minutes before continuing.) Position the dough so that the fold is on your left. Lightly press the dough out with the rolling pin, then finish rolling into a rectangle 8" x 16". Fold the 2 short ends of the dough into the center, leaving a small (about ¼") space between them. Fold one half over the other half. Cover the dough with plastic wrap and place the dough in the freezer for 30 minutes. Refrigerate the dough for at least 2 hours, or overnight.

Roll the dough into a 9" x 18" rectangle (this slightly larger size will make it easier to measure for making individual croissants). Trim the short ends with a sharp knife or pastry wheel. Turn the dough so that the longer side is facing you. Fold ⅓ of the dough towards the center. Fold the other third over to cover the center, as if folding a letter. Cover with plastic wrap and freeze the dough block for 15 minutes.

Cut the dough in half, forming 2 rectangles 4 ½" x 6". Place parchment paper between the 2 blocks and wrap them loosely in plastic wrap. Place in the refrigerator for at least 2 hours, or overnight (up to 24 hours). Dough may be kept in the freezer for up to 1 week. Thaw the dough overnight in the refrigerator before using. The dough may now be rolled out for baking or frozen for future use.

To shape the dough for traditional croissants, place half of the dough onto a lightly floured work surface. Roll the dough into a 9" x 18" rectangle. Place the dough so the long edge is facing you. Measure across the bottom dough and mark every 3". Cut the dough into 6 even rectangles, 3" x 9". Cut each rectangle in half diagonally, forming 2 even triangles (12 in total).

Line 2 baking sheets with parchment paper. Hold 1 dough triangle up at the wide end and gently stretch the dough 1-2" longer. Place the dough onto a work surface with the wide end facing you. Roll the dough up, lightly pressing outward as you roll so that the sides extend slightly. Place the rolled dough on a parchment-lined baking sheet, tucking the pointed tip underneath (you can tuck the points in together if you prefer a tighter crescent shape). Press down lightly to secure the tip underneath and flatten the bottom. Repeat with the remaining pieces of dough, placing 6 finished rolls at least 3" apart on each baking sheet.

Whisk together the egg with 1 tsp. water and the remaining ½ tsp. salt. Lightly brush the croissants all over with the egg wash. Refrigerate the remaining egg wash. Place the sheet pans inside unscented plastic bags, placing empty glasses or cups on it as necessary to prevent the plastic from touching the croissants. Allow the croissants to proof and rise for 2–2 ½ hours, until croissants are puffy. (When you lightly press the dough, you should still see the impression.)

Preheat the oven to 375 degrees F. Lightly brush the croissant with egg wash and bake for 15 minutes. Rotate the pans and brush the croissants again with egg wash. Bake for 5–10 minutes longer, until golden brown all over. Cool the croissants on a rack at least 5 minutes before serving.

Chef's Tip: For chocolate croissants, roll the dough a little larger than a 20" x 20" square (so you can trim off the edges and still have a 20" x 20" square). Trim the sides to form straight edges. Cut the dough into 4 (10") squares. Cut each of those squares into 3 rectangles (about 10" x 3 ¼" each) to form a total of 12 rectangles. Place about ½ tablespoon of chopped chocolate in the upper third of each one. Fold that third of the dough over the chocolate. Place about another ½ tablespoon of the chocolate along one seam of the folded dough. Brush the edge of the dough with egg wash. Fold the bottom third of the dough over the chocolate and seal the edge.

Transfer to the prepared baking sheets seam-side down, brush with egg wash and proceed with proofing and baking as above.

Simple Croissant Dough

This simpler recipe for croissant dough involves spreading the softened butter on the dough for layering instead of incorporating it as a block. You will still get a flaky croissant, but not quite the lift of the traditional recipe.

MAKES 24 SMALL TRADITIONAL-SHAPED CROISSANTS OR 1 RECIPE OF CROISSANT DOUGH

- 3 ½ cups (15.4 oz.) plus 2 tbsps. all-purpose flour
- 2 tsps. instant yeast
- ¼ cup (1.8 oz.) granulated sugar
- 1 tsp. salt
- 1 ¼ cups (10 fl. oz.) whole milk
- 22 tbsps. unsalted butter (11 oz.)

Combine 3 ½ cups (15.4 oz.) flour, yeast, sugar and salt in a medium bowl. Pour the milk into the bowl of a stand mixer. Add the flour mixture and mix at low speed until a ball of dough forms. Add 2 tbsps. butter, 1 tbsp. at a time, to the dough and mix to combine. Switch to the dough hook and knead for 4–5 minutes, until the dough forms a ball and clears the sides of the bowl. Place the dough in a bowl and cover with plastic wrap. Allow the dough to rise at room temperature for 1 hour, then refrigerate the dough for at least 2 hours, or overnight.

Cut the remaining butter into 1" pieces. Toss the butter with 2 tbsps. flour in a medium bowl. Flatten the pieces of butter into disks. Turn the dough out onto a floured work surface. Roll dough out into a 9" x 18" rectangle, short ends at top and bottom. Sprinkle the butter pieces evenly over the bottom ⅔ of the dough. Fold the unbuttered third over the center to encase the butter. Then fold the remaining buttered third up over the center, like a folding a letter. Press the seam together.

Roll the dough into a 9" x 18" inch rectangle. Trim the short ends. Fold one short end ⅔ of the way up. Fold up the other short end over top. Turn the dough so a short end is facing you. Repeat the rolling and folding. If any butter breaks through, lightly dust the spot with flour. Cover the dough with plastic wrap and freeze it for 20 minutes.

Repeat the rolling and folding a final time. Wrap the dough loosely in plastic wrap. Place the dough in the freezer for 1 hour, then move to the refrigerator for at least 1 hour (up to 24 hours). Dough can be kept in freezer for up to 1 week. Thaw the dough overnight in the refrigerator before using.

CHAPTER SIX
Pantry

- Almond Paste
- Apricot Fruit Spread
- Raspberry Jam
- Applesauce
- Cream Cheese Glaze
- Lemon Glaze
- Vanilla Glaze
- Chocolate Glaze
- Chocolate Ganache
- Peanut Butter Glaze
- Salted Caramel Glaze
- Maple Glaze
- Peanut Crunch Topping

Almond Paste

- 1 cup (4 oz.) almonds, finely ground
- ½ cup (2.11 oz.) confectioners' sugar
- 1 large egg white
- 1 tsp. almond extract

Combine almonds, sugar, egg white and almond extract in a food processor or with a mixer until smooth. Divide the dough in half. Form each half into a log 1" x 12" and wrap in plastic wrap.

Store in the refrigerator for up to 1 week or in the freezer for up to 1 month.

Apricot Fruit Spread

MAKES 1 CUP

- 1 lb. ripe apricots, peeled, pitted and quartered (about 8)
- ½ cup (3.5 oz.) granulated sugar
- 1 tsp. lemon juice

In a medium saucepan or Dutch oven, combine the apricots, sugar and 1 tbsp. water. Bring to a simmer over medium-high heat, stirring to dissolve the sugar. Simmer the jam until thickened but some chunks of fruit remain, 10–12 minutes (or until temperature reaches 220 degrees F). Stir in the lemon juice and remove the pan from the heat. Let cool, transfer to a plastic container with a tight fitting lid and refrigerate.

Chef's Tip: To peel the apricots, fill a large saucepan with water and bring to a boil. Fill a large bowl with ice and water. Make an X in the bottom of each apricot with a sharp paring knife. Turn off the heat and submerge the apricots in the boiling water for 30 seconds. Transfer the apricots to the ice bath to cool quickly. Peel off the skins.

Raspberry Jam

MAKES 1 ½ CUPS

- 2 cups (9.2 oz.) fresh raspberries
- 2 cups (14.1 oz.) granulated sugar
- 1 tbsp. lemon juice

Combine the raspberries, sugar and lemon juice in a large saucepan. Mash the berries lightly to release their juices. Cook the mixture over medium heat, stirring until the sugar is melted. Bring the mixture to a boil over medium-high heat. Simmer, stirring often, until the mixture reaches 220–225 degrees F and the jam is slightly thickened, about 6–7 minutes (or use the plate test below). Remove from the heat and allow to cool. Refrigerate for up to 1 week.

Chef's Tip: To check for the proper consistency without a thermometer, place a small plate in the freezer for 20 minutes. Pour a small amount of the boiling jam onto this plate and let it sit in the refrigerator for 1 minute. If the mixture gels and wrinkles when you push it with your finger, it's done. If it doesn't, then continue to cook the jam for few more minutes and repeat.

Applesauce

MAKES 2 CUPS

- 6 large Granny Smith or other cooking apples, peeled, cored and coarsely chopped
- 2 tbsps. lemon juice
- ¼ cup granulated sugar
- ½ tsp. ground cinnamon (optional)

In a large saucepan, combine apples, lemon juice, ¾ cup water, sugar and cinnamon (if using). Cover and cook over medium heat for 20–25 minutes, or until apples are soft, stirring occasionally. Allow the mixture to cool, then mash to the desired consistency or puree in a food processor or blender. Refrigerate for up to 1 week.

Cream Cheese Glaze

- 2 tbsps. cream cheese
- ½ cup (2.11 oz.) confectioners' sugar
- 1 tbsp. heavy cream
- 1 tsp. vanilla extract

Combine the cream cheese and half of the confectioners' sugar in a medium bowl. Beat in the heavy cream and vanilla. Stir in the remaining confectioners' sugar until smooth. Refrigerate until ready to use.

Lemon Glaze

- 2 tbsps. lemon juice
- 1 cup (4.3 oz.) confectioners' sugar
- 1 tbsp. unsalted butter, melted
- 1 tsp. finely grated lemon zest

Combine the lemon juice, confectioners' sugar and 1 tbsp. warm water in a medium bowl. Whisk until smooth. Stir in the butter and lemon zest.

Vanilla Glaze

MAKES 1 CUP

- 1 cup (4.3 oz.) confectioners' sugar
- 2 tbsps. whole milk
- ½ tsp. vanilla extract

Whisk together all ingredients until smooth.

Chocolate Glaze

MAKES 1 CUP

- 1 cup (4.3 oz.) confectioners' sugar
- 3 tbsps. Dutch process cocoa powder
- ¼ tsp. espresso powder (optional)
- 3 tbsps. whole milk
- 2 tbsps. unsalted butter, melted

Whisk all the ingredients together until smooth.

Chocolate Ganache

Thicker and richer than the chocolate glaze, this ganache is delicious as a topping or served warm for dipping.

🌀 MAKES 1 CUP

- ½ cup heavy cream
- 8 oz. chopped bittersweet chocolate
- 1 tsp. espresso powder (optional)

Heat the heavy cream until hot but not boiling. Remove from the heat and stir in the chocolate until it's completely melted. Stir in the espresso powder if using. If a lighter texture is desired, cool the mixture completely and whip it for 3–4 minutes.

Peanut Butter Glaze

🌀 MAKES 1 CUP

- 2 tbsps. unsalted butter
- 4 tbsps. creamy peanut butter
- 1 cup (4.3 oz.) confectioners' sugar
- 1 tbsp. whole milk

Melt the butter in a small saucepan over medium heat. Stir in the peanut butter until melted. Remove from the heat and stir in the sugar and milk until smooth.

Salted Caramel Glaze

MAKES 1 CUP

- ¼ cup granulated sugar
- 4 tbsps. unsalted butter, melted
- 1 tsp. vanilla
- ¾ cup heavy cream
- 1 tsp. coarse sea salt
- 1 cup confectioners' sugar

Combine the granulated sugar and 1 tbsp. water in a medium saucepan. Bring to a boil over medium-high heat and simmer, without stirring, until medium golden brown, about 5–7 minutes (temperature should read 360 degrees F). If sugar crystals form on the sides of the pan, wash them down with a wet pastry brush. Swirl the pan gently to make sure the color is even throughout, then remove from the heat. Carefully stir in the butter (use caution, as the mixture will bubble up and is extremely hot). Whisk in the vanilla, cream and salt. Stir in the confectioners' sugar until smooth.

Maple Glaze

Sprinkle cooked crumbled bacon over this glaze for a sweet and salty treat.

MAKES 1 ½ CUPS

- 4 tbsps. maple syrup
- 2 tbsps. unsalted butter
- 1 ½ cups (6.35 oz.) confectioners' sugar
- 2 tbsps. heavy cream

Warm the maple syrup and butter over low heat in a small saucepan until the butter is melted. Remove from the heat and stir in the confectioners' sugar until dissolved. Stir in the cream until smooth. Refrigerate if not using immediately.

Peanut Crunch Topping

Here is a sweet peanut topping that's delicious on donuts and muffins.

- 1 ½ cups (10.6 oz.) granulated sugar
- 2 cups (8.8 oz.) salted roasted peanuts

Grease a baking sheet and set aside.

Combine the sugar and ¾ cup water in a medium saucepan. Bring the mixture to a boil. Lower to a simmer and cook without stirring until medium golden brown, about 5-7 minutes (temperature of 360 degrees F). If sugar crystals form on the sides of the pan, wash them down with a wet pastry brush. Remove from the heat and stir in the peanuts. Spread the mixture onto the baking sheet and cool completely. Break the brittle into small pieces and process in a food processor until crumbled.

Donuts

- Donut Making Tips
- Butter Pecan Crunch Cake Donuts
- Glazed Vanilla Yeast Donuts
- Beignet Fritters
- Crullers
- Raspberry Jelly-Filled Donuts
- White Cream-Filled Donuts
- Peanut Butter Cream-Filled Donuts
- Lemon Cream-Filled Donuts
- Maple-Glazed Bacon Fritters
- Vanilla-Glazed Chocolate Cake Donuts

Donut Making Tips

Although this started out strictly as a baking book, I couldn't imagine a comprehensive cookbook for breakfast treats that didn't include fried donuts. So this BONUS chapter includes a variety of recipes.

Here are some tips for successful donut making:

Donut dough should be sticky, even for fried donuts. Don't overwork the dough or add too much flour.

Choose a neutral vegetable oil like canola for frying. You can also use solid shortening, preferably trans-fat free.

Consistent oil temperature is the key to having your donuts not absorb the oil. Use a deep fry/candy thermometer to ensure your oil is at a constant temperature, and to make sure the oil does not exceed its smoke point, where it becomes flammable (400 degrees F for canola).

To transfer the donuts to the frying oil, slide a bench scraper or thin spatula underneath. Slide the donut from the bench scraper onto the palm of your other hand, without touching the top. For very soft doughs, place each donut on an individual square of foil. Place the donut foil-side up into the hot oil. The foil should easily release from the dough, keeping the shape intact. Remove the foil with tongs and discard.

Only add 2–3 donuts to the hot oil at a time to keep the oil temp from dropping excessively.

Always keep a kitchen fire extinguisher on hand whenever you are deep-frying donuts.

The dough for many of these recipes may be allowed to rise in the refrigerator overnight, making morning prep easier. Yeast donuts typically require a second rising in the morning before frying, so plan on extra time. If you want to be able to shape and fry the donuts first thing in the morning, choose a recipe for cake donuts instead.

These recipes include specific toppings and glazes, but feel free to make your own variations. Recipes for a variety of glazes and toppings are included in the Pantry section.

Butter Pecan Crunch Cake Donuts

Topped with a crunchy topping, these fried donuts are best consumed the day they are made.

MAKES 12 DONUTS

- 6 tbsps. unsalted butter, melted
- ¼ cup (2 oz.) light brown sugar
- 3 ¾ cups (16.5 oz.) all-purpose flour
- ½ cup (1.6 oz.) sweetened shredded coconut
- ½ cup (2 oz.) finely chopped pecans
- 4 tsps. baking powder
- 1 tsp. salt
- ½ tsp. ground nutmeg
- 1 cup (7 oz.) granulated sugar
- 4 tbsps. solid shortening
- 1 large egg
- 1 large egg yolk
- 1 cup (8 fl. oz.) buttermilk
- Canola oil for frying
- 1 cup (4.23 oz.) confectioners' sugar

To make the coating, preheat oven to 400 degrees F. Line a 9" x 9" baking pan with parchment and lightly grease the parchment.

Combine 6 tbsps. butter, brown sugar, ¾ cup (3.3 oz.) flour and coconut in a medium bowl. Stir in the pecans. Spread the mixture in an even layer on the parchment. Bake for 12–15 minutes, until the mixture is lightly browned and bubbling. Allow to cool completely. Combine the coconut mixture and pecans in a food processor and pulse until just crumbly.

Combine the remaining 3 cups (13.2 oz.) flour, baking powder, salt and nutmeg in a medium bowl and set aside.

Combine the granulated sugar and shortening in the bowl of a stand mixer. Beat for 1 minute. Add the egg, egg yolk and 1 tsp. vanilla extract and mix until fluffy and lemony, about 1–2 minutes. Add half the flour mixture and beat to combine. Add the buttermilk and beat to combine. Mix in the remaining flour until just combined. Cover the dough with plastic wrap and refrigerate for 1 hour, or overnight. (The dough may also be shaped and refrigerated on baking sheets overnight.)

Turn the dough onto a floured surface and roll it out to ½" thickness (about a 10" circle), adding flour as necessary. Flour a 3" donut cutter (or a 3" round and ½" round pastry cutter) and cut out as many donuts as possible. Place the donuts on a floured surface. Reshape and roll out the dough until 12 donuts are complete.

Pour at least 2" oil into a deep-fryer or Dutch oven. Heat until the oil reaches 370 degrees F. Line a cooling rack or baking sheet with paper towels. Add the donuts 2–3 at a time and fry until golden brown, about 1 ½ minutes. Turn the donuts and fry 1–2 minutes longer until golden brown all over. Transfer the donuts to the paper towels and continue until all are fried. Allow the donuts to cool.

Whisk the confectioners' sugar with 1 tbsp. water to make a glaze in a shallow bowl. Spread the butter pecan mixture on a plate or shallow dish. Dip the top of each donut into the glaze, allowing any excess to drip off. Dip the glazed side of the donut in the butter pecan mixture to coat. Set the donuts with the topping up on a rack to allow the glaze to set before serving.

Make Ahead Tip: The topping may be made a day ahead and stored in an airtight container. The dough may be refrigerated to rise overnight and then shaped in the morning.

Glazed Vanilla Yeast Donuts

The recipe for these fried donuts features a simple glaze, but your imagination is the limit for how to top them.

MAKES 12 DONUTS

- ¾ cup (6 fl. oz.) whole milk
- 3 tbsps. solid shortening
- 3 cups (13.2 oz.) plus 3–5 tbsps. all-purpose flour
- 1 tbsp. instant yeast
- ⅓ cup (2.35 oz.) granulated sugar
- ½ tsp. salt
- 1 tsp. freshly ground nutmeg
- 2 large eggs
- Canola oil for frying
- 1 cup (4.23 oz.) confectioners' sugar
- 1 tsp. vanilla extract

Warm the milk in a small saucepan over medium heat. Stir in the shortening until melted, then set aside.

Combine 3 cups (13.2 oz.) flour, yeast, granulated sugar, salt and nutmeg in the bowl of a stand mixer. Mix in the milk mixture until smooth. Add the eggs 1 at a time and beat until combined. Add flour 1 tbsp. at a time until the dough just begins to pull away from the sides of the bowl but is still tacky. Turn the dough onto a lightly floured work surface and knead for 3-4 minutes, until smooth. Gather the dough into a ball. Transfer the dough to a large greased bowl and cover. Allow the dough to rise until doubled in size, about 1-1 ½ hours, or in the refrigerator for at least 8 hours (or overnight). (The dough may also be allowed to rise, then shaped and refrigerated on baking sheets overnight.)

Turn the dough onto a floured surface and roll it out to ½" thickness (about a 10" circle). Flour a 3" donut cutter (or a 3" round and ½" round pastry cutter) and cut out as many donuts as possible. Place the donuts on a floured surface. Reshape and roll out the dough until 12 donuts are complete. Cover the donuts with plastic wrap or a large unscented bag and allow them to rise in a warm place until soft and puffy, about 1 hour.

Pour at least 2" oil into a deep-fryer or Dutch oven. Heat until the oil reaches 360 degrees F. Line a cooling rack or baking sheet with paper towels. Add the donuts 2–3 at a time and fry until golden brown, about 1 ½ minutes. Turn the donuts and fry 1–2 minutes longer until golden brown all over. Transfer the donuts to the paper towels and continue until all are fried.

Whisk the confectioners' sugar, vanilla and 1 tbsp. water together in a shallow bowl. Dip the donuts into the glaze to coat, allowing any excess to drain off. Place the donuts on a rack and allow the glaze to set 10 minutes before serving.

Make Ahead Tip: The dough may be placed in the refrigerator overnight and then shaped in the morning for the final rise.

Beignet Fritters

These fritters are made with yeast dough in the New Orleans style. If you are looking for the French-style made with the lighter choux pastry, see the recipe for Crullers on p. 327.

⭕ MAKES 24–30 FRITTERS

- 3 cups (13.2 oz.) plus 3–5 tbsps. all-purpose flour
- 1 tbsp. instant yeast
- 3 tbsps. granulated sugar
- ¼ tsp. salt
- ½ cup (4 fl. oz.) evaporated milk
- (or heavy cream)
- 1 large egg
- 1 tsp. vanilla
- 3 tbsps. solid shortening
- Canola oil for frying
- ½ cup confectioners' sugar

Combine 3 cups (13.2 oz.) flour, yeast, sugar and salt in a large bowl and set aside. Combine the milk, ½ cup (4 fl. oz.) water, egg and vanilla in the bowl of a stand mixer. Add half the flour mixture and beat until combined. Add the shortening and beat to combine. Beat in the remaining flour mixture. Add flour 1 tbsp. at a time until the dough pulls away from the sides of the bowl. Switch to the dough hook and knead until smooth, about 3–4 minutes. Gather the dough into a ball. Transfer it to a lightly greased bowl and cover with plastic wrap. Refrigerate the dough at least 1 hour, or overnight. (The dough may also be shaped and refrigerated on baking sheets overnight.)

Transfer the dough to a floured work surface and pat it into a rectangle about 22" x 15" and ¼" thick. Slice it on the diagonal to form 2" strips. Slice again on the opposite diagonal into 2" strips, to form diamonds.

Pour at least 2" oil into a deep-fryer or Dutch oven. Heat until the oil reaches 360 degrees F. Line a cooling rack or baking sheet with paper towels. Add the beignets 2–3 at a time and fry until golden brown, about 1 ½ minutes. Turn the beignets and fry 1–2 minutes longer until golden brown all over. Transfer the beignets to the paper towels and continue until all are fried. Place the confectioners' sugar in a paper bag and toss the warm beignets to coat. Serve warm.

Crullers

These donuts are made with choux pastry and have a delightful, airy texture. Because the dough is very soft, briefly freezing the dough before frying makes the shaped crullers easier to handle.

MAKES 8–10 CRULLERS

- 4 tbsps. unsalted butter
- 1 tsp. granulated sugar
- ½ tsp. salt
- ½ cup (2.2 oz.) all-purpose flour
- 2 large eggs
- 1 cup (4.23 oz.) confectioners' sugar
- 3 tbsps. whole milk
- Canola oil for frying

Combine ½ cup (4 fl. oz.) water, butter, sugar, and salt in a large saucepan. Bring to a boil over medium-high heat. Immediately remove the pan from the heat and stir in the flour all at once, stirring until the dough forms a ball. Return the pan to low heat and stir to evaporate excess moisture, about 3-4 minutes.

Transfer the mixture into the bowl of a stand mixer. With the mixer running on low, add the eggs 1 at a time. Increase the speed to medium and mix until the dough is just smooth and glossy, about 1–2 minutes.

Line a baking sheet with parchment. Using a pastry bag fitted with a large star tip, pipe the dough into 2 ½" rings on the sheet pan (you can also do these in twists). Freeze the rings on the pan for 15 minutes to harden them slightly.

In the meantime, stir together the confectioners' sugar and milk in a small bowl to make a glaze.

Pour at least 2" oil into a deep-fryer or Dutch oven. Heat until the oil reaches 375 degrees F. Line a cooling rack or baking sheet with paper towels. Add the crullers 2-3 at a time and fry until golden brown, about 1 ½ minutes. Turn the crullers and fry 1-2 minutes longer until puffed and golden brown all over. Transfer the donuts to the paper towels and continue until all are fried. Dip the crullers in the glaze to completely coat them. Transfer the crullers to a baking rack and allow the glaze to set, about 5 minutes.

Raspberry Jelly-Filled Donuts

I vary the dough for filled donuts to balance the filling, instead of using the same dough for all filled donuts. This jelly-filled version is light and not overly sweet. Frying filled donuts at a slightly lower temperature for a longer time allows the centers to cook all the way through. I like filled donuts to have filling in every bite! If you prefer less filling, simply adjust the amount used.

MAKES 12 DONUTS

- 3 cups (13.2 oz.) plus 3–5 tbsps. all-purpose flour
- ½ cup (3.5 oz.) plus 3 tbsps. granulated sugar
- 1 tsp. salt
- 2 ½ tsps. instant yeast
- ¾ cup (6 fl. oz.) whole milk, warmed
- 2 large eggs
- 4 tbsps. unsalted butter, melted
- Canola oil for frying
- 1 ½ cups raspberry jam (see recipe p. 307)

Combine 3 cups (13.2 oz.) flour, 3 tbsps. sugar, salt and yeast in the bowl of a stand mixer. In a separate bowl, whisk together the milk, eggs and butter. Add the milk mixture to the dry ingredients and mix until just combined. Add flour 1 tbsp. at a time until the dough just pulls away from the sides of the bowl but is still slightly tacky. Transfer the dough to a floured work surface and knead until the dough is smooth, about 3-4 minutes. Transfer the dough to a large greased bowl and cover. Allow the dough to rise until doubled in size, about 1–1 ½ hours, or in the refrigerator for at least 8 hours (or overnight). (The dough may also be allowed to rise, then shaped and refrigerated on baking sheets overnight.)

Line a baking sheet with parchment and grease the parchment. Transfer the dough to a lightly floured work surface and roll it to ½" thickness. Use a 3" round pastry cutter to cut out as many rounds as possible. Transfer the donuts to the baking sheet with a spatula. Gather up the remaining dough and roll it out again to ½" thickness. Continue to cut rounds until 12 donuts are formed. Cover with a large unscented plastic bag and allow the donuts to rise until puffy and soft, about 1 hour.

Pour at least 2" oil into a deep-fryer or Dutch oven. Heat until the oil reaches 350 degrees F. Line a cooling rack or baking sheet with paper towels. Add the donuts 2–3 at a time and fry until golden brown, about 2–3 minutes. Turn the donuts and fry 2–3 minutes longer until golden brown all over. Transfer the donuts to the paper towels and continue until all are fried.

Spread the remaining ½ cup (3.5 oz.) sugar on a plate or shallow bowl. Roll the donuts in sugar to coat both sides. Allow the donuts to cool completely before filling.

Spoon the jelly into a pastry bag fitted with a ¼" round tip. Make a small (½") slit in the side of a donut. Place the end of the tip inside the slit and pipe in filling. Continue until all donuts are filled. Serve immediately.

Make Ahead Tip: Make the dough the day before and refrigerate overnight to rise before cutting.

White Cream-Filled Donuts

Also known as Holland cream, this white cream filling is sweet and buttery. Since I prefer my filled donuts completely filled, I cut these fried beauties in half so I can sandwich the filling into every bite.

MAKES 12 DONUTS

- 4 tbsps. solid shortening
- 8 tbsps. unsalted butter, melted
- 2 ½ cups (10.6 oz.) confectioners' sugar
- 1 ¼ cups (10 fl. oz.) plus 1 tbsp. whole milk, warmed
- ½ tsp. vanilla extract
- 3 cups (13.2 oz.) plus 3–5 tbsps.
- all-purpose flour
- ¼ cup (1.8 oz.) granulated sugar
- ½ tsp. salt
- 2 ½ tsps. instant yeast
- ¾ cup (6 fl. oz.) whole milk
- 2 large eggs
- 4 tbsps. unsalted butter, melted
- Canola oil for frying

To make the filling, blend the shortening, 4 tbsps. butter and 2 cups (8.5 oz.) confectioners' sugar in a medium bowl. Add 1 tbsp. milk and vanilla and beat until smooth. Refrigerate until ready to use.

Combine 3 cups (13.2 oz.) flour, sugar, salt and yeast in the bowl of a stand mixer. In a separate bowl, whisk together the milk, eggs and remaining 4 tbsps. butter. Add the milk mixture to the dry ingredients and mix until just combined. Add flour 1 tbsp. at a time until the dough just pulls away from the sides of the bowl but is still slightly tacky. Transfer the dough to a floured work surface and knead until the dough is smooth, about 3–4 minutes. Transfer the dough to a large greased bowl and cover. Allow the dough to rise until doubled in size, about 1–1 ½ hours, or in the refrigerator for at least 8 hours (or overnight). (The dough may also be allowed to rise, then shaped and refrigerated on baking sheets overnight.)

Line a baking sheet with parchment and grease the parchment. Transfer the dough to a floured work surface and roll it to ½" thickness (about a 10" circle). Use a 3" round pastry cutter to cut out as many rounds as possible. Transfer the donuts to the baking sheet with a spatula. Gather up the remaining dough and roll it out again to ½" thickness. Continue to cut rounds until all the dough is used. Cover with a large unscented plastic bag and allow the donuts to rise for 1-1 ½ hours, until soft and puffy.

Pour at least 2" oil into a deep-fryer or Dutch oven. Heat until the oil reaches 350 degrees F. Line a cooling rack or baking sheet with paper towels. Add the donuts 2–3 at a time and fry until golden brown, about 2–3 minutes. Turn the donuts and fry 2–3 minutes longer until golden brown all over. Transfer the donuts to the paper towels and continue until all are fried. Toss the donuts with the remaining ¼ cup granulated sugar (this will help the confectioners' sugar to stick to the filled donut).

Allow the donuts to cool completely before filling. Slice a donut in half to form a top and bottom. Spoon 2 tbsps. filling into the bottom half. Place the second half on top and press to flatten the filling. Continue until all donuts are filled. Dip the donuts in the remaining ½ cup (2.1 oz.) confectioners' sugar to coat. Serve immediately.

Make Ahead Tip: Make the cream filling up to 2 days ahead and refrigerate. The dough may be placed in the refrigerator to rise overnight and then shaped in the morning for the final rise.

Peanut Butter Cream-Filled Donuts

Rich peanut butter cream fills these fried donuts. Dip them in chocolate glaze (see recipe p. 311) for an even more decadent treat.

MAKES 12 DONUTS

- 1 cup (8 fl. oz.) half and half
- ½ tsp. vanilla bean paste
- 3 large egg yolks
- 1 ¼ cups (8.8 oz.) granulated sugar
- 2 tbsps. cornstarch
- 5 tbsps. unsalted butter

- 2 tbsps. creamy peanut butter
- ¼ cup (2 fl. oz.) whole milk
- 5 tbsps. unsalted butter, softened
- 3 ½ (15.4 oz.) cups plus 3–5 tbsps. all-purpose flour
- ½ tsp. salt
- 2 ½ tsps. instant yeast

To make the filling, combine the half and half and vanilla bean paste in a medium saucepan and heat on low until just steaming. Whisk the yolks and ¼ cup (1.8 oz.) sugar in the bowl of a stand mixer until fluffy and lemony. Stir in the cornstarch. With the mixer running, pour about ⅓ of the hot half and half mixture into the egg. Whisk the tempered egg mixture back into the remaining hot mixture and return the saucepan to medium heat. Lightly whisk the mixture until it comes to the boil. Reduce the heat and simmer for about 1-2 minutes until thickened, whisking constantly. Remove from heat and whisk in 2 tbsps. butter and peanut butter. Spoon the mixture into a small bowl and allow to cool slightly. Place plastic wrap on the surface and chill completely.

To make the dough, combine the milk and remaining 3 tbsps. butter in a small saucepan. Heat over low until milk is just warm and butter is melted. Set aside.

Combine 3 ½ cups (15.4 oz.) flour, ½ cup (3.5 oz.) sugar, salt and yeast in the bowl of a stand mixer. Add the milk mixture and beat until combined. Add flour 1 tbsp. at a time until dough just begins to pull away from the sides of the bowl but is still tacky. Transfer the dough to a floured work surface and knead until the dough is smooth, about 3-4 minutes. Transfer the dough into a large lightly greased bowl and cover with plastic wrap. Allow the dough to rise until almost doubled in size, about 1 –1 ½ hours, or in the refrigerator for at least 8 hours (or overnight). (The dough may also be allowed to rise, then shaped and refrigerated on baking sheets overnight.)

Line a baking sheet with parchment and grease the parchment. Transfer the dough to a floured work surface and roll it to ½" thickness (about a 10" circle). Use a 3" round pastry cutter to cut out as many rounds as possible. Transfer the donuts to the baking sheet with a spatula. Gather up the remaining dough and roll it out again to ½" thickness. Continue to cut rounds until all the dough is used. Cover with a large unscented plastic bag and allow the donuts to rise for 1-1 ½ hours, until soft and puffy.

Pour at least 2" oil into a deep-fryer or Dutch oven. Heat until the oil reaches 350 degrees F. Line a cooling rack or baking sheet with paper towels. Add the donuts 2-3 at a time and fry until golden brown, about 2-3 minutes. Turn the donuts and fry 2-3 minutes longer until golden brown all over. Transfer the donuts to the paper towels and continue until all are fried. Toss the donuts with the remaining ½ cup (3.5 oz.) sugar to coat both sides. Allow the donuts to cool completely before filling.

Spoon the filling into a pastry bag fitted with a ¼" round tip. Make a small (½") slit in the side of a donut. Place the end of the tip inside the slit and pipe in filling. Continue until all donuts are filled. Serve immediately.

Make Ahead Tip: Make the cream filling up to 2 days ahead and refrigerate. The dough may be placed in the refrigerator to rise overnight and then shaped in the morning for the final rise.

Lemon Cream-Filled Donuts

These round bite-size donuts are filled with a slightly tart creamy filling. As in all filled donuts, allow the donuts to cool completely before filling.

◯ MAKES 24–30 DONUTS

- 1 ½ cups (10.6 oz.) granulated sugar
- 5 large egg yolks
- 3 tbsps. cornstarch
- 1 cup (8 fl. oz.) plus 2 tbsps. lemon juice
- 3 tsps. lemon zest
- ½ tsp. vanilla extract
- 8 tbsps. unsalted butter, at room temperature, cut into bits

- 2 cups (8.75 oz.) all-purpose flour
- 2 tsps. baking powder
- ¼ tsp. salt
- ½ cup (4 fl. oz.) sour cream
- 2 large eggs
- 1 tbsp. solid shortening
- ½ cup (4 fl. oz.) heavy cream

To make the filling, whisk together ¾ cup (5.3 oz.) sugar and egg yolks in a medium bowl until light and lemony. Whisk in the cornstarch. Combine 1 cup (8 fl. oz.) lemon juice, 1 tsp. lemon zest and vanilla in a small saucepan over medium-high heat. Bring just to a boil. Whisk in half of the warm juice to temper the egg-yolk mixture, then pour all the tempered mixture back into the saucepan. Heat the mixture over low, whisking constantly for about 5 minutes, until the mixture thickens to the consistency of pudding. Remove from the heat.

Add the butter 1 tbsp. at a time, whisking to thoroughly incorporate each addition. Place plastic wrap directly on the surface of the lemon filling and refrigerate until ready to use.

Combine the flour, baking powder and salt in a medium bowl and set aside. In a separate medium bowl, whisk ½ cup (3.5 oz.) sugar, sour cream, eggs, the remaining 2 tbsps. lemon juice, 1 tsp. zest and shortening until smooth. Stir in the flour mixture until combined.

Cover the bowl with plastic wrap and refrigerate for at least 1 hour, or overnight.

Pour at least 2" oil into a deep-fryer or Dutch oven. Heat until the oil reaches 350 degrees F. Line a cooling rack or baking sheet with paper towels. Drop 1 tbsp. batter into the oil. Repeat until 3-4 more donuts are formed. Fry, turning as necessary, until golden brown on all sides, about 3-4 minutes. Drain on paper towels and continue until all the batter is used. Toss the donuts with the remaining ¼ cup granulated sugar to coat. Cool completely before filling.

Whip the heavy cream to stiff peaks. Fold the heavy cream into the chilled lemon custard. Spoon the lemon filling into a pastry bag fitted with a ¼" round tip. Make a small (½") slit in the side of a donut. Place the end of the tip inside the slit and pipe in filling. Continue until all donuts are filled. Serve immediately.

Make Ahead Tip: Make the lemon cream the day before and refrigerate. Make the dough the day before and refrigerate overnight.

Maple-Glazed Bacon Fritters

The sweet and salty combination of maple and bacon are delicious in this fried donut. The batter for fritters requires little planning ahead, since it can be mixed and fried right away.

◯ MAKES 20-24 FRITTERS

- 2 cups (8.75 oz.) all-purpose flour
- ⅓ cup granulated sugar
- 2 tsps. baking powder
- ½ tsp. salt
- ½ tsp. ground nutmeg
- 8 slices bacon, cooked crisp and crumbled
- ½ cup (4 fl. oz.) whole milk
- 1 large egg
- 8 tbsps. unsalted butter, melted
- ½ cup (5.6 oz.) plus 1 tbsp. maple syrup
- Canola oil for frying
- 2 cups (8.46 oz.) confectioners' sugar

Combine the flour, granulated sugar, baking powder, salt and nutmeg in a medium bowl. Stir in the bacon. In a separate medium bowl, whisk together the milk, egg, 2 tbsps. melted butter and 1 tbsp. maple syrup. Pour the milk mixture into the dry ingredients until just combined. Stir in the bacon.

Pour at least 2" oil into a deep-fryer or Dutch oven. Heat until the oil reaches 360 degrees F. Line a cooling rack or baking sheet with paper towels. Drop a heaping tablespoon of batter into the hot oil. Repeat to add 3-4 more fritters. Fry until golden brown, about 1 ½ minutes. Turn the fritters and fry 1-2 minutes longer until golden brown all over. Transfer the fritters to the paper towels and continue until all are fried. Allow the fritters to cool.

To make the glaze, heat the remaining 6 tbsps. butter in a small saucepan over medium heat until the butter just turns brown and fragrant. Remove from heat and allow to cool. Combine the confectioners' sugar and butter in a medium bowl. Whisk in the remaining ½ cup maple syrup. Dip the fritters into the glaze and turn to coat. Transfer the glazed fritters to a rack to allow the glaze to set for 5 minutes before serving.

Make Ahead Tip: Make the bacon the day before and refrigerate.

BAKING FOR BREAKFAST

Vanilla-Glazed Chocolate Cake Donuts

These tasty chocolate cake donuts are fried and then glazed with vanilla.

MAKES 12 DONUTS

- 2 ¼ cups (10 oz.) all-purpose flour
- ½ cup (1.5 oz.) Dutch-process cocoa powder
- ½ tsp. espresso powder (optional)
- 1 ¾ tsps. baking powder
- ¼ tsp. salt
- 2 large eggs
- 1 cup (7 oz.) granulated sugar
- ¼ cup (4 fl. oz.) whole milk
- 4 tbsps. unsalted butter, melted
- 2 tsps. vanilla extract
- Canola oil for frying
- 3 tbsps. heavy cream
- 1 cup (4.23 oz.) confectioners' sugar

Combine the flour, cocoa powder, espresso powder (if using), baking powder and salt in a medium bowl and set aside. Whisk the eggs and sugar together in a large bowl until fluffy and lemony. Whisk the milk, butter and 1 tsp. vanilla until combined. Pour the milk mixture into the egg mixture and beat to combine. Add the flour mixture and beat until a soft dough forms. Place the dough in a greased bowl, cover and refrigerate for at least 1 hour, or overnight.

Turn the dough onto a floured surface and roll it out to ½" thickness (about a 10" circle). Use a 3" donut cutter (or a 3" round and ½" round pastry cutter) to cut out as many donuts as possible. Reshape and roll out the dough until 12 donuts are complete. Lightly brush the tops of the donuts to remove any excess flour.

Pour at least 2" oil into a deep-fryer or Dutch oven. Heat until the oil reaches 350 degrees F. Line a cooling rack or baking sheet with paper towels. Add the donuts 2–3 at a time and fry until golden brown, about 1 ½ minutes. Turn the donuts and fry 1–2 minutes longer until golden brown all over. Transfer the donuts to the paper towels and continue until all are fried.

To make the glaze, combine the remaining 1 tsp. vanilla and heavy cream in a small saucepan. Heat the mixture over low until steaming but not simmering. Whisk in the confectioners' sugar until smooth. Dip the donuts in the glaze and place them on a rack to allow the glaze to set up before serving.

Make Ahead Tip: The dough may be placed in the refrigerator overnight and then shaped in the morning.

Index

Thank you!

I appreciate you purchasing this book and hope you've enjoyed the recipes. I know you could have picked dozens of other cookbooks, so to show my appreciation I'd like to offer you a bonus: *Ten Delicious Donut Recipes*. Simply sign up on my website www.donnaleahy.com and I will send you the PDF. I will also include you on my list for free stuff, and periodically send you exclusive special offerings.

Finally, I need to ask you for a favor. If you have a moment to post an online review of this book on a book retailer site, I'd really appreciate it. This type of feedback will help me continue to write the kind of cookbooks that you want to use. Thanks again, I look forward to hearing from you.

Chef Donna

CPSIA information can be obtained at www.ICGtesting.com
Printed in the USA
BVOW05s1532310716

457018BV00031B/37/P